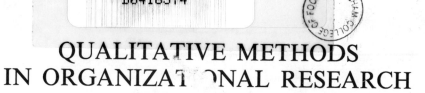

QUALITATIVE METHODS
IN ORGANIZATIONAL RESEARCH

QUALITATIVE METHODS IN ORGANIZATIONAL RESEARCH

A Practical Guide

edited by

Catherine Cassell and Gillian Symon

SAGE Publications
London • Thousand Oaks • New Delhi

Editorial arrangement and Chapter 1 © Catherine Cassell
and Gillian Symon 1994
Chapter 2 © Nigel King 1994
Chapter 3 © Anne Rees and Nigel Nicholson 1994
Chapter 4 © Graham I. Johnson and Pamela Briggs 1994
Chapter 5 © John G. Gammack and Robert A. Stephens
1994
Chapter 6 © Harriette Marshall 1994
Chapter 7 © David Waddington 1994
Chapter 8 © Chris Steyaert and René Bouwen 1994
Chapter 9 © Nick Forster 1994
Chapter 10 © Pat Hornby and Gillian Symon 1994
Chapter 11 © John G. Burgoyne 1994
Chapter 12 © Jean F. Hartley 1994
Chapter 13 © David Fryer and Norman T. Feather 1994

First published 1994

SAGE Publications Ltd
6 Bonhill Street
London EC2A 4PU

SAGE Publications Inc
2455 Teller Road
Thousand Oaks, California 91320

SAGE Publications India Pvt Ltd
32, M-Block Market
Greater Kailash – I
New Delhi 110 048

British Library Cataloguing in Publication Data

A catalogue record for this book is available from the British
Library.

ISBN 0–8039–8769–2
ISBN 0–8039– 8770–6 (pbk)

Library of Congress catalog card number 94–066701

Typeset by Mayhew Typesetting, Rhayader, Powys
Printed in Great Britain by Redwood Books, Trowbridge,
Wiltshire

Contents

Acknowledgements

The editors wish to thank the contributors for their hard work and commitment to this project over the last two years. We would also like to thank the following people who have supported, advised or entertained us (in some cases all three) during the duration of this project:

Bob Cox, Brian Parkinson, Matthew Cassell, Danny Cox, Susan Walsh, Chris Clegg, Shireen Agnew, Jane Bird, Rashmi Biswas, Edward Border, Peter Border, Stephanie Cassell, Norman Cassell, Ged Cassell, Laurie Cohen, John Downes, Judi Ellis, Julie Elliot, Steve Evans, Eileen Green, Maureen Houldsworth, Phil Johnson, Ruth Krascum, Karen Long, Alan Milne, Carlton Palmer, Row T. Owls, Angela Semple, Andrew Semple, Helen Sharp, Ken Smith, Peter Totterdell, Chris Waddle, Clare Warnock, Jane White, Raquel Wolstenhulme.

Catherine Cassell and Gillian Symon
Sheffield and Cardiff

Notes on Contributors

René Bouwen is Professor at the Catholic University of Leuven (KU Leuven), where he teaches Organizational Behaviour and Group Dynamics to students in Organizational Psychology and Educational Sciences, and Behavioural Decision-Making and Organizational Behaviour Special Topics on the MBA programme. His research, based on qualitative methodology, focuses on organizational innovation, group effectiveness and conflict management. He has published several articles on these topics from a social constructionist perspective. He acts as a consultant to companies and non-profit-making organizations in change projects and management development.

Pamela Briggs is Principal Lecturer in Psychology at the University of Northumbria at Newcastle. Her research interests are primarily concerned with the acquisition of computer-based skills, although she has also published articles on comparative human resource management and on the processes involved in word recognition.

John G. Burgoyne is Professor in (and founding member of) the Department of Management Learning in the School of Management, University of Lancaster, where he has been since 1974. His work there has focused on the design of management development programmes and the nature of managerial behaviour and competencies – topics he has explored through pure and applied research and the provision of development programmes for management educators. In recent years, his interests have broadened into the areas of career management and management development policy. He is currently working on projects relating management development to corporate performance, creating the 'learning company' and defining the competencies of human resource development.

Catherine Cassell graduated in Social Psychology from the London School of Economics, thereafter completing an MA and a PhD in Occupational Psychology at the University of Sheffield. She is currently a Senior Lecturer in Organizational Behaviour at Sheffield Business School, part of Sheffield Hallam University, where she teaches on a range of undergraduate and postgraduate programmes. She has published in the areas of information technology and organizational change and gender at work, and her current research interests focus on women's experiences of organizational cultures; gender and technology; business ethics and ethical behaviour; and the interface between clinical and organizational psychology. She is co-editor (with Rob Davies) of the British Psychological Society magazine, *The Occupational Psychologist.*

Norman T. Feather is Foundation Professor of Psychology at the Flinders University of South Australia in Adelaide. He is past-President of the Australian Psychological Society. He is a graduate of the University of Sydney, the University of New England, and the University of Michigan, where he received the Donald G. Marquis Award for his doctoral dissertation. He has published widely in the areas of achievement motivation, expectancy-value theory, attribution theory, gender roles, the psychology of values, social attitudes, justice-related behaviour and the psychological impact of unemployment. He has authored or edited five books, including *Expectations and Actions: Expectancy-Value Models in Psychology* (1982) and *The Psychological Impact of Unemployment* (1990).

Nick Forster is a Lecturer in Organizational Behaviour and Human Resource Management at the Cardiff Business School, University of Wales, College of Cardiff. He is co-author (with J. Altman, L. Greenbury and A. G. Munton) of *Job Relocation: Managing People on the Move* (1993). His current research interests include international career pathing and job mobility, and human resource management in multinational firms.

David Fryer is a Senior Lecturer in Psychology at the University of Stirling, where he is engaged in research into links between unemployment, relative poverty and mental health. He is the joint editor (with P. Ullah) of *Unemployed People* (1987) and Guest Editor of a Special Edition of the *Journal of Occupational and Organizational Psychology* (December 1992) which is devoted to the psychological consequences of unemployment.

John G. Gammack has a background in psychology and computing and carried out his PhD in Experimental Psychology at the MRC Applied Psychology Unit, Cambridge. He has published in the areas of information systems, knowledge elicitation, and knowledge-based systems. He is currently a Senior Lecturer in Business IT in the Computer Science Department at Paisley University.

Jean F. Hartley is a Senior Lecturer in the Department of Organizational Psychology, Birkbeck College, University of London. Her research interests are in the fields of employment relations and in organizational change. She has used case study strategy in research into a major strike, into job insecurity, and currently in research into organizational change in local authorities. She is the (co-) author/editor of three books: *Steel Strike* (with John Kelly and Nigel Nicholson: 1983), *Job Insecurity* (with Dan Jacobson, Bert Klandermans and Tinka van Vuuren: 1991), and *Employment Relations* (with Geoffrey Stephenson: 1992).

Pat Hornby is a Teaching Fellow in the Department of Management at the Manchester Metropolitan University. Her research interests include decision-making in systems design and, more recently, management career decisions. She is particularly keen to explore and develop field research methods for investigating complex organizational processes.

Graham I. Johnson is a Senior Consultant Cognitive Engineer for AT&T's Self-Service and Financial Systems Division based in Dundee. His work involves the integration of usability concerns in the development and evaluation of concepts, products and systems. His main research interests include usability evaluation methods, particularly those that are user-centred or participatory in nature, and users' mental models of everyday devices.

Nigel King graduated in Social Psychology from the University of Kent in Canterbury and obtained his PhD from the MRC/ESRC Social and Applied Psychology Unit, University of Sheffield. His research interests include creativity, innovation and change in organizations, occupational psychology in the National Health Service, relationships between patients and health practitioners, and the development of qualitative methods in applied psychology. He is currently a Lecturer in Psychology at the University of Huddersfield.

Harriette Marshall is a Senior Lecturer in Social Psychology in the Psychology Department at the University of East London. Her research interests include the social construction of gender and 'race', feminist psychology and the relationship between psychology and inequality.

Nigel Nicholson is Chair of the Organizational Behaviour Group and Director of the Centre for Organizational Research at London Business School. Prior to this, he was a Senior Research Fellow at the MRC/ESRC Social and Applied Psychology Unit, University of Sheffield, leading a team studying individual and organizational change. He has published numerous books and articles on a variety of topics including absenteeism, psychological aspects of industrial relations, career transitions and corporate culture change. Recently, he has embarked on studies of business ethics.

Anne Rees is currently at the MRC/ESRC Social and Applied Psychology Unit, University of Sheffield, working in psychotherapy research. Her other research interests include: women's experiences in organizations, particularly in junior and middle management; adaptability and effectiveness of organizations in periods of environmental uncertainty; and the measurement of personal change over time.

Robert A. Stephens has a background in social science and computing and is currently completing a PhD in knowledge-based systems. He has published mainly in the areas of knowledge-based systems and information systems. He is at present a Lecturer in the Transputer Centre, Faculty of Computer Studies and Mathematics, University of the West of England.

Chris Steyaert is working at the Catholic University of Leuven (KU Leuven), Department of Psychology. He is preparing a PhD on an organizational analysis of small high-tech firms based on in-depth case studies. His publications focus on organization theory and human resource management for small and medium enterprises (SMEs). Other research interests and publications concern work motivation, and organizational change and intervention.

Gillian Symon is a Lecturer in Organizational Psychology in the School of Psychology, University of Wales, College of Cardiff. Her research interests are in the area of the design of information technology – more particularly in the organizational processes which constitute this activity. In exploring this issue, she adopts a longitudinal case study approach utilizing a number of qualitative techniques. A more general interest is in the methods of psychological research and the nature of the research process itself.

David Waddington is a Senior Lecturer in Communication Studies at Sheffield Hallam University. He has published widely in the fields of industrial relations, public disorder and the sociology of mining communities. He is author of *Trouble Brewing: a Social Psychological Analysis of the Ansells Brewery Strike* (1987) and *Contemporary Issues in Public Disorder: A Comparative and Historical Approach* (1992); and co-author of *Flashpoints: Studies in Public Disorder* (with Karen Jones and Chas Critcher: 1989), and *Split at the Seams? Community, Continuity and Change after the 1984–5 Coal Dispute* (with Maggie Wykes and Chas Critcher: 1991).

1

Qualitative Research in Work Contexts

Catherine Cassell and Gillian Symon

This book is about conducting qualitative research in organizations. It is about the variety of qualitative methods available and how these methods can be used in practice to provide quality research data. We came together to produce this book as a result of our own research experiences. We share the view that qualitative methods are more appropriate to the kind of research questions we want to ask in our own work, that is: focusing on organizational processes, as well as outcomes, and trying to understand both individual and group experiences of work. However, as organizational psychologists we were trained, like most psychology students, in the use of quantitative methodologies, and have often bemoaned how difficult it is to access information about the application of qualitative methods, particularly in work psychology. The use of qualitative methods is becoming more widespread within work settings, but is, we suspect, under-reported. We wanted to know more about how our colleagues are using such approaches and how we can access and utilize this rich diversity of methods in practice. The result is this book.

Specifically, we see this book as having three important aims. First, to document a variety of qualitative methods currently used in organizational research, particularly, although not solely, in our own area of occupational and organizational psychology; second, to provide the researcher and the practitioner with an outline of how to use such methods in practice; and third, to contribute to raising the profile of qualitative methods within organizational research. In this introduction we explain why we felt these three aims were important and how the book sets out to achieve them.

It would be inappropriate here to give a *comprehensive* account of the ongoing debate concerning suitable methodological and philosophical viewpoints to take in understanding human behaviour. The division between qualitative and quantitative methods has had a long history in the social sciences and is dealt with in detail in other sources (for example, Bryman, 1988; Cook and Reichardt, 1978; Henwood and Pidgeon, 1992; Lincoln and Guba, 1985). Our focus is firmly on qualitative approaches to organizational research. However, in preparing the book we found ourselves continually discussing what we meant by qualitative methods and we feel it is important to make some general points about definition at this stage. We have found it impossible to do this without comparing qualitative methods with quantitative methods, which in itself is a reflection of the pervasiveness of the debate. A key starting-point is the recognition that the two different approaches rely on different underlying epistemologies.

Positivism and phenomenology

Henwood and Pidgeon (1992) suggest that there is a confusion in defining qualitative techniques which emerges from the narrow association of such techniques with particular modes of data-gathering. As Bogdan and Taylor point out, 'most debates over methods are debates over assumptions and goals, over theory and perspective' (1975: 1). Thus debates focus on the meta-theoretical – theory about theory.

It is argued that adopting qualitative (phenomenological) approaches implies taking a different perspective on human behaviour from that adopted in utilizing quantitative (positivist) approaches (Giorgi, 1970; Spiegelberg, 1972). The philosophies behind the two sets of techniques are very different. To summarize: the assumption behind the positivist paradigm is that there is an objective truth existing in the world which can be revealed through the scientific method where the focus is on measuring relationships between variables systematically and statistically. Hollway (1991) claims that quantification is at the heart of the social sciences' claim to scientific method. The key concerns are that measurement is reliable, valid and generalizable in its clear predictions of cause and effect. In psychology, for example, the 'discovery' of the general laws that govern human behaviour occurs through this process. It is the application of the methods of the natural sciences to social phenomena. Qualitative techniques emerge from phenomenological and interpretive paradigms. Typically, the emphasis is on constructivist approaches where there is no clear-cut objectivity or reality. Social life emerges from the shared creativity of individuals (Filstead, 1978). As Fryer suggests:

> Qualitative researchers are characteristically concerned in their research with attempting to accurately describe, decode and interpret the precise meanings to persons of phenomena occurring in their normal social contexts and are typically pre-occupied with complexity, authenticity, contextualization, shared subjectivity of researcher and researched and minimization of illusion. (1991: 3)

The perception that different methods emerge from different philosophies has important implications. First, theory is generated differently depending on the paradigm. In the positivist approach, theory is deduced as a result of testing hypotheses. In phenomenological and interpretive approaches, theory is generated from the data collected, that is, it is 'grounded' in the data (Glaser and Strauss, 1967). Second, there are key differences in what is perceived to be the nature of knowledge. As Henwood and Pidgeon suggest: 'Framing the distinction between quantitative and qualitative research in terms of these two epistemological poles is important in alerting us to the fact that there are competing claims regarding what constitutes warrantable knowledge' (1992: 99). This is important when considering the criteria by which the outputs of research are evaluated, an issue we return to later.

Bryman points out that there have been two distinct explanations of the differences between qualitative and quantitative research. There is the epistemological account outlined above but there is also the technical account: 'The alternative standpoint is to suggest that quantitative and qualitative research are each appropriate to different types of research problem, implying that the research issue determines (or should determine) which style of research is employed' (1988: 106). Taking this perspective implies that both quantitative and qualitative methods can be used together in the same study – researchers taking the pragmatic view that whatever 'tools' are available and seem appropriate should be adopted (Crompton and Jones, 1988; Patton, 1988). However, this does not really avoid the epistemological issue (Gill and Johnson, 1991). Hartley (Chapter 12) argues that techniques are not of themselves positivist or phenomenological – it is how they are used and how the data are interpreted that defines the epistemological assumptions on which they are based. Similarly, King (Chapter 2) emphasizes that the degree of structure imposed on the research interview is dependent on the underlying philosophy adopted by the researcher.

Having briefly outlined the underlying epistemology of qualitative approaches as opposed to quantitative, we are still concerned with the problem of what adopting a qualitative approach implies in methodological terms.

Qualitative methods: what's in a name?

There does not seem to be an agreed definition of what constitutes a qualitative method. As Van Maanen suggests:

> The label qualitative methods has no precise meaning in any of the social sciences. It is at best an umbrella term covering an array of interpretive techniques which seek to describe, decode, translate and otherwise come to terms with the meaning, not the frequency, of certain more or less naturally occurring phenomena in the social world. (1979: 520)

This quote draws directly on the epistemological account given above. However, perhaps the search for a 'one best' definition is a misguided endeavour? Some authors have instead attempted to isolate defining *characteristics* of qualitative research (for example, Bryman, 1988). In a similar fashion, this book illustrates how the *general characteristics* of qualitative research are applied *specifically* in organizational research. Contributors tend to emphasize different aspects of using qualitative methods in terms of what they themselves perceive to be important facets.

Some of the themes recur in different chapters, some are peculiar to individual chapters. Below, we outline the major emergent themes.

On a superficial level, the immediate assumption is that qualitative methods do not involve numbers, or, rather, the quantification of phenomena. Qualitative methods are often associated with the collection and analysis of written or spoken text or the direct observation of behaviour. Most of the contributors to this book seem to agree that we should 'count the countable' (Burgoyne, Chapter 11) – that is to say, count what it makes sense to reduce to quantifiable terms. In organizations, it may make 'sense' to count numbers of employees in different departments, profits, numbers of computers in use, numbers of products processed. However, when looking beyond these data for explanations of the behaviours surrounding this differential distribution of 'facts', counting may well become inappropriate.

Qualitative research is less likely to impose restrictive a priori classifications on the collection of data. As a result of the underlying epistemology, research is less driven by very specific hypotheses and categorical frameworks and more concerned with emergent themes and idiographic descriptions. In the chapters that follow, the authors describe how the ways in which their respondents constructed and reported *their* views of the phenomena under investigation were crucial to the research process. Thus, one of the cornerstones of the qualitative approach is its acceptance of the inherent subjectivity of the research endeavour (Bryman, 1988). The argument is that the search for objectivity is to some extent misguided for it is the participants' perspectives on and interpretations of the situation which are of value in understanding behaviour.

Qualitative methods allow flexibility in the research process. Thus the responsiveness to the individual's and organization's conceptualizations of themselves is also related to a willingness to formulate new hypotheses and alter old ones as the research progresses, in the light of emerging insights. Many qualitative methods (because they are less rigidly defined) allow the researcher to change the nature of his or her intervention as the research develops in response to the changing nature of the context. With respect to organizational research – where we always have to be responsive to the organizational circumstances – this is crucial: not just in terms of what we are allowed to do, but also because the fact that we are working in complex situations means we cannot define exactly what we are interested in or how to explore the issue at the outset. With similar regard to flexibility, qualitative researchers are also more likely to take advantage of other (non-psychological) sources of data in interpreting events. Many of the contributors to this book emphasize the use of the method they describe in conjunction with other sources of data – for example, documentary evidence or economic data. The triangulation of data by multi-method approaches is essential to answer many of the most important questions in organizational research, where we are concerned with very complex processes involving a number of actors over time.

Only qualitative methods are sensitive enough to allow the detailed analysis of change. In organizational research organizational dynamics and change are major areas of interest. ❧With quantitative methods we may be able to assess that a change has occurred over time but we cannot say how (what processes were involved) or why (in terms of circumstances and stakeholders)! 'Qualitative methods are sensitive to issues of this kind. On a more theoretical level, most of the contributors to this book conceptualize the respondent (individual or organization) as an active shaper of situations and events, and argue that the methods they describe are more able to encompass this dynamic situation than quantitative methods.❧

It has been argued that qualitative research in general can take place only in naturalistic settings (Denzin, 1971; Lincoln and Guba, 1985; Marshall and Rossman, 1989). This means that topics for study focus on everyday activity as 'defined, enacted, smoothed, and made problematic by persons going about their normal routines' (Van Maanen, 1983: 255). Taking an explicitly contextual perspective recognizes the influence that the situation has on behaviour and that behaviour has on situations. In organizational research particularly, considerations of context should be paramount – the field itself is defined by the context of organizational life.

Closely related is the view that an important characteristic of qualitative approaches is that they seek to provide a holistic view of the situations or organizations that researchers are trying to understand (Bogdan and Taylor, 1975; Patton, 1980). Individual or organizational behaviour is perceived not as the outcome of a finite set of discrete variables (some of which should be rigorously controlled), but rather as a 'lived experience' of the social setting – a Gestalt of meanings (Ashworth, 1993, personal communication). The focus within qualitative studies is with understanding the individual's 'life-world' (Giorgi, 1970). Hartley focuses on this point in her description of the use of case studies in organizational research (Chapter 12), where the whole organizational situation is explored and is formative in explaining specific processes and behaviours.

An example of the everyday understanding of the advantages of such a holistic approach became apparent to us recently while watching a soap opera on British television *(Coronation Street*, episode broadcast on Wednesday, 24 February 1993). Rita Sullivan's husband has died of a brain tumour and a legal action has been brought by his relations concerning whether he was of 'sound mind' when he made his will (in which the widow receives most of the money). When gathered in court, the prosecuting lawyer describes Rita's husband as 'a man who couldn't do up his own buttons, whose writing and speaking would lead you to believe he was drunk and who in the ordinary run of things was sometimes confused about his wife's identity', and asks Rita 'would that be a fair picture?' Rita replies: 'No, I would say it were more like one of them games where you join t' dots up to make a face – you just don't get a true impression.' In the positivist tradition we are concerned with establishing what the dots (or variables) are and drawing lines (causal links) between them – a reductionist view of the situation. In the interpretivist tradition however, we are concerned with taking a holistic viewpoint – where context and behaviour are interdependent.

The final key characteristic shared by qualitative approaches which we outline here is the role of the researcher and the researched. Because such methods are used in 'natural' settings, Kirk and Miller (1986) suggest that qualitative researchers are engaged in interacting with people in their own language and on their own terms, as would be expected on someone else's territory. Consequently, the participants in such studies should be proactive in defining their own key issues in relation to the investigation. It is argued by many of the contributors that this therefore makes the research process 'transparent' to the respondents and hence more accessible. This is similar to the point made earlier concerning subjectivity, but goes further – employees are *participants* (in the proper sense of the word) in the research endeavour not *subjects* of it (the objects of our scientific curiosity). In some cases this has led to the development of participative or more collaborative research, though, as Reason and Rowan (1981) point out, qualitative methods, as they have been traditionally used, can be quite different from the participative or collaborative styles that characterize new paradigm research. However, the perception of individuals as active constructors of meaning rather than passive observers of events (as we have suggested earlier) does imply assigning a more proactive role to the participants in the research process.

There is not only a recognition of the autonomy of the participant, but also a recognition of the part that the researcher plays in the research. Rather than being an uninvolved bystander observing the organizational action, the researcher is a social being who has an impact on the behaviour of those around. The research process is conceptualized as a social process which is heavily influenced by the choices made by the researcher as the research progresses. Consequently, the researcher is seen as a craftsperson – skilled not just in the nuts and bolts of research but in his or her ability to interact with others.

Thus, the reflexive character of social research is actively considered by qualitative researchers. As Hammersley and Atkinson state:

> We are part of the social world we study. . . . This is not a matter of methodological commitment, it is an existential fact. There is no way in which we can escape the social world in order to study it; nor fortunately, is that necessary. We cannot avoid relying on 'common-sense' knowledge nor, often, can we avoid having an effect on the social phenomena we study. (1983: 15)

Indeed, understanding the role of the researcher within the research process can form an important part of a research study (Cassell, 1989; Cassell and Fitter, 1992). Because qualitative methods are frequently more interactive, more intensive and involve a longer-term commitment, researchers are likely to build up a social relationship with the organizational members and therefore gain more insights into their collective understanding by actively sharing that experience.

Within this book reflexivity is illustrated in a number of ways. In Burgoyne's chapter on stakeholder analysis (Chapter 11) the researcher is perceived as a stakeholder in the outcome of the research and usually a representative of another's (often management's) interest (as well as his or her own). In Chapter 6 on discourse analysis, Marshall outlines the importance of the nature of the social interaction between interviewed and interviewer in constructing the situation. In Waddington's analysis of participant observation (Chapter 7), he outlines the extent to which he was aware that his own values guided his actions in the research situation. In Chapter 13, Fryer and Feather outline the strategy of intervention research which is directly concerned with impacting a situation to bring about change and in which it is important that intervention researchers assess the difference they are making to an ongoing event in a practical sense – that is, 'has anything changed for the better as a result of this research?'.

In summary, qualitative research can be said to have a number of defining characteristics which include: a focus on interpretation rather than quantification; an emphasis on subjectivity rather than objectivity; flexibility in the process of conducting research; an orientation towards process rather than outcome; a concern with context – regarding behaviour and situation as inextricably linked in forming experience; and finally, an explicit recognition of the impact of the research process on the research situation.

There may seem so far to be distinct advantages to using qualitative methods; however, such methods are not extensively reported. We believe that the determination of research method is not just one of appropriateness or philosophy but of ideology – what constitutes 'valued' research?

Evaluating qualitative research

Clearly, issues of value and ideology are important in determining 'acceptable' research. In the social and human sciences, value is placed on research which is perceived to be methodologically rigorous. Not infrequently, this is equated with quantitative approaches: hard and scientific. Useful and appropriate knowledge is produced by orthodox techniques Clearly this has implications for qualitative researchers, particularly in an area such as organizational psychology. In choosing to focus on qualitative approaches, researchers are taking a risk. Not for them is the credibility of the hard-nosed scientist searching for the truth, but rather a vulnerability and uncertainty as to how their research will be interpreted and evaluated which arises primarily as a result of their choice of method.

In our experience, there is a high level of expectation that qualitative researchers can and will account for the methodological approach of their work. This is in stark contrast to positivist work, where the legitimacy and relevance of the fundamental method adopted is rarely questioned. On the other hand, much time *is* spent in this paradigm in debating the validity of the research design, which courts the danger (particularly with statistical methods) of being obsessed with the intricacies of the measuring instrument and becoming alienated from the actual behaviour of interest. Qualitative researchers are more likely to be aware of (and to feel they have to explain) the epistemological stance they are taking; whereas few researchers working in the positivist tradition would feel the need to explain or justify their chosen paradigm – it is simply how research is conducted. The upshot of this unbalanced view is that qualitative researchers may find themselves having to justify their research in terms of an inappropriate paradigm. Consequently, most qualitative researchers have become well practised in defending their research in the context of positivist notions of reliability, generalizability and validity. This creates a number of different responses from researchers. Hollway describes her experiences:

> Breaking out of the orthodoxy was difficult. . . . It was difficult, not only because of the dominant values of psychologists, not just because there were few alternatives, certainly not legitimate ones, but also because psychological theories have been produced in the shadow of these methods and their capacity to embrace people's diversity, depth, richness and creativity has been consequently depleted. (1991: 10)

David Waddington (Chapter 7) discusses the implications of focusing his doctoral research primarily on qualitative approaches, the risks he was perceived to be taking by 'advisers' who urged him to do otherwise. Choosing research methods that go against the prevailing orthodoxy can clearly have an impact on individual careers. Brookfield points to some of the difficulties that face researchers in the field of education who 'abandon the elegance, precision and clarity afforded by "scientific" modes of enquiry in favour of qualitative or participative research methods' (1983: 7). He suggests that this approach 'can place a promising academic career in jeopardy, place a researcher in isolation, and require a measure of professional courage' (1983: 7).

Our own experience in psychology departments has been of qualitative PhD researchers being informed by staff members that their research is 'nothing but journalism' (this was meant to be derogatory) and a visiting discourse analyst giving a seminar being told by staff members in the audience that her methodology 'came out of a Blue Peter annual'. As universities have to search for money to fund research, it becomes impossible for researchers to 'take risks' (as taking a qualitative approach would be interpreted). Perhaps this explains the seeming defensiveness of those social scientists working within the positivist paradigm. As Punch puts it (quoting Reiss, 1979):

the more 'journalistic' social science becomes, the easier it is for its opponents to dismiss it as non-scientific. This leads to social science being seen as trivial in its results and dangerous in its techniques, making it 'simultaneously impotent and threatening'. (1986: 82)

In work psychology efforts to legitimize psychology as a scientific endeavour (in the positivist sense) have been translated as the search for the 'natural (field) experiment' or the adoption of 'quasi-experimental' techniques (Cook and Campbell, 1979). In contrast, this book has the objective of legitimizing the use of *qualitative* methods in organizational research by illustrating the insights which can be achieved through their use.

These issues are not just confined to the academic environment, however. Organizational research is fundamentally a practical endeavour. Researchers address the very real problems that organizations are facing in the 1990s and often require a wide range of techniques at their fingertips depending on the demands of the clients with whom they deal. What, then, do client organizations regard as useful data? Most of the contributors emphasize that qualitative techniques are much more time-consuming – both in data collection and analysis. Indeed many of the methods described here tend to assume a longitudinal research design. In terms of organizational research this may be considered problematic, as clients tend to desire immediate answers. Just as journals declare themselves unable to accept the (necessarily) lengthy output of qualitative research (see Marshall, Chapter 6 and Forster, Chapter 9), so organizations may balk at uncategorized data:

Many policy-makers find descriptive accounts more palatable than an avalanche of figures and tables. However, the length of most ethnographic appraisals inhibits the most diligent sponsors and evaluators from even approaching a qualitative report of research findings. Simply put, few individuals have the time to read, absorb and assimilate lengthy narratives – let alone sift out the data specifically relevant to pressing policy concerns of the day. (Fetterman, 1988: 15–16)

However, the problem is not just a practical one. Organizations are impressed by numbers, regarding these as 'accurate' data. One of our colleagues reported attempting to set up a research study in a major UK company in which he wanted to conduct a questionnaire survey. The company argued for a series of interviews instead, claiming that quantifying phenomena would be too 'real', would be inescapable, would be accepted as 'true'. They are not alone in this assumption: such incidents illustrate the power of quantification in our western culture. Many of the contributors to this volume, as we have already outlined, have emphasized the 'richness' of qualitative data and the insights they provide which would be impossible to access through other means. Our recent experiences with organizations who have specifically requested detailed qualitative data (as being more informative) suggest that things may be changing.

The important point to recognize here is the manifold demands that are placed upon the researcher from the various stakeholder groups. Reflecting the interests of: clients; funding organizations; professional assessors; and the researcher her/himself is one of the key dilemmas of the research process. Within this context, the criteria by which stakeholders evaluate qualitative methods are clearly crucial in determining what kind of research is undertaken.

Overview of the book

In describing qualitative methods, commentators (particularly in sociological texts) often refer to the 'big three': interviews; participant observation/ethnography; and document analysis. We wanted to broaden this perspective by providing a variety of methods in this book, thus revealing the diversity of methods available and the subtle distinctions between them. We are presenting a number of methods here; however, we are aware of many more which we did not have room on this occasion to include. It is a rich field and one which we hope will provide a stimulus for readers to consider alternative approaches to investigating their chosen research areas.

The chapters each take a qualitative method as their theme. The authors outline the method, describe how it is administered, delineate and analyse a study they have conducted using the technique, and evaluate the advantages and disadvantages of its use. We recognize that this structure can in practice create an artificial distinction between the technique and the research context; however, it was our intention to provide clear accounts of the methods which would then encourage others to consider how such methods may benefit their work in other contexts.

We also came to realize that there are a number of different views as to what constitutes 'methods' (see Burgoyne's discussion of this point, Chapter 11). Consequently, we were led to make a distinction between 'techniques' and 'frameworks' and to see these as lying on a continuum. We define techniques as specific ways of gathering data (for example, interviews, Twenty Statements Test, repertory grids) and frameworks as more 'holistic' strategies of approaching the study of organizational behaviour, which may encompass a number of specific techniques (for example, case studies, stakeholder analysis, intervention research). This book is organized to reflect this continuum – beginning with the more specific techniques and moving towards the more general frameworks. There is clearly some overlap between operating at an individual or at a group/organizational level in making this distinction. Consequently, the chapters also tend to move from research at an individual level to research at the organizational level.

As well as illustrating the variety of techniques and frameworks available in this area, the contributions to this book also highlight the range of (work) issues and environments in which qualitative methods can provide useful and informative insights. The chapters cover the well-known areas of: (individual) decision-making (Chapter 2); personality assessment (Chapter 3); usability analysis (Chapter 4); knowledge elicitation (Chapter 5); working practices (Chapter 6); conflict (Chapter 7); innovation processes (Chapter 8); relocation and staff development (Chapter 9); systems analysis and organizational decision-making (Chapter 10); training and development (Chapter 11); employee relations (Chapter 12); and unemployment (Chapter 13). The methods outlined here have been utilized in health care environments, government bureaucracies, trades union organizations, the retail trade, engineering firms and multinational corporations. However, all the contributors would argue that the study they describe is only an example and not restricted to any particular field of interest.

Although the techniques described here are quite distinctive, and the research projects located in a wide variety of organizations, there are a number of similarities in the way the authors provide their accounts of their research strategies. In each chapter, the authors outline why their chosen method was appropriate to the research question they were addressing. Van Maanen (1983) describes how there is more than a little pontification involved when researchers describe their own chosen methods. We shamelessly recognize that this volume is guilty in that respect. In each of the chapters a conviction and commitment to the techniques of research is written between the lines if not made explicit. For us this adds to, rather than detracts from, the quality of the contributions.

Conclusions: raising the profile of qualitative methods

We believe the contributions to this book raise some important issues concerning the conceptualization of qualitative methods (including what is meant by both 'qualitative' and 'method'), which arise specifically because of the work context in which they have been applied and the pragmatic problems associated with investigating 'real world' problems. Contributors to this book emphasize that there is no one best way to utilize the methods they describe and the need to be responsive to the context and emerging data. Consequently, we see this volume as a *guide* rather than a set of instructions. We are keen to raise the profile of qualitative methods and our view is that this can only be done by giving people the tools to use such methods for themselves. In this sense, we agree with Reason and Rowan that 'we need to establish some degree of legitimacy and credibility for this way of inquiry, and we need to establish some political support' (1981: 486).

Acknowledgement

We would like to thank Peter Ashworth, Phil Johnson and Nigel King for their helpful comments on earlier drafts of this chapter.

References

Bogdan, R. and Taylor, S.J. (1975) *Introduction to Qualitative Research Methods.* New York: Wiley.

Brookfield, S. (1983) *Adult Learners, Adult Education and the Community.* Milton Keynes: Open University Press.

Bryman, A. (1988) *Quantity and Quality in Social Research.* London: Unwin Hyman.

Cassell, C.M. (1989) 'The use of information technology in the community: an evaluation'. PhD Dissertation, University of Sheffield.

Cassell, C.M. and Fitter, M.J. (1992) 'Responding to a changing environment: an action-research case study', in D.M. Hosking and N. Anderson (eds), *Organizational Change and Innovation.* London: Routledge.

Cook, T.D. and Campbell, D.T. (1979) *Quasi-experimentation: Design and Analysis Issues for Field Settings.* Boston: Houghton Mifflin.

Cook, T.D. and Reichardt, C.S. (1978) *Qualitative and Quantitative Methods in Evaluation Research.* Beverley Hills, CA: Sage.

Crompton, R. and Jones, G. (1988) 'Researching white-collar organizations: why sociologists should not stop doing case studies', in A. Bryman (ed.), *Doing Research in Organizations.* London: Routledge.

Denzin, N.K. (1971) 'The logic of naturalistic inquiry', *Social Forces,* 50: 166–82.

Fetterman, D. (1988) 'A qualitative shift in allegiance' in D. Fetterman (ed.), *Qualitative Approaches to Evaluation in Education.* New York: Praeger.

Filstead, W.J. (1978) 'Qualitative methods: a needed perspective in evaluation research', in T.D. Cook and C.S. Reichardt (eds), *Qualitative and Quantitative Methods in Evaluation Research.* Beverley Hills, CA: Sage.

Fryer, D. (1991) 'Qualitative methods in occupational psychology: reflections upon why they are so useful but so little used', *The Occupational Psychologist,* 14 (Special Issue on Qualitative Methods): 3–6.

Gill, J. and Johnson, P. (1991) *Research Methods for Managers.* London: Paul Chapman.

Giorgi, A. (1970) *Psychology as a Human Science: a Phenomenologically Based Approach.* New York: Harper & Row.

Glaser, B. and Strauss, A.L. (1967) *The Discovery of Grounded Theory: Strategies for Qualitative Research.* Chicago: Aldine.

Hammersley, M. and Atkinson, P. (1983) *Ethnography Principles in Practice.* London: Routledge.

Henwood, K.L. and Pidgeon, N.F. (1992) 'Qualitative research and psychological theorizing', *British Journal of Psychology,* 83: 97–111.

Hollway, W. (1991) 'Objectivity and subjectivity', *The Occupational Psychologist,* 14 (Special Issue on Qualitative Methods): 10–13.

Kirk, J. and Miller, M.L. (1986) *Reliability and Validity in Qualitative Research (Qualitative Research Methods Series, Vol. 1).* Beverley Hills, CA: Sage.

Lincoln, Y.S. and Guba, E.G. (1985) *Naturalistic Inquiry.* Beverley Hills, CA: Sage.

Marshall, C. and Rossman, G.B. (1989) *Designing Qualitative Research.* Newbury Park, CA: Sage.

Patton, M.Q. (1980) *Qualitative Evaluation Methods.* Beverley Hills, CA: Sage.

Patton, M.Q. (1988) 'Paradigms and pragmatism', in D. Fetterman (ed.), *Qualitative Approaches to Evaluation in Education.* New York: Praeger.

Punch, M. (1986) *The Politics and Ethics of Fieldwork* (*Qualitative Research Methods Series, Vol. 3*). Beverley Hills, CA: Sage.

Reason, P. and Rowan, J. (1981) *Human Inquiry: a Sourcebook of New Paradigm Research.* Chichester: Wiley.

Reiss, A.J. (1979) 'Governmental regulation of scientific enquiry: some paradoxical consequences', in C.B. Klockars and F.W. O'Connor (eds), *Deviance and Decency.* Beverley Hills, CA: Sage.

Spiegelberg, H. (1972) *Phenomenology in Psychology and Psychiatry: a Historical Introduction.* Evanston, IL: Northwestern University Press.

Van Maanen, J. (1979) 'Reclaiming qualitative methods for organizational research: a preface', *Administrative Science Quarterly*, 24: 520–6.

Van Maanen, J. (ed.) (1983) *Qualitative Methodology.* Beverley Hills, CA: Sage.

2

The Qualitative Research Interview

Nigel King

Without doubt, the most widely used qualitative method in organizational research is the interview. It is easy to see why this should be the case: it is a highly flexible method, it can be used almost anywhere, and it is capable of producing data of great depth. Above all, it is a method with which most research participants feel comfortable; when a researcher tells them 'I would like to interview you about . . .' most people have a reasonable idea of what to expect. This is not necessarily the case with other qualitative methods, such as participant observation or the Twenty Statements Test. The consequent danger for qualitative researchers using interviews is that they may feel the method is so familiar and straightforward as not to require much thought about what they are doing. In fact, at least as much thought needs to go into the design and execution of a qualitative research interview study as into one using any other methodology – as I hope this chapter will demonstrate.

Types of research interview and their uses

The first question to address is that of definition: what types of interview can be considered qualitative? As is often the case with qualitative methods, terminology is a problem: the types of interview which fit this label are variously referred to as 'depth', 'exploratory', 'semi-structured' or 'unstructured'. Rather than become involved in semantic wranglings, in this chapter I use the general term 'qualitative research interview'. This covers a range of approaches to research interviewing, as will become apparent, but all qualitative research interviews have certain characteristics in common.

Kvale defines the qualitative research interview as 'an interview, whose purpose is to gather descriptions of the life-world of the interviewee with respect to interpretation of the meaning of the described phenomena' (1983: 174). He adds that 'neither in the interview phase nor in the later analysis is the purpose primarily to obtain quantifiable responses' (1983: 175). The goal of any qualitative research interview is therefore to see the research topic from the perspective of the interviewee, and to understand how and why he or she comes to have this particular perspective. To meet this goal, qualitative research interviews will generally have the following characteristics: a low degree of structure imposed by the interviewer; a preponderance of open questions; a focus on 'specific situations and action sequences in the world of the interviewee' (1983: 176) rather than abstractions and general opinions.

Qualitative research interviews vary in their focus – from a broad focus on the individual's whole life-world, as seen in ethnographic research (Fetterman, 1989), to a narrower focus on particular topics and how they are perceived and understood by interviewees. Though never highly structured, they also vary in the degree of structure imposed, from relatively spontaneous, unstructured discussions used during the course of a participant observation study, to quite detailed (though still flexible) interview guides, as used in the example I discuss later. These differences reflect the different social scientific disciplines which use qualitative research interviews (social anthropology, sociology, psychology, etc.), and their different underlying philosophies, which range from what Miles and Huberman (1984) call 'soft-nosed' positivism to phenomenology and radical humanism. I return to this issue in my examination of approaches to the analysis of qualitative research interview data.

A key feature of the qualitative research interview method is the nature of the relationship between interviewer and interviewee. In a quantitative study using structured interviews, the interviewee is seen as a research 'subject' in much the same way as he or she would if completing a questionnaire or taking part in an experiment. The researcher's concern is to obtain accurate information from the interviewee, untainted by relationship factors. The interviewer therefore tries to minimize the impact of interpersonal processes on the course of the interview. In contrast the qualitative researcher believes that there can be no such thing as a 'relationship-free' interview. Indeed the relationship is part of the research process, not a distraction from it. The interviewee is seen as a 'participant' in the research, actively shaping the course of the interview rather than passively responding to the interviewer's pre-set questions.

The diametrical opposite to the qualitative research interview is the structured interview. In this the interviewer uses a detailed schedule with questions asked in a specific order. Every effort is made to control the way these questions are asked in order not to bias the responses of different interviewees. Questions are mostly closed, and will use numerical rating scales, and/or tick-boxes. A small number of open-ended questions may be used to allow the interviewee to expand upon particular points or make general comments about the research topic, but the emphasis is heavily on easily quantifiable information. The interview will rarely be taped; instead, the interviewer will record responses by hand. The structured interview method is squarely in the positivist camp, alongside such techniques as postal or telephone surveys, and laboratory or field experiments.

A third type of research interview lies somewhere between the qualitative research interview and the structured interview in terms of its degree of imposed structure and balance of open and closed questions. It uses an interview schedule which is in format rather like the structured interview, with questions included in a set order. However, many more of the questions will be open-ended, and there may be flexibility to allow variation in the order in which groups of questions are asked. There is no generally used term to describe interviews of this type; I will refer to them as *structured open-response interviews*. They tend to focus on factual information, and general evaluative comments – 'was *x* a good or bad thing?' – without exploring deeper layers of meaning. It is hard to locate the structured open-response interview within a particular philosophical tradition; it shares assumptions of both positivist and more humanistic approaches, which creates problems for the method. It is generally not structured enough to allow detailed statistical analyses and hypothesis-testing, but not flexible and responsive enough to allow exploration of anything beyond surface meanings. Also, its 'neither fish nor fowl' nature can create difficulties for the interviewer–interviewee relationship, as the interviewee needs to alternate between the 'participant' and 'subject' roles discussed above.

It should go without saying that the type of interview to be used in a study depends on the nature of the research question to be addressed. Unfortunately, it is all too common to come across studies in which decisions about methodology seem to have preceded any careful consideration of the research question, leaving the researcher with data which do not properly address his or her question. The guide-lines below suggest the kinds of circumstances to which each of the types of research interview is best suited.

The *qualitative research interview* is most appropriate:

1   Where a study focuses on the meaning of particular phenomena to the participants.

2   Where individual perceptions of processes within a social unit – such as a work-group, department or whole organization – are to be studied prospectively, using a series of interviews.

3   Where individual historical accounts are required of how a particular phenomenon developed – for instance, a new shift system.

4   Where exploratory work is required before a quantitative study can be carried out. For example, researchers examining the impact of new technology on social relationships in a workplace might use qualitative interviews to identify the range of different types of experience which a subsequent quantitative study should address.

5   Where a quantitative study has been carried out, and qualitative data are required to validate particular measures or to clarify and illustrate the meaning of the findings. For instance, people with high, medium and low scores on a new measure of stress at work might be interviewed to see whether their experiences concur with the ratings on the measure.

The *structured interview* is most appropriate:

1 Where testing of a formal hypothesis (or hypotheses) is desired.
2 Where data gathered can be readily (and meaningfully) quantified.
3 Where factual information is to be collected and the researcher knows in advance the type of information the participants will be able to provide.
4 Where a postal survey would be likely to produce a very poor response rate – for instance, in market research into product awareness.
5 Where the generalizability of previously obtained qualitative findings is to be tested.

The *structured open-response* interview is most appropriate:

1 Where a quick, descriptive account of a topic is required, without formal hypothesis-testing.
2 Where factual information is to be collected, but there is uncertainty about what and how much information participants will be able to provide.
3 Where the nature and range of participants' likely opinions about the research topic are not well known in advance, and cannot easily be quantified.

Description of the method

This section describes the main practical issues involved in using the qualitative research interview method. I cover constructing and using an interview guide, conducting the interview itself, approaches to analysing transcript data (including issues of reliability and validity), and the use of computerized aids to analysis. To help bring the issues to life, I illustrate my main points with a study using qualitative research interviews in which I am currently involved.

A real-life example: decision-making by general practitioners

The study I am using as an illustration is part of an ongoing programme of research at the Centre for Primary Care Research, University of Manchester, looking at aspects of the general practitioner (GP) referral system in the British National Health Service (NHS). Referral is the main mechanism by which patients pass from the primary care sector to the secondary (hospital) care sector. In most cases, the GP sends a letter to a consultant, asking him or her to see the patient; in urgent cases, referral may be carried out over the telephone. The decision to refer or not refer a patient is of great importance: to the patient, as it determines what type of care he or she receives, and to the NHS more widely, as secondary care is considerably more expensive than primary care.

The present study involved qualitative interviews with twenty-nine GPs in the north-west of England, carried out by myself and my colleague Dr Jacqueline Bailey (King et al., 1994). It focused on individual/affective, interpersonal and organizational influences on the referral decision, as well as the narrowly clinical. As such, the study can be seen to fall into an area of overlap between occupational/organizational and health psychology, but the points it illustrates are applicable to more mainstream occupational/organizational topics.

Constructing and carrying out qualitative research interviews

The process of constructing and using qualitative research interviews can be split into four steps:

1 defining the research question;
2 creating the interview guide;
3 recruiting participants;
4 carrying out the interviews.

I discuss the first three of these here, and look at the practical issues involved in carrying out interviews in the next section.

Defining the research question   Most of the issues involved in defining the research question have been raised in the introductory section of this chapter. To recap: the research question should focus on how participants describe and make sense of particular element(s) of their lives. The primary concern should not be to quantify individual experience, and the researcher should be wary of framing the research question in a way which reflects his or her own presuppositions or biases. A research question like 'In what ways is unemployment a bad thing?' is inappropriate for a qualitative research interview study, because although focusing on participant perceptions and non-quantitative, it makes the assumption that unemployment is a bad thing for participants. If researchers were to start from this assumption, they might fail to explore ways in which unemployment is not a bad thing for at least some of their interviewees. There may of course be a number of research questions for any one study.

In the GP referrals study we set out to address two principal research questions:

1 What factors influence GPs when they are making decisions about referring patients to specialists?
2 How do individual GPs differ in their referral decision-making styles?

The focus of the first question is upon what happens in real cases for individual GPs. It requires participating GPs to reconstruct and explain the processes involved in referral decisions, producing data of a type which cannot be obtained from large-scale survey studies (Newton et al., 1991; Wilkin and Smith, 1987). For instance, it allows us to obtain accounts of how the history of the GP's relationship with an individual patient – perhaps over many years and many episodes of illness – influences the decision he or she makes. The second question, if used in a quantitative study, would involve the testing of a hypothesis that factor y is associated with decision style x. However, it is used here in an exploratory way, without preconceptions as to the dimensions on which GPs will differ in referral decision styles.

Creating the interview guide   The qualitative research interview is not based on a formal schedule of questions to be asked word-for-word in a set order. Instead it uses an *interview guide*, listing topics which the interviewer should attempt to cover in the course of the interview. There are three sources for topics to be included in an interview guide: the research literature; the interviewer's own personal knowledge and experience of the area; and informal preliminary work such as unstructured discussions with people who have personal experience of the research area. The development of the interview guide does not end at the start of the first interview. It may be modified through use: adding probes or even whole topics which had originally not been included, but have emerged spontaneously in interviews; dropping or reformulating those which are incomprehensible to participants or consistently fail to elicit responses in any way relevant to the research question(s).

In the GP referrals study, we identified the main topics to be included in the interview guide from the research literature, from the advice of academic colleagues working in the area, and (perhaps most importantly) from the anecdotal evidence of many GPs we spoke to. We then conducted a preliminary study involving eight GPs, each interviewed on four separate occasions about recent referral decisions (King and Bailey, 1992). The guide was modified on the basis of our experiences in the preliminary study. The topics included were placed in four sections, covering 'information-gathering', 'details of the referral decision', 'relationship with the patient' and 'uncertainty and risk'. The following extract is taken from the second of these sections: 'details of the referral decision'.

f)   **Q**   At what point did you first consider referral? Why then? (if not already stated)

g)   **Q**   Did you consider any action instead of referral?
      prompt – e.g. refer to practice nurse or paramedic, treat or manage yourself, ask patient to come back in a week (review), etc.
      IF YES, why did you decide not to do it?
      IF NO, why no other action considered?
      probe – were any other options possible?

h) **Q**   Who first suggested referral?
            If GP suggested referral:
            At what point did you suggest a referral to the patient?
            What was his/her reaction?

i) **Q**   What do you expect will be the consequences of the referral?
            probe – at hospital, in the longer term (future patient presentation)

j) **Q**   Has anything actually happened yet?
            probe – patient has been seen by specialist

As the extract shows, the guide consisted of main questions, sometimes with subsidiary or conditional questions ('IF YES . . ./IF NO . . .'). There were also probes, reminding the interviewer to explore certain areas in more depth. Finally, some questions were followed by prompts. These were only to be used where the GP required some illustration of what the interviewer meant by a question, and care was taken that they did not lead the GP's responses in a particular direction – for instance, by giving a number of illustrative examples rather than a single example. In keeping with the recommendation that qualitative research should concern itself with specifics rather than abstractions and generalizations (Kvale, 1983), the main part of the guide focused on actual recent examples of referral decisions, six of which were discussed in each interview. A short section of more general questions concluded the interview guide.

Recruiting participants for the study   The recruitment of participants to a qualitative interview study will of course depend on the study's aims. For instance, if researchers wished to examine the impact of a training programme on a single work-group, then it would be desirable to interview all its members. If the aim was to explore experiences of and needs for training generally within a large organization, representatives of different occupational groups would be chosen.

In deciding how many participants to recruit, the amount of time and resources available is a critical factor. It is very easy for an inexperienced qualitative researcher to underestimate seriously the time needed to undertake a study based on qualitative research interviews. It is worth noting that even an experienced transcriber is unlikely to be able to transcribe more than one one-hour interview in a working day. To analyse such a transcript in any depth two or three working days will often be needed. To these figures must be added the time taken to develop the interview guide and recruit participants, to carry out the interviews, and to travel to and from them, and to feedback findings (in verbal or written form) to participants and funding bodies. In designing a qualitative research interview study, time and resources must be budgeted for all these areas.

Participants for our study were selected from a much larger sample who had taken part in a survey of referrals about 18 months earlier. They were selected to include roughly equal numbers of GPs with relatively high and relatively low referral rates, and to cover a variety of geographical settings – urban inner city, suburban and semi-rural. On the basis of the preliminary study, we estimated that we could carry out and analyse about 30 interviews in the time available to us. In the event, we initially recruited 32 GPs, three of whom dropped out before the start of the study. One interview was not recorded, due to a malfunction of the cassette recorder (a serious hazard for this method!), leaving a total of 28 interviews included in the main analyses.

As in any type of social scientific research, potential participants must be assured of confidentiality, and should be told clearly for whom the research is being carried out and what it hopes to achieve. These points should be repeated at the start of the interview itself, and permission to tape-record the interview must be obtained. The interviewee should be told what kind of feedback about the study he or she will receive and be given at least a rough idea of when he or she is likely to receive it.

Practical issues in carrying out qualitative interviews

Flexibility is the single most important factor in successful qualitative interviewing. It is likely that a common opening question will be used to start all interviews in a study, but beyond that topics need not be addressed in the order in which they appear in the interview guide, or in any other predetermined sequence. As an interviewer, you may allow them to be raised by the interviewee or introduce them yourself at points where they fit naturally into the course of the interview. Similarly, probes need not be used in any particular order, and may not be required at all if the interviewee introduces the areas concerned.

Starting the interview   It is normally best for the interviewer to open with a question which the interviewee can answer easily and without potential embarrassment or distress. More difficult or sensitive questions should be held back until some way into the interview, in order to give time for both interviewer and interviewee to relax and feel they are getting to know each other. Requests for factual or descriptive information can be useful opening questions. In our study, we usually started the interview by asking the GP to give a descriptive account of how the patient presented him- or herself at the beginning of the consultation under discussion.

Phrasing questions   The way in which questions are asked during the interview has a major bearing on how useful the responses are likely to be. It is advisable to avoid multiple questions, such as: 'How did the patient's family circumstances and her poor English affect the way she presented herself to you, and what you decided to do for her?' This is, in fact, four questions, and in attempting to reply to them as a single question, the interviewee may give only a partial answer, or may just become confused as to what question he or she is supposed to be answering. It is best to ask questions singly and phrase them as simply as possible. Leading questions – 'So you felt angry about the patient demanding to be referred, did you?' – should be avoided, as they impose your own perceptions on the interviewee, who may agree out of a wish to please you, or just to be polite. In the example just given, it would be better to say; 'How did you feel when the patient demanded to be referred?' This would not give a cue to the interviewee that you expect a certain reply.

You need to beware of assuming that the answer to a question is so obvious that it need not be asked. For instance, while promotion might well be a significant goal for most middle managers in a large corporation, it would be wrong to assume that it would be so for any one manager. In a qualitative study, you would need to ask whether, and to what extent, promotion was important to each individual participant. You should not tell the interviewee what his or her answers mean – 'So what you're really saying is . . .'; again, your perception may be wrong, but the interviewee may not feel able or willing to challenge the misinterpretation. It is, however, sometimes useful to repeat an answer back to the interviewee in order to seek clarification.

Ending the interview It is important that you avoid ending the interview on a topic which is difficult, threatening or painful. If possible, the concluding questions should steer the interview towards positive experiences; in any event the interviewer should not pack up and leave immediately after probing the interviewee about some highly negative, distressing or personal experience or feeling. Sometimes it is useful to finish by giving the interviewee the opportunity to make any comments about the subject at hand which have not been covered in the rest of the interview.

'Difficult' interviews Not all interviews will progress smoothly. Occasionally you will come away from an interview feeling dissatisfied with your own performance, or irritated, angry or upset by the interviewee. While it is impossible to specify all the ways in which interviews can be difficult, there are some situations where difficulties are rather more common than usual, and by being aware of these it is possible to have coping strategies to hand if and when they do occur. These include the uncommunicative and the over-communicative interviewee, high-status interviewees, interviews on highly emotionally charged topics, and interviewees who try to swap roles and become the interviewer. Some tips about how to deal with each of these are given below.

The uncommunicative interviewee. There are some interviewees who seem unable, or unwilling, to give anything more than monosyllabic answers. The reasons for this vary widely: they may be defensive about the topic being discussed; they may be trying to get the interview over with as quickly as possible; they may think that brief answers are what you want; they may just be habitually laconic. The risks of monosyllabism can be reduced before the interview begins by being quite clear about how much time you require – and that the interviewee has the time available – and by stressing the anonymity of all answers. If the interviewee is unresponsive despite such precautions, the first thing to check is that you are phrasing questions in as open a way as possible. 'How useful did you find the course?' may well lead to a one or two word answer ('Quite useful'). 'In what ways – if any – did you find the course useful?' would be more likely to elicit expansive replies, with the added advantage that it would be likely to lead the respondent on to giving specific, concrete examples of how he or she found it useful (or not useful). If you are succeeding in framing questions in a very open manner, and still getting brief, shallow answers, a useful strategy is silence. Instead of moving on to your next question when the interviewee provides another terse response, pause for a few seconds. Very often this will serve as a cue to the interviewee that you would like to hear more on the subject, and is less likely to annoy him or her than repeated probes of the 'Tell me more' type.

The over-communicative interviewee. The opposite problem to that discussed above is the interviewee who repeatedly indulges in long-winded digressions from the interview topic. Some degree of digression should be tolerated; sometimes it can lead you to areas that are of genuine interest which you had not anticipated when compiling the interview guide. However, if it is clear that the interviewee is repeatedly straying far from your questions without adding anything of significant interest, you need to attempt to impose more direction on the course of the interview. Of course, this should be accomplished as subtly as possible, to avoid causing offence. It is also important to ensure that you are not resorting to leading questions in your eagerness to keep the interview within your control. A good strategy is to interrupt the digression politely at a natural pause or break and refer back to an earlier point made by the interviewee which was relevant to your research question; 'That's very interesting. Could we go back to what you were saying earlier about . . . as I'd like you to tell me more about that . . .'.

The high-status interviewee. When interviewing people of high status (such as senior managers and professionals), who are used to being treated with a degree of deference in most of their daily interactions, it is important to set your relationship with them at an appropriate level. If you are over-familiar, or appear to show off your knowledge in their domain, you may cause offence. Conversely, if you are overly nervous or submissive you are likely to be patronized. Either way, it might be difficult for you to obtain anything other than the most shallow, surface level of answers to your questions. You need to be respectful – especially in regard to their areas of professional or expert knowledge – but at the same time confident of the worth of what you are doing and of *your* own expertise.

Interviews on emotionally charged subjects. Perhaps the most difficult situation for an interviewer to cope with (particularly if inexperienced) is when the interviewee becomes visibly upset as a result of questioning. It is perfectly natural to feel uncomfortable in such circumstances, but they do not necessarily mean that you have been insensitive, or that the interview must be terminated. The possibility of such reactions from interviewees can often be predicted where the topic of a study is self-evidently emotionally charged. Examples in occupational psychology include subjects like the impact of redundancy, sexual harassment at work, and accidents at work. When interviewees are finding an area difficult to talk about because of their emotional reactions to it, make sure that you give them the time they require to answer your questions. Be particularly careful to avoid non-verbal cues that might be taken as indicating impatience: looking at your watch, fidgeting and so on. If their distress is great, let them known that it is perfectly all right for them to leave the question altogether, or to return to it later if they feel able to. You will probably find that people will often want to come back to questions which address issues of real importance to them, and just need time to muster their feelings. For the interview to be abruptly terminated can be the most hurtful option of all.

The would-be interviewer. Some interviewees persistently ask the interviewer questions about their own opinions, experiences and so on. While this can be a good sign, showing that rapport has been established, as the interviewer you need to maintain control over the situation. The main danger if you simply concur and state your views is that you may bias the interviewee's subsequent responses in the same way as can happen with leading questions – by implying that certain answers are more acceptable to you than others. A useful strategy is to say to interviewees that you will be happy to answer any of their questions at the end, but for now you would like to concentrate on their views.

By being aware beforehand of some of the ways in which problems can arise in interviews, and of techniques for handling them, you are less likely to be thrown out of your stride by a difficult interviewee. That said, there really is nothing to beat experience in gaining confidence and competence as an interviewer. Happily, novices almost always find that their skills improve rapidly over the first few interviews they carry out, especially if able to review what went wrong (and what went right) with a supervisor or colleague as soon as possible after an interview. Perhaps the single most important rule is – to quote from *The Hitchhiker's Guide to the Galaxy* – 'DON'T PANIC!'

Analysing data from qualitative interviews

There is no single set of rules for the analysis of data from qualitative research interviews. Indeed, as Hycner (1985) points out, the notion of producing a 'cookbook' of instructions is entirely at odds with the aims of flexibility and openness to the data that are at the heart of qualitative research. However, it is possible to identify common features in the methods of analysis used across different studies, and to offer guidelines for the main approaches to analysis which exist. As there is not the space in this chapter to cover them in great detail, I have given references to other texts which the reader may consult to follow up particular topics in more depth.

This discussion of data analysis makes the assumption that the researcher has available full transcripts of interviews. Difficult and time-consuming though transcription is, there really is no satisfactory alternative to recording and fully transcribing qualitative research interviews. It is impossible for the interview to progress smoothly and without self-consciousness on both sides if the interviewer has to stop after each question to write by hand what was said. If tape-recording is impossible, for instance if a participant refuses to allow it, the best the interviewer can do is make brief memory-jogging notes during the interview and reconstruct as much as possible immediately afterwards.

Familiarization with the data It is essential that the researcher is thoroughly familiar with the data before commencing any kind of analysis. This will certainly involve reading through all the transcripts more than once, but I would also strongly recommend that the researcher listens to each interview as well in order to take into account nuances of speech, tone of voice, hesitations and other such 'paralinguistic' information. In addition to familiarization, this gives the researcher the opportunity to correct any mistakes which may have been made in transcribing.

Approaches to analysing data Earlier I pointed out that there are a range of approaches to using the qualitative research interview, varying in their breadth of focus and degree of imposed structure. This leads to a corresponding variation in approaches to analysing data. In fact, because qualitative methods have evolved separately within many social scientific disciplines, the number of different data analysis techniques is large. Miller and Crabtree (1992) provide a useful framework for summarizing the various approaches to data analysis. They propose four main approaches into which individual analytical techniques can be categorized: quasi-statistical, templates, editing and immersion/crystallization. I outline each of these approaches below.

Quasi-statistical. This kind of analysis seeks to turn the textual data into quantitative data which can be manipulated statistically. The approach is best illustrated in the technique of content analysis (Weber, 1985). The content analyst selects a suitable unit of measurement – single words, phrases or themes – and then categorizes each unit found. Statistical analyses can then be carried out comparing individuals or groups on the distribution of units across categories. Kassarjian states that content analysis has three distinguishing features: objectivity, systemization and, above all, quantification: 'A measurement of the extent of emphasis or omission of any given analytic category is what content analysis is all about' (1977: 9). It is clear from this that content analysis is firmly within the quantitative, logical-positivist tradition, concerned with hypothesis-testing, generalizability and the separation of the researcher from the data for the sake of objectivity. As such, it should not be used to answer research questions which are essentially qualitative – 'What does x mean to the interviewee, and why?' However, elements of content analysis can be usefully applied in the early stages of some qualitative analysis. For instance, if a study were interested in comparing men's and women's experiences of training in an organization, it could be helpful to count the overall frequency with which each group mentions particular themes. Such a comparison, however, would not involve testing for statistical significance, and would serve as just one way in which to help focus subsequent purely qualitative analyses on key themes.

Template. In the template approach, text is analysed through the use of an analysis guide, or 'codebook' (Crabtree and Miller, 1992), consisting of a number of categories or themes relevant to the research question(s). In this it is similar to classical content analysis. Where it differs – and what makes it a truly qualitative approach – is in two characteristics. First, the codebook is revised, perhaps many times, through exposure to the textual data. Second, the pattern of themes emerging is interpreted qualitatively, rather than statistically. The GP referrals study used a template analysis technique, which I describe in detail below.

Template techniques vary in the extent to which the codebook is built upon existing knowledge (a priori) or is developed from initial analysis of the interview data (a posteriori). Miles and Huberman (1984) advocate a largely a priori codebook derived from the literature and the content of the research question. At the other end of the scale, in Altheide's (1987) 'ethnographic content analysis', the codebook is developed during initial analysis. But in both cases, the notion that codebooks may be modified through use remains crucial.

Editing. Miller and Crabtree explain their use of the term 'editing' as follows: 'This style is termed editing because the interpreter enters the text much like an editor searching for meaningful segments, cutting, pasting and rearranging until the reduced summary reveals the interpretive truth in the text' (1992: 20).

The best-known example of the editing approach is Glaser and Strauss' (1967) grounded theory, which presents guidelines for developing theory grounded in qualitative data (see Strauss, 1987, for a recent account). A key feature of most editing techniques is their cyclical nature; interpretations emerging from analysis of a particular theme or category are repeatedly compared with the original textual data. In grounded theory this process is called 'constant comparison': its goal is to achieve a point of 'theoretical saturation' where 'additional analysis no longer contributes to discovering anything new about a category' (Strauss, 1987: 21).

The editing approach has its roots in the philosophical tradition of phenomenology, which seeks to understand the experiences of individual life-worlds (Husserl, 1931). In phenomenological investigation the researcher 'brackets' – sets to one side – his or her own preconceptions about the phenomena being studied. Hycner (1985) and Kvale (1983) therefore argue that recognizing and explicitly stating preconceptions is an essential step in the process of phenomenological analysis of interview data.

Immersion/crystallization. In this fourth approach researchers immerse themselves in the research subject over a prolonged period of time, and produce an account of their findings through analytical reflection and intuitive crystallization of meaning. An example of this approach is Moustakas' (1961) study of loneliness using what he calls a 'heuristic research' method. This kind of research requires immersion in the subject at every possible level: qualitative research interviews – in the form of spontaneous and naturalistic conversations – would constitute only one strand of information/experience-gathering. Others could include observation, introspection and reading of non-academic literature – Moustakas, for instance, examined poetic and autobiographic accounts of loneliness.

Analysing the interview data

Analysis of the data from the GP referrals study, which is still in progress, followed the template approach. This was suited to the relatively focused nature of the study, examining one specific type of decision made by one professional group. The procedure we followed was towards the more formal and structured end of the spectrum; in other studies a template might be used more loosely as an aid to extracting meaningful themes from the data. Below I show how our template was developed, and present some preliminary findings from its application.

Developing the template for the GP referrals study The template used in our study was developed from one designed in the preliminary study involving eight GPs. This began with 30 influencing factors identified on an impressionistic basis from half of the preliminary study transcripts. These factors were then applied to the full set of transcripts in a more rigorous manner, with new factors suggested where none of the existing ones seemed applicable. At the end of the preliminary study analysis, a total of 67 different influencing factors were included in the template. The development of the template in the main referral decisions study took place in six stages, as shown in Figure 2.1.

The first step taken was to select four full interview transcripts – two conducted by each researcher – which Jackie Bailey and I coded using the preliminary study template. We both added any new codes we felt necessary as we went along, and at the end the codings were compared, disagreements discussed, and decisions made about the inclusion of

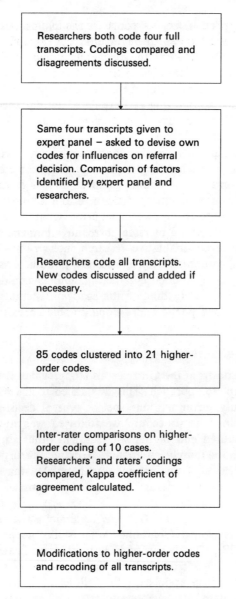

Figure 2.1   *Development of the template for the GP referrals study*

proposed new codes. The same four transcripts were then given to an 'expert panel' consisting of a psychologist, a GP and a consultant psychiatrist, all with relevant research experience. The aim was to assess the validity of the approach we were taking by seeing whether independent experts with different perspectives would identify the same kind of factors as ourselves. They were not given our template but were asked to devise their own codes for influences they identified – in effect to compile their own templates. These were then compared to the template we had developed, and the similarities and differences discussed face-to-face with expert panel members. As a result, five new codes were added to the template, and the working definitions of several more were modified (further discussion of validity in qualitative research interviews follows in a later section of this chapter).

Following the expert panel exercise, we coded all 28 interview transcripts, adding new codes where necessary. At the end of this, a total of 85 codes were included in the template. Clearly this was an unmanageably large number of different codes to use in analysis, and collapsing them into a smaller number of higher-order codes was necessary (what Hycner [1985] calls 'clustering'). One of the best ways of doing this – and one we employed – is to write or print the original codes on cards and arrange and rearrange them on a desk or floor into clusters which appear to fit together by virtue of similar meanings. In our study, for example, the single higher-order code of 'judgements of clinical risk' was compiled from lower-order codes relating to 'risks associated with patient's condition', 'risks associated with treatment and/or investigation', and 'considerations of side-effects of specific treatments'. It is important not to begin clustering lower-order codes too early in the coding process, as it is easy to succumb to the temptation to squeeze potentially important and distinct new codes into existing higher-order codes for the sake of tidiness. For this reason we left clustering until we had coded all the transcripts with the lower-order codes. In the GP referrals study clustering produced a total of 21 higher-order codes.

The fifth stage of coding addressed the issue of inter-rater reliability. We followed a formal, statistical approach using the Kappa coefficient of agreement (Cohen, 1960) to compare ratings by ourselves and three independent raters across 10 cases – one selected from each of 10 randomly chosen transcripts. Once this analysis was completed, and we were satisfied that the template of higher-order codes could be used reliably, we recoded all the transcripts. Minor modifications to the code definitions continued up to the very end of the process, in response to problems thrown up by the data.

At the time of writing, analysis of the interview data is still in progress. However, the first of our research questions – 'What are the factors influencing referral decisions?' – has already been addressed in compiling the template. We have been able to draw out 21 higher-order factors which are able to encompass all the influences on GP referral decisions apparent in our interviews. As a further step in exploring in greater depth the meanings behind referral decisions, we have looked at ways in which differences and similarities between the higher-order factors can be understood. We have explored a number of ways of classifying the factors, such as by 'influence source': GP, patient, organization, etc. In

A Episode-specific/Clinical	B Background/Clinical
C. Episode-specific/Non-clinical	D Background/Non-clinical

Figure 2.2 *The quadrants of influencing factors in the GP referrals study*

doing so, we have always borne in mind the importance of not becoming too distanced from the data; any classification system must be meaningful at the level of individual interviews and the decision cases of which they are comprised. Presently, we have found a two-way classification of the factors to be useful in highlighting meaningful differences between GPs. Factors can be seen to vary according to whether they relate to largely 'clinical' or 'non-clinical' aspects of the referral decision. They also vary in whether they are related to the specific problem as presented by the patient on this occasion ('episode-specific') or are of a more long-term or general nature ('background'). Cross-tabulating these two dimensions produces a quadrant framework for exploring differences between individual GPs' referral decision-making styles (see Figure 2.2).

We will explore whether there are distinctive characteristics of GPs who appear to be influenced particularly strongly by factors associated with one or other quadrant. The framework is thus a means of focusing further analyses on cases which may be especially valuable in increasing our understanding of how GPs make referral decisions.

Issues of reliability and validity

Quantitative research in occupational and organizational psychology places great emphasis on the need for reliability and validity in the measures it uses. Not surprisingly, methods developed to assess reliability and validity in quantitative research cannot be applied directly to qualitative research. Nevertheless, the underlying issues involved are as important in qualitative research.

Reliability Quantitative researchers are concerned that the measures they use will produce the same results when applied to the same subjects by different researchers: 'The same "yardstick" applied to the same individual or object in the same way should yield the same value from moment to moment, provided that the thing measured has itself not changed in the meantime' (Guilford and Fruchter, 1978: 407). For characteristics of the researcher to influence the way in which 'subjects' respond to the instruments in a structured interview would be considered a flaw in the research method. Qualitative research, in seeking to describe and understand how people make sense of their world, does not require researchers to strive for 'objectivity' and to distance themselves from research participants. Indeed, to do so would make good qualitative research impossible, as the interviewer's sensitivity to 'subjective' aspects of his or her relationship with the interviewee is an essential part of the research process.

Kvale argues that it is an advantage if different interviewers using the same interview guide vary in their sensitivity to particular themes, as this will yield a broader and richer overall picture of a topic: 'The requirement of standardized objectivity here yields to the aim of individual sensitivity' (1983: 189). This does not mean that in analysing qualitative interview data, the issue of possible researcher bias can be ignored. It is just as important as in a structured quantitative interview that the findings are not simply the product of the researcher's prejudices and prior expectations. This can be guarded against in two ways. First, researchers should explicitly recognize their presuppositions and in the analysis of the data make a conscious effort to set these aside (as in the technique of 'bracketing' in phenomenology, mentioned earlier). They should allow themselves to be surprised by the findings. Second, at the stage of coding for themes or categories, inter-rater comparisons can be used. Co-researchers can code 'blind' (that is, independently, without consultation), and afterwards explore the reasons for any disagreements. Similarly, independent raters not associated with the study may be used.

Where coding schemes use exclusive categories, it may be appropriate to use a statistical test of inter-rater reliability such as Kappa (Cohen, 1960; see also Fleiss, 1981). This was the approach we followed in the GP referrals study. We felt that as our work represented quite a radical departure from the bulk of past research on referrals, we needed to be able to present persuasive evidence that the influences we identified were not purely idiosyncratic to us. Our joint codings of 10 cases were compared with those of three independent raters (a psychologist, a GP and a health economist). Agreements on each of the 21 codes were established. From these the Kappa coefficient for the coding template was calculated, using the HANDY KAPPA program (Jackson, 1983). This produced an overall Kappa of 0.52, indicating a satisfactory level of inter-rater reliability (Fleiss [1981] cites a coefficient of 0.4 as the minimum acceptable level of agreement).

Validity In quantitative research, a valid instrument is one which actually measures what it claims to measure. Similarly, in qualitative research, a study is valid if it truly examines the topic which it claims to have examined. In essence, then, the concept of validity is the same in both research traditions. Where the traditions differ is that in quantitative research, notions of validity centre on methods – for instance, the validity of rating scales used in a structured interview. In qualitative research, the concern is for the validity of interpretations – whether a researcher's conclusion that x is the main theme to emerge from an interview is valid.

The involvement of other people – colleagues, interviewees, expert judges and so on – is crucial to considerations of validity in interpreting data from qualitative research interviews. Reason and Rowan make the point that 'the only criterion for the "rightness" of an interpretation is *inter-subjective* – that is to say, that it is right for a group of people who share a similar world' (1981: 243, original emphasis). This was the rationale behind our use of the expert panel to help validate the approach we had taken in the patterns of referral study. It should be recognized, however, that the use of multiple viewpoints is not the only technique for ensuring validity in qualitative research interview analysis. Reason and Rowan's chapter on the subject in their comprehensive introduction to 'new paradigm' research (1981: xiv–xv) offers a set of eight guidelines for tackling the validity question. These include: the need for 'high-quality awareness' in co-researchers, to be maintained through systematic methods of 'personal and interpersonal development'; the use of 'feedback loops' – returning to interviewees with interpretations and developing theory; actively seeking contradictions in the data (a process equivalent to conventional attempts at falsification); and convergent validation through triangulation of different methods or comparison with the findings of similar studies.

The use of computers in qualitative analysis

Ten years ago the analysis of qualitative research interview data was almost entirely a paper-based task. Typically the researcher would annotate and perhaps colour-code transcripts, use 'cut-and-paste' techniques to gather together information on themes across transcripts, and accumulate large piles of notes to help find where particular themes were referred to in particular interviews. Since then, and particularly in the last five years, there has been something of a revolution in analysis techniques. A range of computer packages aimed at assisting qualitative text analysis have appeared on the market, and a growing number of social scientists are using them. The best known and most widely used is THE ETHNOGRAPH; others include NUDIST, QualPro, Word Match, TAP and WordCruncher.

Typically, computerized aids to qualitative analysis offer the researcher the chance to carry out sophisticated and rapid searches through textual data which has been entered from a word-processing package such as Word Star or Word Perfect. In THE ETHNOGRAPH, for example, the researcher produces an ASCII version of each interview transcript, which is line-numbered by the program. The researcher then enters line numbers indicating where particular themes have been identified in the text. Overlapping and nesting (that is, themes within themes) of codes is allowed. Once all codes are entered, the researcher can search for selected codes, or combinations of codes, across all or a selected sub-set of the interviews.

Despite many advantages, there are some drawbacks and potential pitfalls in the use of computers. The greatest danger is that researchers may design their studies and analysis techniques on the basis of what the program they happen to own can best handle. Some of the packages on the market are quite expensive, though not more so than quantitative packages. Also, many produce large numbers of subsidiary files in the course of analysis; conscientious disk management is essential. (For a good overview of issues involved in computer-assisted qualitative analysis, see Fielding and Lee's [1991] edited volume on the subject.)

Advantages and disadvantages of the method

Most of the main strengths and weaknesses of qualitative research interview will have become apparent in the course of my description of the method. I draw them together here, with special reference to the context of applied psychological research in organizations.

Advantages

Different types of qualitative research interview can be used to tackle different types of research question in organizations, making it one of the most flexible methods available. It can address quite focused questions about aspects of organizational life: for instance, specific decision-processes such as selection decisions, or decisions about innovation adoption. Similarly, it can focus on experiences of a particular training or development programme, perhaps as part of a wider assessment process. At the other end of the scale, qualitative research interviews can be used to examine much broader issues, in areas such as gender, organizational culture and the effects of unemployment.

The qualitative research interview is ideally suited to examining topics in which different levels of meaning need to be explored. This is something that is very difficult to do with quantitative methods, and problematic for many other qualitative techniques. One area where qualitative interviews may be of great use is in studying organizational and group identities in large organizations such as the National Health Service, where a complex pattern of organizational, work-group, professional and interpersonal loyalties exists.

Finally, the qualitative research interview is a method which most research participants accept readily. As I mentioned at the start of this chapter, this is partly due to familiarity with interviews in general. However, as important is the fact that most people like talking about their work – whether to share enthusiasm or to air complaints – but rarely have the opportunity to do so with interested outsiders. Feedback I have received suggests that interviewees enjoy being interviewed, and in some cases find that it has helped them clarify their thoughts on a particular topic.

Disadvantages

Developing an interview guide, carrying out interviews, and analysing transcripts are all highly time-consuming activities for the researcher. It is essential that the researcher does not attempt to take on more interviews than he or she has time for in a study (see my early estimates of the time taken to transcribe and analyse interviews). Qualitative research interviews are also tiring to conduct, as they involve considerable concentration from the interviewer. I would certainly recommend a maximum of three hour-long qualitative interviews in a day, and two would be preferable. Interviews are also time-consuming for interviewees, and this may cause problems in recruiting participants in some organizations and occupations. The best recruitment strategy is probably to send a letter with basic details of the study's aims and what will be required of the interviewee, with a follow-up phone-call in which the researcher can explain his or her aims in more depth and answer any queries. A firm time and date for the interview should be fixed as soon as possible. Once people have made such a commitment, it is rare for them to drop out of the study subsequently.

Occasionally, the researcher will experience 'difficult' interviewees – defensive, hostile or unable/unwilling to focus on the research topic(s). To be told to your face 'That was a ridiculous question!' or 'I can't see why you're asking me these things' is much more uncomfortable than receiving a questionnaire back from a survey participant with 'Stupid question!' scrawled across it. The researcher may be able to use interpersonal skills (above all, patience) to defuse awkward situations, and must ensure that his or her research questions are likely to be relevant to the people being interviewed. But in the end, there will always be a minority of interviewees who intentionally or unintentionally make life difficult for you as an interviewer. These should be balanced against the many interviews which will be a positive experience, giving the researcher the opportunity to learn directly how other people see their world.

A difficulty faced by many researchers using qualitative research interviews is the feeling of data overload as a result of the huge volume of rich data produced by even a moderate-sized study. It is easy for the researcher, particularly if inexperienced in the method, to feel that he or she is lost and sinking in a quagmire. This is most likely to happen when the researcher is alone as a qualitative methods user in an institution dominated by traditional quantitative techniques. In these circumstances, I would suggest that there are three directions in which the researcher can turn for a rope to pull him- or herself out of the swamp. First, there are the original aims of the study. If beginning to feel lost in a particular line of exploration, the researcher should ask: 'Is this adding to my understanding of the topics I set out to study? If not, is it raising new and related topics which are of interest?' If the answer to both questions is 'no', then the researcher should change the direction of the analysis. Second, the inexperienced researcher can turn to literature describing other studies using qualitative research interviews, to provide examples of how problems in data analysis were tackled, including material outside his or her own area. Third, personal networking is of great importance. If there is no one even sympathetic to qualitative methods in the researcher's own department, try other departments – for instance, Sociology or Social Anthropology. As the number of occupational and organizational psychologists using qualitative research interviews grows, the opportunities for such networking increase.

Concluding remarks

There is no one way of using qualitative research interviews, as I have sought to make clear in this chapter. Equally, not all my suggestions will be relevant to any single qualitative interview study, nor will all of them meet with agreement from all qualitative researchers. Nevertheless, I hope that this chapter has been able to provide some useful guidance as to how to get the best out of one of the most flexible and rewarding methods in applied psychology. There is no doubt that the qualitative research interview (as with other qualitative methods) is gaining a higher profile within occupational and organizational psychology. As more people use the method and more journals are willing to publish their work, I believe we will begin to see the evolution of distinct forms of the qualitative research interview, adapted to the special demands of carrying out psychological research in organizations. There is still a long way to go, especially in teaching students at the undergraduate and postgraduate levels about the method, but the future for the qualitative research interview in applied psychology looks bright.

References

Altheide, D.L. (1987) 'Ethnographic content analysis', *Qualitative Sociology*, 10: 65–77.
Cohen, J.A. (1960) 'A coefficient of agreement for nominal scales', *Educational and Psychological Measurement*, 20: 37–46.
Crabtree, B.F. and Miller, W.L. (1992) 'A template approach to text analysis: developing and using codebooks', in B.F. Crabtree and W.L. Miller (eds), *Doing Qualitative Research*. Newbury Park, CA: Sage.
Fetterman, D.M. (1989) *Ethnography: Step by Step (Applied Social Research Methods Series, Vol. 17)*. Newbury Park, CA: Sage.
Fielding, N.G. and Lee, R.M. (1991) *Using Computers in Qualitative Research*. London: Sage.

Fleiss, J.L. (1981). *Statistical Methods for Rates and Proportions*. New York: Wiley.

Glaser, B. and Strauss, A.L. (1967) *The Discovery of Grounded Theory: Strategies for Qualitative Research*. Chicago: Aldine.

Guilford, J.P. and Fruchter, B. (1978) *Fundamental Statistics in Psychology and Education* (6th edn). Kogakusha, Tokyo: McGraw-Hill.

Husserl, E. (1931) *Ideas: a General Introduction to Pure Phenomenology*. New York: Humanities Press.

Hycner, R.H. (1985) 'Some guidelines for the phenomenological analysis of interview data', *Human Studies*, 8: 279–303.

Jackson, P.R. (1983) 'An easy to use basic program for agreement amongst raters', *British Journal of Clinical Psychology*, 22: 145–6.

Kassarjian, H.H. (1977) 'Content analysis in consumer research', *Journal of Consumer Research*, 4: 8–18.

King, N. and Bailey, J. (1992) 'Referral decision-making: an exploratory study in two Health Centres', paper presented at the Annual Scientific Meeting of the Association of University Teachers in General Practice, Manchester, July.

King, N., Bailey, J. and Newton, P. (1994) 'Analysing general practitioner referral decisions: I. Developing an analytical framework', *Family Practice*, 11: 3–8.

Kvale, S. (1983) 'The qualitative research interview: a phenomenological and a hermeneutical mode of understanding', *Journal of Phenomenological Psychology*, 14: 171–96.

Miles, M.B. and Huberman, A.M. (1984) *Qualitative Data Analysis: a Sourcebook of New Methods*. Beverly Hills, CA: Sage.

Miller, W.L. and Crabtree, B.F. (1992) 'Overview of qualitative research methods', in B.F. Crabtree and W.L. Miller (eds), *Doing Qualitative Research*. Newbury Park, CA: Sage.

Moustakas, C. (1961). *Loneliness*. Englewood Cliffs, NJ: Prentice-Hall.

Newton. J., Hayes, V. and Hutchinson, A. (1991) 'Factors influencing General Practitioners' referral decisions', *Family Practice*, 8: 308–13.

Reason, P. and Rowan, J. (1981) *Human Inquiry: a Sourcebook of New Paradigm Research*. Chichester: Wiley.

Strauss, A.L. (1987) *Qualitative Analysis for Social Scientists*. Cambridge: Cambridge University Press.

Weber, R.P. (1985) *Basic Content Analysis*. Beverly Hills, CA: Sage.

Wilkin, D. and Smith, A. (1987) 'Explaining variation in General Practitioner referrals to hospital', *Family Practice*, 4: 160–9.

3

The Twenty Statements Test

Anne Rees and Nigel Nicholson

I am an independent-minded person; I am committed to personal improvement; I am competitive; I am gentle; I am good at many things, brilliant at
none; I am an entrepreneur; I am inconsistent; I am enthusiastic; I am not very
gregarious; I am deceptive in business dealings; I am fair; I am intolerant of
superiors; I am a risk-taker; I am excited by personal business; I am not
motivated by a career pattern; I am a planner; I am not materialistic; I am a
sportsman; I am easy to get on with; I am a family-orientated person.

These are the 20 self-identifying statements made by one of our respondents. Rich data indeed. Viewed holistically, these definitions are a self-
portrait the individual had offered by making conscious choices about
what really matters to him about himself – what might be called a 'desert
island discs' of the personality. Although our aim here will be to demonstrate the potential of the Twenty Statements Test (TST) as a qualitative
research tool which can also yield codeable and quantifiable assessments,
a significant implicit assumption of our methodology is that each response
gains meaning from the others. The example above, at one level, tells an
irreducible story, yet what respondents provide when they complete the
TST is not simply a straightforward reflection of some underlying 'truth'.
We shall argue that such self-identifications make explicit how individuals
mediate their social environment in different, more or less adaptive, ways.
Additionally, by using the methods we describe, themes can be extracted
in ways which allow for meaningful comparison with others, or of the
same self over time.

Once 20 statements about the self are obtained, the possibilities for
qualitative analysis are endless. As a researcher, how do you go about
collecting such data, and once you have them, what can you do with
them? What sort of hypotheses might you test using this kind of material?
Is it possible to derive indices or measures from such qualitative self-
description that would allow comparative assessment of how individuals'
self-images differ or change over time? This chapter aims to answer these
questions and persuade the reader that the TST can be a powerful
alternative or addition to standard psychometric techniques, offering the
possibility of quantifiable assessment hand-in-hand with rich, qualitative,
freely elicited material.

Background

The TST was developed within a symbolic interactionist perspective, a framework with a pedigree of writing and research (usually case-based ethnographies) long before the instrument itself came into use. This theoretical perspective locates the self as a crucial element in the analysis of social behaviour, with identity dependent upon symbolic mediation for its interior meanings and control of action. Agents are seen as framing their actions in terms of internalized social definitions and self reflections. Within the broad spectrum of adherents to symbolic interactionism, some would resist any methodology which constrains the forms of interpretable behaviour or expression to be collected. Others have taken a more eclectic approach, such as Ziller's (1981) use of subject-generated photographic material. It was in the latter spirit that Kuhn looked for an empirical means of assessing the self in society, and began the first work on the TST in the late 1940s.

The first time the current version of the TST was used was in 1950 when students at the University of Iowa completed it as part of a study of the effects on the self-concept of unfavourable evaluations by others. The study documented the initial administration of the TST, conceptual categories for coding, and scoring techniques. The instrument was used extensively in the 1950s and 1960s, and is comprehensively reviewed in Spitzer et al.'s manual *The Assessment of the Self* (1973).

Individuals think of themselves in terms of what they do and how they do it, whether this is 'mother', 'designer', 'athlete' or whatever. They also identify themselves in terms of values and moral attitudes, which locate the self within a shared cultural frame of norms and constructs, and provide a symbolic system for action. Therefore the aim of measurement is to allow sufficient statements to be made for individuals to articulate the most salient aspects of the symbolic system they apply to themselves. An underlying assumption is that the 'self' depends on 'others' – self-classifications have to be culturally shared if they are to be a feature of an individual's social behaviour with others. Related to this is the idea that the individual is not just a passive agent, responding to external stimuli, but that the process of self-identification helps to determine which objects are given attention, what interpretations are made of them, and what behaviours they elicit.

General description of the method and its analysis

In its early days, the TST was used in the United States in varied settings with differing populations in order to test many hypotheses. It was also used in different formats. In most instances, a maximum of 20 statements was requested, with an overall mean of over 15 statements per respondent. The standard format for instructions was:

In the spaces provided below, please give twenty different statements in answer to the question, 'Who am I?' Give these answers as if you were giving them to yourself, not to somebody else. Write fairly rapidly, for the time for this part of the questionnaire is limited. (Kuhn, 1950)

Categorizing the statements

As described in Spitzer et al. (1973: 15ff.), many different procedures were developed for classifying statements on the TST, mostly falling into a 'specific category approach' or a 'total domain approach'. The latter classifies every statement available, whereas the former only classifies specific types of statement. The originator of the total domain approach was McPartland, who in 1965 devised a fourfold comprehensive schema of 'referential frames'. This system recognized that statements made in response to the question 'Who am I?' reflect the different relationships people have with their objective world; his classification of self-definitions places any statement in one of four mutually exclusive categories:

- category A: conceptions of the self as a physical structure in time and space ('I am six feet tall'), termed 'physical';
- category B: the self identified in terms of position within social roles and structures ('I am a psychologist'), termed 'social';
- category C: as a social actor abstracted from social structure ('I am not very self-confident'), termed 'reflective';
- category D: conceptions of the self as abstracted from physical being, social structure and social action, that is to say, non self-identifying statements ('I am a human being'), termed 'oceanic'.

All statements defining the self can be fitted into one of these four categories, although special classes may have to be constructed for ambiguous statements.

McPartland suggested that A-type/physical statements do not imply an awareness of others, yet they identify self in consensual terms:

> The use of this mode of self-identification defines self as a physical organism moving in time and space without reference to, or involvement in, social relations or socially consequential action. These statements indicate the person refers to the self by the use of conventional labels but do not implicate the self with others. (1965: 16)

Statements about physical characteristics, age, home location and similar attributes fall into this category.

Those which identify the self in relation to social groupings, including norms of behaviour, are classed as B-type/social. Identifications of role, status, occupation or membership of groups belong here. Such statements locate the individual in a network of statuses and interpersonal relationships, within which specific behaviours or expectations are implicit. They imply an interactive context by referring to positions in defined social settings in which roles are established, performed and maintained.

When statements imply or make specific reference to a pattern of behaviour, attitudes, needs or values, they are characterized as C-type/ reflective. These also include *styles* of behaviour which respondents attribute to themselves within a situational reference. Qualified statements of type B therefore also properly belong in this category, for example, 'I am an effective administrator', since it is clearly the performance which is qualifying the role, not vice versa: that is, the individual is making a reflective statement about personal qualities, manifested in a current context. Therefore, any reflections on mood, motivation, temperament, style or ability fall into this category.

Identifications of self so vague or abstract that they cannot be classed as physical, social or self-reflective are classed as D-type/oceanic. Here, 'there are no others implied or the implicit others are beyond the possibility of consensual validation or even verifiable communication' (McPartland et al., 1961: 115). Such self-definitions do not lead to any reliable expectations about behaviour.

For most individuals, the majority of statements fall into a single class, A, B, C or D, which suggests that these four categories may be used to describe not only responses, but also *respondents*. On the evidence available at the time, Spitzer stated that seven out of 10 respondents were clearly characterized by self-definitions of one of the four types. Through the use of the TST in the United States in the 1950s, researchers came to the conclusion that the vast majority of Americans were firmly anchored socially, because respondents from all kinds of research populations gave statements falling mainly in the B category, and could therefore be characterized as 'social selves'. Hartley (1968) hypothesized that the majority of students would be B-mode, with membership in, and identification based on, stable social structures, and, in a random sample of 1,653 undergraduate students, found that 2 per cent were A-mode, 51 per cent B-mode, 31 per cent C-mode and 16 per cent D-mode. Her subsequent research confirmed that B-mode individuals had a greater chance of completing four years of study, and that they had the best chance of succeeding in work organizations, especially bureaucracies.

In 1970, Zurcher, working in Texas, was puzzled when his research amongst a student sample proved unable to replicate Hartley's findings, and instead found that 68 per cent of respondents were C-mode, 'reflective selves' (Zurcher, 1977). He postulated that if symbolic interactionist theory was correct, a B-mode self-definition would need relatively stable social forms and interactions upon which the individual could base his or her sense of identity. A C-mode self-definition would be more adaptive to, perhaps even parallel the development of, socio-cultural conditions of low stability. A C-mode individual's self-concept could be positioned more independently of any given unstable social structure, and protected from the need for self-definition in unreliable externalities. His subsequent research demonstrated that in populations undergoing abnormal or temporary instability, individuals were predominantly C-mode. Zurcher proposed the concept of a 'mutable self' to characterize this phenomenon, in which 'all four components of self are balanced and synthesized, purposefully and productively for the individual and for society' (1977: 14).

Much of the current research using the TST is in the field of cross-cultural comparisons (Bond and Cheung, 1983; Cousins, 1989; Kitayama and Markus, forthcoming) as well as in more specific areas such as gender comparisons of self-imagery and self-esteem (Mackie, 1983), and, along with other methods, including repertory grids, a case study of a woman's changing identity during her first pregnancy (Smith, 1993). Recently, a variant on the method was used by Locatelli and West (1991) when they compared the capacity of different measures, including the TST in a modified version, to collect images of organizational culture, and concluded that the TST yielded the richest and most usable data.

Application of the referential frames method

Our own research focused on the changes in self-identity which accompanied the career entry of a group of graduate entrants into a large technically based organization (Arnold and Nicholson, 1991; Nicholson and Arnold, 1989a, 1989b, 1990). In developing our methodology for the research, we sought measures which would reflect transformations in aspects of self-identity over the course of the entry transition. We assembled a battery of methods for this purpose, including repertory grids, interviews and standardized questionnaires. Many of these methods tend to bias towards stability ('retest reliability' in testing jargon), and we wanted to be sure that, even over a short period of time, we would include instrumentation highly sensitive to subtle shifts in identity, through which we would be able to test differential predictions about personal change.

We hypothesized that, over time, there would be an increase in frequency and saliency of occupational self-identifications; for example, reference to their specialist roles in engineering, computing or marketing, and increasing endorsement of organizational values and norms. We also expected a decreasing proportion of C-type/reflective statements, and an increase in B-type/social statements. Zurcher's work suggested the suitability of the TST for this purpose. We were especially attracted by the possibilities it offered for revealing empirically degrees of change in free-floating reflective constructions versus more socially anchored self-perceptions through this period of early career role adoption and professional identity development.

Administering the TST alongside other psychological assessment measures also had the manifest advantage of allowing us to triangulate on respondent characteristics with open-ended and fixed response measures, allowing richer scope for interrogating the meaning of convergencies and apparent contradictions in the data. (The covariates of the TST data are the subject of a separate article: Rees and Nicholson, forthcoming.)

The group of 97 graduate entrants was made up of 33 1982 entrants, all of whom completed the TST within two weeks of joining the organization, and a further 16 (four from each of four departments) who had joined the organization in each of the years 1978 to 1981. Of the 97 who completed the standard TST in autumn 1982, 94 completed it again a year later. We felt that an atmosphere of trust, developing over the course of intensive interviews, was important for the successful administration of an instrument such as the TST, which requires respondents to be unconstrained in their choice of self-definitions. Individuals completed the form in privacy, and then handed it to us for analysis. Confidentiality was assured and guaranteed by a system of unique codes. Our sample consisted of 32 women and 62 men. At the first phase, respondents produced an average of 19.7 responses; and at the second phase, an average of 19.5 responses. This yielded a total of 3,774 statements to classify and analyse.

The system we used for rating statements was multi-level, providing three classifications: response type (referential frame); for C-type/reflective statements only, we constructed our response content level (the SICV – Skills, Interests, Character and Values System); and response value (self-evaluation). Our primary system was the A–B–C–D method, described above. Spitzer et al. (1973) suggest that all statements can be placed in A, B, C or D, apart from statements which (a) relate to completing the instrument itself; (b) indicate that the question itself has been rejected or misunderstood; or (c) are intended to trivialize the exercise. We used an 'uncodeable' category for all such statements, accounting for 3 per cent of the total.

We predicted that most of the new graduate entrants, at the point of entry into the organization, would be modal category C, demonstrating definitions of self not relating primarily to social structure, occupation or organization. It should be added that our other instrumentation, and the kinds of assessments habitually made in organizations via selection and appraisal methods, tended to reinforce this use of reflective constructs. With these considerations in mind, we were particularly interested in respondents' shifts over time from their own baseline levels, described below.

To demonstrate better the range of responses typically produced, and some of the analytical problems they pose, we give here two actual examples of completed TST protocols, followed by a brief interpretative commentary. So that the reader can get the full flavour of these employees' self-descriptions, we show responses from both phases, one year apart. A common progression through their 20 statements was for our respondents to give two or three A- and/or B-type statements, and devote the rest, the bulk of their self-descriptions, to C-type/reflective statements (54 of the 97 at phase 1 took this form). In the case illustrated

Table 3.1   *The most common pattern of response: a slight shift away from reflective*

Phase 1		Phase 2
1	I am married [B]	I am married [B]
2	I am broad-minded [C]	I live in (name of place) [A]
3	I am friendly [C]	I am social [C]
4	I am interested in the environment [C]	I am career-minded [C]
5	I am of a nervous disposition [C]	I am outgoing [C]
6	I am not very self-confident [C]	I am not very self-confident [C]
7	I am fairly intelligent [C]	I am always considering alternatives [C]
8	I am outgoing [C]	I tend to worry [C]
9	I am ambitious [C]	I am moderately ambitious [C]
10	I am not always articulate [C]	I am moderately materialistic [C]
11	I am a worrier [C]	I enjoy travelling [C]
12	I enjoy the arts [C]	I tend to be discontented [C]
13	I am not a sportswoman [C]	I am cautious about acting on new ideas [C]
14	I enjoy living in London [C]	I like to be popular [C]
15	I am interested in travel [C]	I am efficient (generally) [C]
16	I am close to my parents [C]	I enjoy the theatre [C]
17	I am moderately efficient [C]	I am very happy with my home [C]
18	I enjoy socializing [C]	I enjoy an intellectual challenge [C]
19	I can be lethargic [C]	I sometimes over-react [C]
20	I tend to jump to conclusions [C]	I try to be perfectionist [C]

in Table 3.1, the slight shift from 19 C-mode statements at the first phase to 18 after a year was a fairly typical pattern for these graduate entrants.

Clearly, this 24-year-old woman, working in the organization for three years in a technical capacity, demonstrates some stability in self-description over the year. Six of her 20 statements remain unchanged, almost word for word. On balance, her self-image is positive, although both sets of responses indicate some ambivalence in self-presentation.

The second most common pattern, illustrated in Table 3.2, was a sequence of wholly reflective self-definitions, which we found in 26 of the 97 cases at phase 1. This 'mode stability' was more typical of graduates who had been working in the organization for more than a year than it was for new entrants.

These are the self-identifications of a 26-year-old man, working in a technical department during his four years in the organization. It is noticeable here how different the statements are from one year to the next, yet recurring *themes* are evident: self-confidence, political awareness, intellectual characteristics, for example. He demonstrates a mixture of positive and negative self-evaluation, and overall a coherent self-image.

Twelve of the 97 respondents gave responses more or less equally distributed across the physical, social and reflective categories. Again, this pattern was more typical of people who had worked in the organization for several years, and demonstrates a striking stability of self-definition, an outcome which is partly due to the high level of physical and social

Table 3.2 *The second most common pattern of response: 100 per cent reflective*

Phase 1		Phase 2
1	I am careful [C]	Uncertain [C]
2	I am anxious to please [C]	Ambitious for power [C]
3	I am shy [C]	Ambitious for love/respect [C]
4	I am quiet [C]	Capable [C]
5	I am patient, but not indefinitely so [C]	Sensitive to personal criticism [C]
6	I am gradually getting a clearer idea of what I want [C]	Impatient of stupid ideas/arguments [C]
7	I am intellectually intolerant [C]	Hardworking [C]
8	I am otherwise fairly easy-going	Easily involved [C]
9	I am very stable [C]	Reluctant to take on long-term commitments [C]
10	I am self-motivating [C]	Sensitive to other people's feelings [C]
11	I am often frustrated [C]	Sceptical [C]
12	I am usually cheerful [C]	Easily frustrated [C]
13	I am not very confident on a personal level, except with people I know well [C]	Fairly easily intimidated [C]
14	I am usually tactful [C]	Quick to learn new skills [C]
15	I enjoy a good argument [C]	Slower to understand interpersonal politics [C]
16	I am awkward if forced into difficult situations [C]	Motivated by a desire to get a clear idea of things [C]
17	I am becoming politically (personally) alert [C]	Not given to instant emotional responses [C]
18	I am easy to get on with [C]	Basically unconfident, but becoming aware of a long-term increase in confidence [C]
19	I am independent [C]	Fairly sociable [C]
20	I am self-critical [C]	Not without a sense of humour, the ridiculous [C]

description. But even reflective definitions tended not to change over time. Typically, we found that people identifying themselves as equally A-, B- and C-mode made no negative evaluations, projecting an unproblematic, objective, 'this is how others see me and this is how I am' image. These individuals were closest to Zurcher's 'mutable selves'. Part of our continuing research will be to examine whether such individuals are more likely to be successful in an organizational context.

Reliability of referential frame scoring

Agreement between the two raters on the primary cut made on this rich qualitative data, the referential frames A–B–C–D + uncodifiable category, was 94 per cent, in line with the level of agreement reported for various studies by Spitzer et al. (1973). However, agreement in some cases

Table 3.3 *Resolving competing interpretations: ambiguity between social and reflective classes*

		Rater 1	Rater 2
1	I am an Englishman at heart	C	uc[1]
2	I am half-foreign by ancestry and it does affect me	C	uc[1]
3	I am a Christian still learning what it means to be one	C	C
4	I am a loyal friend	C	C
5	I am sometimes almost mediaeval in my moral judgements	C	C
6	I enjoy being a host and sharing with people	C	C
7	I am uncertain of my future	C	C
8	It does not worry me that I do not know what is coming	C	C
9	I have many of the trappings of a student	C	B[2]
10	I have not yet become a working man	C	C
11	I am a liberal intellectual	C	C
12	I am sceptical about many new ideas	C	C
13	I am a democrat	C	C
14	I am a patriot	C	B[2]
15	Even though I have finished studying I feel like a historian	C	B[2]
16	I am a would-be playwright	C	C
17	I am an actor	B	B
18	I am a runner at heart, even though I am not training at present	C	B[2]
19	Many of my choices are still dictated by social pressures	C	C
20	I am fairly self-sufficient, and do not depend on any particular person	C	C

[1] Uncodeable.
[2] Competing interpretations.

fell to 12 or 14 out of the 20 statements given. Clearly, even on this primary A–B–C–D cut, some sets of responses proved much easier to code than others, typically those involving conventional single-phrase self-descriptions. The minority of respondents who provided more extended multi-phrase and qualified expressions presented more difficulties. However, the general rule adopted for multiple single responses ('a keen sportsman and supporter of the arts') was to code the first clause only, though there may be the need for some flexibility in applying this rule.

In general, we achieved less reliability on the first-phase responses given by new entrants. One reason for this was that, on the whole, they used more complex linguistic constructions. Another was that they expressed more uncertainty about their current working state. In Table 3.3, we show a case which illustrates a degree of ambivalence, a 21-year-old man who had entered a technical environment within the previous two weeks. Our purpose in selecting this case is also to demonstrate some of our difficulty in resolving competing interpretations.

The disagreements here nearly all arise from ambiguity between the social (B) and reflective (C) classes, a confusion most often generated by responses which add some qualification to stated membership of a social class or grouping. Where there is such qualification, we work on the principle that the statement is primarily reflective rather than social. So, although 'I am a student' would be (B) social, 'I have many of the trappings of a student' is a (C) reflective statement. The use of the word 'patriot' in statement 14 illustrates a different kind of ambiguity. Rater 2 understandably classified this as a B-type response, on the implicit reasoning that it connoted a distinct set of social attitudes. But even though patriotic attitudes might turn out to be associated with particular social groups (for example, a political party or interest group), 'patriot' itself denotes no identifiable social role or grouping. Thus beliefs and values clearly anchored in social norms and associated with social categories are reflective unless the respondent's social position is the explicit frame for them. Again, Rater 2 chose to use the 'uncodeable' class for the first two statements, feeling that they were too ambiguous to code, whilst Rater 1 decided that they were in the reflective category, since they seemed to carry overtones of an identification which was situation-free but significant to this individual.

By the time he completed the TST a year later, this man demonstrated less uncertainty, identifying himself more consistently within the work context, and making more B (social) 'other-orientated' statements. In consequence, we achieved higher agreement on his second-phase responses.

Additional coding methods

The overwhelming preponderance of C-type responses convinced us of the need for finer analysis of the content of the reflective data. For this purpose, we initially took Kuhn and McPartland's (1954) 'inclusive categories' as a basis for sub-dividing identity-related constructs:

1 ideological beliefs (individuals' explanations of the cosmos, life, society – and their part in them);
2 interests (approach and avoidance with respect to social objects);
3 ambitions (status and role intentions, anticipations and expectations about positions in social systems);
4 self-evaluations (varieties of pride or self-mortification over the way individuals imagine they appear to others who matter to them).

We extended and systematized Kuhn and McPartland's categories on the following reasoning. It was apparent that the fourth of the authors' categories was not exclusive of the others; for example, one could reflect on one's ambitions in a spirit equally of self-derogation or pride. Therefore we set aside self-evaluation as a completely orthogonal classificatory dimension, which we discuss shortly. The remaining three we augmented to make up a fourfold system of:

1 skills and abilities;
2 interests and needs;
3 character and behavioural style;
4 values and beliefs.

We then analysed responses in terms of the scales, traits and dimensions commonly found in psychometric instruments in each of these areas, collapsing categories where discrimination proved difficult. The purpose here was to evolve a system of rating which could tell us in a standard form something about the *content* of people's responses: for example, how many times did respondents describe themselves in terms of their sociability or lack of it? The system was developed after many iterations with the data and ad hoc rating trials before it was fully developed for test by independent raters. The earliest systems we used proved unwieldy with too many overlapping categories, with which we failed to achieve a reasonable level of reliability. Returning to this issue some time later, another social psychologist joined us as a rater, using the system as described below. All three of us trained together for one week, using six protocols for the purposes of illustrating categories. The second author took on the role of arbiter for the independent ratings of the other two team members.

Table 3.4 describes the rating scheme in detail, and gives typical examples of constructs and their antonyms in each of the system's 31 categories. Readers should note that responses can receive a plus or a minus score for a given category according to whether respondents explicitly state it or its antonym as a self-description.

For all C-mode or reflective statements (2,981) at both phases combined, inter-rater reliability was 78 per cent, which, given the large number of possible classifications, represents a remarkably high level of agreement. This was often associated with the frequency with which a particular type of statement was made. Thus, code 15, our 'outgoing' category, a highly salient dimension for these young people, was used most frequently (95 statements at phase 1 and 110 at phase 2, provided by a total of 77 different individuals), with inter-rater agreement of around 86 per cent. Other salient psychological dimensions for our sample were 'open to experience' (99 and 75, phases 1 and 2 respectively); 'need for affiliation' (94 and 78); 'need for achievement' (86 and 85); 'caring' (83 and 62); 'well-being' (80 and 70); 'self-application' (68 and 52); 'impulsive' (52 and 60); 'emotional' (51 and 47); and 'cognitive skills' (49 and 51). Most statements on these dimensions were positive self-evaluations – considered together, they emphasize the collective psychological strength of these young people. But the point is that they each offered these constructs *independently*.

Just as it is worth looking at the 'outgoing' category for its high reliability, it is also appropriate to consider a category where reliability was lower, though still acceptable. Code 19, 'open to experience', is a case

Table 3.4   *The Nicholson–Rees SICV (Skills, Interests, Character and Values) System for categorizing TST reflective statements*

(a)	Skills, abilities, attainments

01   *Cognitive skills*: being intelligent, quick-witted, good memory, analytical; (antonyms) slow

02   *Social skills*: persuasive, negotiating, relating to others, impression management, verbal fluency, approachable, being well liked, tactful, perceptive; (antonyms) tongue-tied, aloof, tactless

03   *Technical skills*: good at languages, computing, report-writing, numerate, knowledgeable, experienced; (antonyms) poor/bad at specifics

04   *Organizational skills*: administrative skills, methodical, accurate, tidy, persevering, finishes, meets deadlines, decision-making, conscientious; (antonyms) scatterbrained, sloppy, unpunctual

05   *Adaptive*: independent-minded, self-sufficient, innovative, problem-solving; (antonyms) non-creative, lacking initiative, perfectionist

06   *Achieving*: good at job, effective, successful, able, professional; (antonyms) ineffective, failure

07   *Fortunate*: lucky, privileged, wealthy, high-status, non-specific 'talented'; (antonyms) unlucky

(b)	Interests, needs, motives

08   *Need for achievement*: like challenge, competing, achieving, ambitious, determined; (antonyms) non-competitive, unambitious

09   *Need for power*: like controlling, assertive, dominant, argumentative, overbearing; (antonyms) modest, democratic, passive

10   *Need for affiliation*: needing and being interested in other people, liking groups, conforming, in love; (antonyms) only a few intimates, being a loner, liking solitude

11   *Need for growth*: interest in/need for development, learning, growth, interested; (antonyms) not wanting to change
[N.B. use this category to denote desires/motives; use 19 where outlook or style are implied]

12   *Arts, sciences, entertainments*: likes, hobbies, interests in literature, music, sciences [no antonym]

13   *Work orientation*: career-minded, committed, involved; (antonyms) family more important than job [family-orientated, use 10]

14   *Physical, active*: sporty, keen to keep fit, active, athletic; (antonyms) unfit, sedentary, overweight

(c)	Character, style

15   *Outgoing*: lively, easily bored, flirt, humorous, friendly, sociable, trendy, attractive; (antonyms) reserved, quiet, serious, sober, studious

16   *Conceptual*: abstract, theoretical, analytical (types, not skills), critical; (antonyms) practical, scientific, logical

17   *Confident*: self-confident, arrogant, complacent, direct, straightforward; (antonyms) shy, uncertain, awkward

18   *Impulsive*: risk-taking, hasty, romantic, restless, spendthrift; (antonyms) considered, unadventurous, patient

19   *Open to experience*: open-minded, tolerant, expectant, keen to travel, change-orientated, complex; (antonyms) opinionated, obstinate, cynical, suspicious

20   *Caring*: considerate, helpful, sensitive (to others), good listener; (antonyms) self-centred, nasty to people

21   *Well-being*: happy, optimistic, satisfied, relaxed (mood); (antonyms) pessimistic, depressed, anxious, frustrated
22   *Self-application*: energetic, hardworking, fit, a worker, persevering, involved, enthusiastic, busy, proactive; (antonyms) lazy, cowardly, easily tired, unmotivated
23   *Emotional*: changeable, moody, shows feelings, easily hurt, a worrier, nervous; (antonyms) calm, steady, relaxed [type]
24   *Reliable*: good, decent, loyal, trustworthy, sincere, honest; (antonyms) moral self condemnations [neutral = other self statements]
25   *Introspective*: self-critical, self-aware; (antonyms) ignorant about self, unaware of what I want

---

(d)   Values, beliefs

---

26   *Religious*: Christian, member of named religious group; (antonyms) atheist, agnostic
27   *Political*: right-wing, Liberal, radical, Conservative; (antonyms) apolitical
28   *Ethical*: humanistic, environmentalist, other value statements; (antonyms) no moral beliefs
29   *Psychological*: statements of belief about human nature

---

(e)   Others

---

30   *Miscellaneous*: habits, customs, tastes: vegetarian, nail-biter
31   *Expectations*: planning to emigrate, get married

---

in point. Although this, too, was a salient dimension for our sample (99 statements at phase 1 and 75 at phase 2; a self-definition articulated by 66 different individuals), agreement was lower at 68 per cent. Why was the dimension of 'open to experience' more difficult to rate reliably than 'outgoing'? It is interesting to look at the case of one individual who made four statements on this dimension at the first phase, and four at the second phase. Six of his statements were rated as 'open to experience' or its opposite (but still coded 19) by both raters, and two were rated differently. 'Conventional', 'critical', 'suspicious', all at phase 1, and 'fatalistic', 'critical', and 'a conservative person', at phase 2, were the definitions both raters included as 'open/closed to experience'. The two raters disagreed on 'concealing', one rating this as 'outgoing/not outgoing', and 'easy-going', one rating this as code 18, 'impulsive/not impulsive'. It is clear that there are overlaps between dimensions. This also illustrates the importance of taking the whole set of any individual's self-definitions into account when rating responses. Although this *can* lead to over-interpretation on a particular dimension, it is an essential strategy for capturing the spirit of the individual's statements and classifying them appropriately.

Self-evaluation

Our third method of classification was based upon the implicit self-evaluative content of the statements. This method completes the triangle of three complementary analytical approaches: response type (referential frame); response content (the SICV – Skills, Interests, Character and Values System); and response value (self-evaluation). The obvious application of the last of these would be for the TST to be sensitive to the psychological health or adaptive state of the subject, as measured conventionally by such constructs as self-esteem, ego strength, self-efficacy, stress and well-being. Initially we developed a fivefold scoring method to allow us to rate whether any response conveyed not just positive, neutral or negative implicit self-evaluation but also degree: 1 = strongly negative, 2 = negative, 3 = neutral, 4 = positive, 5 = strong positive. Trials with this method revealed that while a high level of agreement could be reached on direction (positive–neutral–negative), extremity was more controversial and significantly reduced inter-rater reliability. The finally adopted system therefore excluded the two extreme categories in favour of a simple threefold coding.

Agreement between raters on the total 2,983 statements was 83 per cent for negative, 62 per cent for neutral and 77 per cent for positive evaluations. The low agreement for the neutral rating was largely due to one rater's reluctance to use the negative rating: disagreements were nearly always in the same direction. For example, if we go back to the case described above where eight possible statements were made on the 'open to experience' dimension, there were three instances ('fatalistic', 'critical' and 'a conservative person') which the first rater scored neutral and the second negative. Taking just the reliably rated C-type statements, 57 per cent at phase 1 and 55 per cent a year later were positive; 23 per cent and 24 per cent were neutral; and 20 per cent and 21 per cent were negative. We interpret this as a further demonstration of stability over time, and suggest that the proportion of negative statements is an indication of the openness of self-disclosure.

Even this response value rating proved to have its difficulties. Our guidance for raters is again to maintain a holistic orientation: look at the whole range of an individual's responses as a meaning-imbued context, within which there are likely to be clues about the evaluative intent in an ambiguous response. Thus a respondent who elsewhere described him- or herself as 'inhibited' and 'humourless' could be inferred to use the term 'serious' as a self-derogation, while another person's set of responses, which included 'dedicated' and 'committed', would imply positive self-evaluation by a self-description of 'serious'. The neutral category should be used where there are conflicting indicators or ambiguities for other reasons, and in all other cases where the *respondent's* intent cannot be clearly discerned. In view of this overriding consideration, one approach to coding for self-evaluation is, as recommended by Spitzer et al. (1973), to ask respondents to evaluate their own statements. Indeed, this method can be used interactively with individuals for all the systems we have described, if appropriate to the context and purpose.

The TST and the study of personal change

Our major aim has been to describe the three-part rating system we developed to capture as much as possible of what was psychologically valid about these employees' self-definitions. Along the way, we have selected data to illustrate the degree of shift or stability in employees' self-identification over one year in their work environment. As we have stated, repertory grids were also used with these graduate entrants (Arnold and Nicholson, 1991), from which one of the major findings was how stable their self-concept proved to be over the year, even for those who had just entered the organization. Through the TSTs, we expected to find evidence of subtle changes in self-identity. To be precise, only taking into account those statements which were reliably rated for referential frame (3,564), the modal classification for *individuals* at the first phase was: none in the A-type/physical category, none in the B-type/social, 90 per cent in the C-type/reflective, and two in the D-type/oceanic category. This had shifted slightly at the second phase: none in the physical category, 3 per cent in the social, 87 in the reflective, and two (the same two individuals) in the oceanic category. The proportion of *statements* in each category across all respondents also changed to a modest but statistically significant degree: overall, at phase 1, 4 per cent of statements were physical; 8 per cent were social; 84 per cent were reflective; and 3 per cent were oceanic. At the second phase, the physical and oceanic had not shifted significantly: 3 per cent and 3 per cent respectively; but the social and reflective had shifted to 10 per cent and 81 per cent respectively. So although the great majority of individuals were still in the reflective mode at phase 2, the percentage of B-type responses had increased. We interpret this as evidence of a shift, particularly amongst new recruits, towards greater stability within explicitly structured situations, often in relation to work. However, the reader has seen from several responses how stable self-definition remained. In Table 3.5, we give the responses of one of our new graduate entrants to illustrate both points: stability and a detectable shift towards greater identification with the work role.

In some cases, the shift from reflective to socially defined self was from two B-type statements at the first phase, to four or five at the second phase. Here, the respondent gave the same physical definition at both phases (his name), two social the first time and seven the second time round, the same oceanic ('familiar face') at both stages, and 16 reflective statements at the first phase and 11 after a year. The whole demonstrates high stability over time, but also relatively high gross change over time. At the start of his work life, he makes two statements directly about his work identity, giving his company number and describing himself as a 'computer artist (as opposed to computer scientist)'. Two other definitions, 'I am on the road to success' and 'I am not keen on routinization' can be interpreted as being related to work values. A year later, he again gives his company number, but now defines himself as 'the computer

Table 3.5   *Stability of self perception over time and a shift towards greater work role identification*

Phase 1		Phase 2
1	I am [name] [A]	I am [name] [A]
2	I am [company number] [B]	I am [company number] [B]
3	I am on the road to success [C]	I am the computer man [D]
4	I am a satisfier rather than an optimizer [C]	I am the only person doing my job [C]
5	I am a fairly familiar face [D]	I am a happily married bachelor [C]
6	I am an adapter [C]	I am unpunctual [C] ,
7	I am the family's first traveller [C]	I am a bit of a joker [C]
8	I am a thinker of profound thoughts [C]	I am the player of the year [C]
9	I am prone to most vices [C]	I am a problem-solver [C]
10	I am a computer artist (as opposed to computer scientist) [C]	I am an Englishman [B]
11	I am lucky [C]	I am open-minded [C]
12	I am open-minded [C]	I am a worrier [C]
13	I am a schemer [C]	I am a familiar face [D]
14	I am a socializer [C]	I am a sailor [B]
15	I am not keen on routinization [C]	I am a smoker [B]
16	I am a snooker player [B]	I am a programmer [B]
17	I am an innovator [C]	I am a driver [B]
18	I am contented [C]	I am an organizer [C]
19	I am useful [C]	I am a socializer [C]
20	I am in love! [C]	I am inquisitive [C]

man', 'the only person doing my job' and 'a programmer' – three definitions directly derived from work; and further sees himself as 'unpunctual' and ' a problem-solver', which can be interpreted as also being work-related self-definitions. Although this is not great change, it does represent a subtle shift towards a clearer work identity, which the TST was able to detect. Another feature of this protocol is a somewhat less uninhibited and responsive framing of self-definitions from phase 1 to phase 2. In many other of the new entrants, a similar shift is detectable towards more 'business-like' and socialized expressions. This can be interpreted as subtle evidence of newcomers acquiring impression management skills and internalizing more professional identities.

Evaluation

The measure's capacity to reflect the saliency of facets of identity is a critical feature favouring the TST over other instruments. The open-ended format allows individuals to determine the type and order of response, and gives them the opportunity to define their personal constructs. This is a special advantage over conventional techniques. Another is its ability to reflect the extent to which individuals locate and evaluate themselves within the social system. These internalized aspects of the self based on social relationships and role identities are largely inaccessible to fixed response self-concept measurement. We found that 28 of the 32 women (or 88 per cent) made a statement about being 'a woman', 'female', 'girl', 'career woman', 'a business woman' or 'an independent woman' within their first three statements, whereas only 22 of the 62 men (36 per cent) identified themselves as 'male' or 'a man' in their first few statements. Undoubtedly, in an organization which is largely technically-based, and in these specific occupational groups, gender is of great salience to women, but for men is more thoroughly internalized and therefore not articulated. This is not surprising. But we do not know of any other measure which would have brought this difference out so clearly, because none other would offer equal scope for individuals to define *their own* identities. Apart from gender for women, occupational and family membership categories were highly salient for this sample of young people.

Projective measures have long been used in clinical practice as diagnostic aids, and found wide acceptance in other applied fields, especially to derive indices of achievement, affiliation and power motivation (McClelland, 1961, 1987). Sentence-completion and draw-a-person techniques (Loevinger, 1976, 1987) have had similar applications, with similar claimed advantages over quantitative methods. These are all valuable techniques, but present analytical difficulties, such as prior investigator interpretation; creating unpredictable demand characteristics; or eliciting responses which may vary on many dimensions – all highlighting familiar problems of reliability and validity. As we have seen, the TST does not completely avoid all these difficulties, but it does have the twin virtues of openness and transparency: openness in that a single direct stimulus instruction produces a specified number of discrete but unconstrained responses; and transparency in the face validity of the task, which elicits self-descriptions directly. Of course, respondents may still wonder what the investigator will do with the material, or how it will be interpreted, but this can be more openly shared, without invalidating the data, than in conventional projective tests.

In some research settings one might imagine classifications being conducted collaboratively with respondents. This method would be especially useful in instructional contexts, where, for example, one wanted to explore with a group of students or managers the meanings and implications of their self-images, or of the specific social environment of interest. In career guidance the method could be imagined as a useful adjunct to the assessment of opportunities and choices. It is also apparent that the TST can be a powerful tool in clinical practice, where a counsellor or therapist wishes to explore with clients the salient constructs they apply to themselves.

In published research, the A–B–C–D method of rating is usually the system exclusively used to quantify results, though, as we have demonstrated here, there are further riches to be extracted by additional analytical frames. In our own research we are undertaking extended analysis and evaluation of reflective statements to reveal their psychological content. Ours is very much a developing system, and we hope that others will be encouraged to use the methodology, and offer suggestions for its extension

References

Arnold, J. and Nicholson, N. (1991) 'Construing of self and others at work in the early years of corporate careers', *Journal of Organizational Behaviour*, 12 (7): 621–39.

Bond, M.H. and Cheung, T. (1983) 'College students' spontaneous self-concept: the effect of culture among respondents in Hong Kong, Japan, and the United States', *Journal of Cross-Cultural Psychology*, 14 (2): 153–71.

Cousins, S.D. (1989) 'Culture and self-perception in Japan and the United States', *Journal of Personality and Social Psychology*, 56 (1): 124–31.

Hartley, W. (1968) 'Self-conception and organizational adaptation'. Paper presented at the Midwest Sociological Association, Omaha, NE.

Kitayama, S. and Markus, H. (eds) (1994) *Emotion and Culture: Empirical Studies of Mutual Influence*. Washington, DC: American Psychological Association.

Kuhn, M.H. (1950) 'Mutual derogation', unpublished manuscript.

Kuhn, M.H. and McPartland, T.A. (1954) 'An empirical investigation of self-attitudes', *American Sociological Review*, 19: 68–76.

Locatelli, V. and West, M.A. (1991) 'On elephants and blind researchers: methods for accessing culture in organizations'. MRC/ESRC SAPU memo no. 1281.

Loevinger, J. (1976) *Ego Development*. San Francisco: Jossey-Bass Inc.

Loevinger, J. (1987) *Paradigms of Personality*. New York: W.H. Freeman & Co.

McClelland, D.C. (1961) *The Achieving Society*. Princeton, NJ: D. van Nostrand Company, Inc.

McClelland, D.C. (1987) *Human Motivation*. Cambridge: Cambridge University Press.

Mackie, M. (1983) 'The domestication of self: gender comparisons of self-imagery and self-esteem', *Social Psychology Quarterly*, 46 (4): 343–50.

McPartland, T.S. (1965) *Manual for the Twenty Statements Problem (Revised)*. Kansas City, MO: Department of Research, Greater Kansas City Mental Health Foundation.

McPartland, T.S., Cumming, J.H. and Garretson [Hartley], W. (1961) 'Self-conception and ward behaviour in two psychiatric hospitals', *Sociometry*, 24: 111–24.

Nicholson, N. and Arnold, J. (1989a) 'Graduate entry and adjustment to corporate life', *Personnel Review*, 18 (3): 23–35.

Nicholson, N. and Arnold, J. (1989b) 'Graduate early experience in a multinational corporate', *Personnel Review*, 18 (4): 3–14.

Nicholson, N. and Arnold, J. (1990) 'From expectation to experience: graduates entering a large corporation', *Journal of Occupational Behaviour*, 12: 413–29.

Rees, A. and Nicholson, N. (forthcoming) 'Covariates of personal change as measured by the TST'.

Smith, J. (1993) 'The case study', in R. Bayne and P. Nicholson (eds), *Counselling and Psychology for Health Professionals*. London: Chapman & Hall.

Spitzer, S., Couch, C. and Stratton, J. (1973) *The Assessment of the Self*. Iowa City, IA: Sernoll Inc.

Ziller, R.C. (1981) 'Orientations: self, social and environmental percepts through auto-photography', *Personality and Social Psychology Bulletin*, 7 (2): 338–43.

Zurcher, L.A. (1977) *The Mutable Self: a Self-concept for Social Change*. Beverly Hills, CA: Sage.

4

Question-Asking and Verbal Protocol Techniques

Graham I. Johnson and Pamela Briggs

The focus of this chapter is upon the moment-to-moment decisions which people make, usually in order to exercise some control over a particular system, product or situation. It deals with two techniques – question-asking and verbal protocols – which are commonly associated with the investigation and analysis of how individuals interact with workplace components or 'tools', typically computer-based systems that require some mental or cognitive effort to operate. Both techniques aim to provide a description of the cognitive aspects of interaction with computer-based systems, making use of elicited verbal comments to assist design and evaluation exercises. Both techniques have their origins in cognitive and human experimental psychology, and are nowadays commonly applied in the areas of human–computer interaction (HCI) and usability engineering. Both techniques are typically viewed as belonging to participative and user-centred approaches to the design of interactive systems.

Throughout the 1980s, there was much discussion of the methodological issues pertaining to research in HCI (for example the 'hard-science/soft-science' debate of Carroll and Campbell, 1986; Newell and Card, 1985, 1986). Since this debate, 'softer' or qualitative methods have been more fully recognized as valuable tools in HCI research. These qualitative methods usually embody an assumption that users of any system bring with them a depth of knowledge and experience which will influence their perception of that system, and which can help to account for their attitudes and performance. While a user's overall impression can often be reliably determined by quantitative methods such as questionnaires, qualitative methods are usually required in order to assess the user's understanding or 'mental model' of any particular system.

Consider, for example, a user with six months' experience of a particular word-processing package, who is retrained in the use of a new system and who then experiences problems in handling many day-to-day jobs. The source of the problem is quite likely to be that the user has inappropriately transferred many of his or her beliefs about the old system on to the new system, with the effect that (1) some of the 'old' functions cannot be identified on the new system and are subsequently neglected; and (2) some of the 'new' functions are never discovered. The extent of the mismatch between old and new beliefs will only be brought to light if the user is given some framework to describe his or her particular mental model of the system. In the sections which follow, we describe two techniques which provide the user with a means of communicating this understanding: question-asking and the verbal protocol technique. While the systems we discuss here as examples are computei-based, the methodologies could be extended to a range of interactive systems.

This chapter is structured as follows. First, we describe the question-asking approach, giving a brief background to the methodology before detailing the steps required in the use and application of the technique, and outlining the advantages and disadvantages of using the method. Then we focus on verbal protocols, again describing the step-by-step procedure, and summarizing its advantages and disadvantages. Finally, we conclude with a broader discussion of the applications of these techniques, and offer our expectations of future developments in this domain.

Question-asking

The question-asking procedure described here is a variant of a method which has been widely used in the field of knowledge elicitation for expert systems (Grover, 1983; Hoffman, 1987). It has been shown to discriminate quite effectively between experts and novices in a variety of domains (for example, Miyake and Norman, 1979), and has been successfully employed in usability assessment (Briggs, 1988, 1990; Kato, 1986; Vries and Johnson, 1992).

With the question-asking method, the user is presented with a novel or unfamiliar system, and is required to generate questions about the operation of that system in order to gain sufficient information to complete a sample task. To develop the example given above: imagine that our user of six months' experience is asked to sit down in front of the word-processing package and given a sample letter to produce – without any training whatsoever. Naturally they would be appalled, but would be told that they would have access to a personal tutor who would give them any information they requested about the system or the structure of the underlying task. Our user would then be in a position to proceed, and we could learn a great deal about his or her 'view' of the system from the questions he or she asks, and the type of information he or she seeks. This, in essence, is the basis of the question-asking method.

The power of the technique is in the fact that people will ask those questions they believe to be relevant (to the task in hand and the system in question), and do so at particular stages in the completion of the task. In this way, a revealing description of the information or knowledge the user seeks is gained in the form of a question-asking protocol.

Question-asking: description of the technique

There are five main steps to using the question-asking method. These are (1) user selection, (2) task selection, (3) procedural aspects (two phases), (4) data-recording, (5) analysis and application. These steps are described below.

Question-asking step 1: user selection   Let us continue with the example of users being retrained in the use of a new word-processing system. If we are to predict the likely sources of difficulty for such users, then we need to select an appropriate sample of users for our investigation, and to do this we need to consider their experience to date. If the 'typical' user is a novice, then this may present difficulties – since users who are complete novices will often find it very difficult to phrase any appropriate questions (Briggs, 1990). Therefore, it may be advisable to select participants who do have some limited experience (although Kato [1986] does report success with total novices).

If, however, the profile of staff (or potential users) is such that they are very experienced, then a small sample of users can be tested whose experience is representative. Note, however, that it is important to differentiate between *extent* and *diversity* of experience – since users who have had experience of a number of different systems have a much more sophisticated understanding of the structure of systems in general (Briggs, 1990). In any case, the participant must not be experienced in the use of the new system under investigation.

Question-asking step 2: task selection   The task should be reasonably familiar to the user. In particular he or she should thoroughly understand the start- and end-points of the task. This is because we are interested in the pattern of actions and commands the user executes in order to achieve a set goal; and not in the user's understanding of the goal itself – which is a rather different issue. Note that some tasks will be contingent upon work done previously – that is, they will involve development of previously prepared work. Under these circumstances it is important to prepare appropriate start- and end-points. In our word-processing example, the task for the user may be to edit a document which had been initially prepared by another member of staff. In this case the format (and style sheet) of the original document should be made clear to the end user, and the final, desired format of the document must also be clearly signalled.

If the task is one in which the user is taking over from a colleague (as would be the case with shift-workers in a process control setting), then the start-point may include a brief report of recent events, and a full description of the state of the system at the point of transfer.

Question-asking step 3: procedure   The respondent is cast in the role of a user given a specific task to complete using an unfamiliar system. The researcher is cast in the role of an 'intelligent talking manual' or tutor who may respond only to relevant user-generated questions, that is, those questions the user could ask of an expert trainer, help system or user manual. Note that it is crucially important that the researcher is thoroughly familiar with both the task and the overall system, and can thus offer quality expert advice. In some respects, the question-asking approach is a form of the 'Wizard of Oz' technique described by Gould et al. (1983) where the researcher plays the role of the support system.

Briggs (1988) recommends breaking down the session into the following two phases:

Phase 1. During the first phase of the study, the start- and end-points of the task are described to the respondent, who is then given an opportunity to ask the researcher (or 'talking manual') for information concerning the operation of the system. Note that the participant should be led to believe that this is the only opportunity they have to ask questions about the task or the system. In our example, the word-processor user may be given an unfinished document and asked to edit it so as to produce a final version. Ideally, they would be given a clear end-point or goal – and this could be achieved by providing them with a hard copy of the finished version.

All types of questions are permitted. Participants may ask either closed or open-ended questions. In the case of closed questions ('Which command is used to print-out?') the relevant response may be obvious. Open-ended questions may take a variety of forms. If the user is asking for procedural information ('How do I format the document?'), the appropriate steps in the procedure have to be explained – however, the researcher should always respond in terms of specific procedures rather than sub-goals. In this case the goal of formatting can be broken down into a number of sub-goals (selection of fonts, paragraph and line spacing, margins, etc.), which can be broken down still further (selecting text, changing text) before specific procedures might be described. However, it is important that the user, and not the researcher, provides information about how they view these different sub-goals, because his or her view may differ considerably from the 'official view'. In other words, the researcher should invite the user to break down higher-level goals into their component sub-goals, before offering information about specific procedures.

Phase 2. In phase 2 of the procedure, the user attempts to complete the specified task, armed with the information acquired during phase 1. An example might be 'using this new word-processing package, edit the document titled "report-A" so that it looks like "report-B"'. At the end of phase 1, the user will have attempted to ask all relevant questions about how to use the system, and is ready to begin. However, it is important to note that the user will almost always encounter some difficulties, unless he or she is given further advice during the attempted task. Thus instructions at the start of phase 2 are important: the user should be asked to try to complete the task without further help, but should be told that he or she can request assistance if it is really needed. With these instructions, we can

Table 4.1 *Question-asking example: questions produced by users with an unfamiliar in-car stereo system*

Phase 1 questions	Phase 2 questions
Does the on/off turn the radio on or the cassette?	So, how do I get back to tape from radio?
What does the 'BAND' button stand for?	How can I go back to the start again?
Does this set play CDs or not?	I didn't think I'd need to change wavelength: where is the button?
Will it work OK inside the building?	

Source: Adopted from Vries and Johnson, 1992

hope to simulate patterns of computer use in the real world, where users are known to be reluctant to seek further advice once they have begun the task-at-hand. Carroll and Rosson (1985) describe this as a motivational paradox, in which the paramount goal of 'throughput' is in direct conflict with the need to spend time learning about a system.

The points at which a user seeks additional information are interesting, since they often indicate that some aspect of the system is causing frustration or confusion. Once again questions may be open-ended: for instance, users may simply wish to be provided with information about a particular function ('what happens if I select the "library" command?'). Users may also seek information by asking why a particular action seems to be associated with more than one outcome – the answer to which may involve a relatively full account of modes, structure of the interactive system, etc. In this case, the researcher will provide information relevant to the task or stage in the task reached by the user.

Example questions asked by users in the question-asking technique are shown in Table 4.1. These example questions are taken from a usability study of a reasonably complex car stereo system (see Vries and Johnson, 1992). In phase 1, prior to embarking upon the task, a different type of question is often asked. Phase 2 questions are generated during the task and represent those issues that users were unaware they would encounter, or where they are unable to remember what was originally said.

The feedback provided to respondents on completion of the exercise must be comprehensive, and related to the introduction to the evaluation. In the context of the debriefing (which could also be given before the study begins), respondents (users) are made aware of the value of their questions and queries in terms of the system's evaluation or development.

Question-asking step 4: data-recording In a strictly limited analysis, only those questions generated by the participants are used as data. However, this information can be complemented by an analysis of errors made in task-execution. Alternative methods of recording this information are available. Video-recording (perhaps combined with a computer-based account of the systems, actions and responses) ensures that little information is lost – but can prove very costly in terms of transcription time. A simpler method is to keep a shorthand log of both questions and actions conducted by the user. Briggs (1988) found this technique to be successful, so long as the researcher had practised the shorthand note form extensively beforehand.

Question-asking step 5: analysis and application The analysis must be clearly linked to the overall goals of the study. For Kato (1986), these were: (1) to understand the problems experienced by participants; (2) to discover what instructional information participants came to need; (3) to rediscover which features of the system proved most difficult to learn; and (4) to detect relative points of understanding and misunderstanding. Kato assumed that in the course of learning, queries will be made about comprehending a current state (of the system), defining a goal, finding a means and predicting the effect of an operation. These four categories provided the basis of his analysis, alongside two categories of 'intent' (exploratory versus confirmatory queries). This refers to whether participants are apparently extending their knowledge via questions to do with 'new' areas (exploratory) or simply confirming some aspect about which they have already been informed (confirmatory).

In contrast, Briggs (1988) was concerned with the extent to which users were able to generate questions about the system given their experience. Rather than assume that the questions would fall into categories such as those used by Kato (1986), the analysis was open-ended – and phrased in terms of the origins of the questions (that is, which cues did participants use to generate questions?). She found marked differences in phases 1 and 2 of the study: questions in phase 1 being explicitly tied to visible aspects of the task, and questions in phase 2 linked primarily with visible aspects of the system. Surprisingly few questions were asked about the 'hidden' aspects of either task or system. In other words, questions were not promoted by past experiences but by information that was visually available there and then.

Advantages and disadvantages of question-asking

This technique has a number of advantages. First, it is wholly user-driven, and is therefore able to provide fairly rich, unconstrained information about a user's expectations. Second, phase 1 can be conducted with a 'dummy' system – or a very early prototype – so that these user expectations can be fed into the design process at an early stage. Third, question-asking is a natural activity: users do request information of tutors, manuals, experienced colleagues, help systems, and the choices they make do determine the mental models they acquire and their subsequent patterns of use.

The method also has a number of limitations. Users can be reluctant to seek out new information and may consequently develop a rather partial or limited view of what a system's capabilities are. The researcher must deal with this issue, encouraging users to ask questions if difficulties are constantly encountered. Question-asking demands a great deal from the researcher in terms of judgements that must be made about the type and amount of information to be provided in response to a user's question. This is perhaps one of the most difficult parts of carrying out a question-asking study.

Finally, the question-asking technique's ability to address those aspects of a task or system with which a user is fairly confident or familiar (irrespective of performance) is also limited. In this case users are unlikely to ask (many) questions, and thus will possibly reveal little about their mental model of these parts of the system. Under such circumstances the technique of protocol analysis (of concurrent verbalizations) is likely to be superior.

Verbal protocols

A verbal protocol is the term given to the commentary or verbalization produced by an individual or small team when asked to describe what they are doing, why they are doing it, what they are about to do, what they hope to achieve, etc. with respect to a particular task or behaviour. In other words, a verbal protocol is a self-report of behaviour which usually includes the individual's reasoning about that behaviour. Verbal protocol analysis offers a means of gaining some insight into the way in which end-users conceive of systems, be they complex power plants, or relatively small software packages. It is a technique which has proved remarkably popular, despite being rather controversial (Ericsson and Simon, 1984). The verbal protocol method is also known as 'think aloud' or 'concurrent verbalization'.

In many respects it is similar to the question-asking approach described above: both are aimed at gaining information about how people approach a system-based problem or task, and the mental processes they employ at the time (for example the types of plans they form, expectations they hold, strategies they adopt, questions they pose, and so on). While question-asking can provide an overview of the kinds of information the user believes is relevant to the task at hand, the verbal protocol method can provide a much finer-grain analysis of a user's understanding of specific interactions. The two methods can be successfully employed in tandem.

It is now some years since verbal protocol methods were proposed in the search for rich information about how people conceive of their actions within specific circumstances (Ainsworth, 1984; Bainbridge, 1979). The technique has been frequently employed within the knowledge elicitation and mental models fields (Gammack and Young, 1985; Johnson and Briggs, 1988; Shadbolt and Burton, 1990) and has been successfully applied to a number of problem-solving and process control environments (for example, Bainbridge, 1990; Kirwan and Ainsworth, 1992).

Recently, verbal protocol analysis has gained popularity in the field of usability analysis and human–computer interaction (HCI). This is particularly the case in the field of software evaluation, where developers and purchasers are charged with responsibility for conducting basic assessments of the overall usability of the products they design or recommend (Wright, 1992). This popularity is, in part, due to the increasing attention paid to usability issues in the development of interactive systems, as well as the global growth of these systems and the features encompassed by them. Other factors probably promoting the increased use of verbal protocol methods are the (early) stages at which evaluations are required and the time-pressure within, say, user interface design projects, where these can conspire to result in the avoidance of lengthy, empirical approaches to appraisal (see Wright and Monk, 1991).

Verbal protocols: description of the technique

This section aims to outline the basic method of verbal protocol analysis. For a fuller treatment of the method, the reader is referred to Bainbridge (1990), Ericsson and Simon (1984) and Kirwan and Ainsworth (1992).

Clearly, this description of the technique, has to be given at a general level. Specific applications of verbal protocol analysis will exercise their own 'tailoring' of the method to take account of the problem addressed, its objectives and its constraints. The description below breaks the approach down into five stages. These are (1) understanding the domain; (2) preparation of materials; (3) recording the verbal protocols; (4) augmenting the data, and (5) analysis of the data and its application. Finally, two variations on the standard approach are briefly described. These are the retrospective protocol and co-discovery approaches.

Verbal protocols step 1: understanding the domain   The first part of the approach is to ascertain whether the verbal protocol approach is the one best suited to the problem under investigation. Whether verbal protocols are appropriate as a means of investigating or assessing a certain behaviour is a judgement based on consideration of a combination of several factors: the work environment; the type of users involved, and their ability to communicate fundamental aspects of their own behaviour (before and) as it occurs; and the ease with which verbal and other types of data can be recorded.

Consider a situation in which a company has 'updated' an electronic mail system – which has led to a sharp decrease in electronic communications. One possible reason for this is that the staff are experiencing problems in operating the new system. However, this is only one out of a range of possibilities. A verbal protocol investigation of the new mail system would help to pin-point any difficulties the users are experiencing – but it would be costly in terms of time and effort, and so it is important that other explanations are ruled out beforehand, so as to be sure that ease of use is the main source of the problem. Even then it is important to consider the feasibility of the exercise in terms of the availability of participants and sites to conduct the study.

Because of the amount and type of data dealt with when using verbal protocols, it is essential that the whole exercise is tightly focused. There should be clarity about why verbal protocols have been chosen as a method, and exactly what the objectives of the study are. An operational definition of the investigation's goals provides a good structure for the investigation, and for the analysis of resulting data.

Verbal protocols step 2: preparation of materials Having investigated the domain, and carried out a feasibility check (above), the next stage is the preparation of the materials. Materials include that instructional information given to users or participants.

The most important area of instruction to participants is that regarding verbalization. Instructions can vary greatly: from requiring of individuals that they comment about what they are doing when convenient to do so, through to the extremely demanding requirement that they describe exactly what they are doing and why, detailing their expectations and plans throughout (see Ericsson and Simon, 1984; Wright, 1992).

In particular, the researcher must ensure that the level of verbalization required is not too demanding (and therefore likely to interfere significantly with behaviour), and that the priorities normally associated with the behaviour under study are retained when verbalizing. In our electronic mail example, the sending and receiving of mail is not time-critical, therefore concurrent verbalization should be possible during the execution of most of the commands. The same would clearly not be true of, say, piloting a flight simulator, where pilots would find their opportunities for verbalization much more limited.

One of the major problems encountered when using the verbal protocol approach is that of individuals who find it difficult to produce a 'natural' commentary. The options open here include practice for individuals, and minimal (non-intrusive) prompting. In advance, a decision must be taken as to how much prompting is to be given and the type of prompting (for example a standard phrase, reminding individuals to 'think aloud'). A related problem can be where users attempt to conform with researchers' expectations, where users are tempted to say what is expected or what they feel they 'ought' to say in given situations.

Wherever possible, investigators should attempt to gather verbal data *in situ*, using real tasks. This demands thorough preparation. Well in advance of any study, the researcher ought to seek the appropriate permission from the individuals involved and from the organization (if relevant), and make arrangements for the collection of any other data which may be relevant. Video-recordings are often useful in such studies, and performance data will usually be required. For example, in the investigation of the mail system, it might be possible to keep a log (electronically) of all of the commands executed throughout the entire system, which would help to pin-point areas of 'neglect'.

Identifying the needed resources (time and equipment) requires careful estimation. Verbal protocol recording and analysis is notorious in terms of the time and effort required for a full investigation. It is wise to clarify at an early stage not just the necessary equipment, but also the time (person-hours) required to administer and analyse. Analysis is especially time-consuming.

The demands on the participants should also be carefully considered: field studies should be planned so as to avoid disruption to their 'normal' work routines. The participants themselves should be carefully chosen on the basis of individual characteristics such as skills, experience and attitude. In our electronic mail investigation, for example, there may be different subsets of mail-users, with widely differing experience – and these should be adequately represented within the participants sampled.

At this stage in the preparation, a short pilot study should be carried out. A pilot study involves a small-scale investigation or trial of the materials and methods adopted in search of the study's general objective(s). In certain circumstances, it is important to determine that the requirement to verbalize does not significantly influence a user's behaviour. In the flight simulator example, we need to be sure that our pilots are behaving exactly as they would under normal flight conditions. As a check, the pilot study could include a control group who are not given the requirement of concurrent verbalization. In this way, it will be possible to make simple comparisons, and assess to what extent behaviour is influenced by the production of the 'think aloud'.

Verbal protocols step 3: recording the verbal protocols   Having established that the approach is appropriate and that the materials prepared are adequate, the next step is to record the verbal data. There are two basic choices for the recording of the protocols – video-tape and audio-tape recordings. In both cases the quality must be sufficiently high to be able to record and reproduce all utterances, including 'um . . .', non-words and audible information within the environment studied. Audible information would include, for example, the noise of a disk drive, an error beep and other action-related machine noises. The playback and analysis of the tapes also ought to be considered when choosing between the two: while audio-tapes may be more convenient and less obtrusive, video-tapes provide a richer source of information, which is useful when the verbal protocols are augmented with descriptions of user behaviour (see below).

It is important that those recording deficiencies encountered in the pilot, for example poor recording of utterances when in a particular location, be rectified. Background noise can have a great effect upon the quality of recordings made, therefore the types of noise expected should be checked in advance of commencing recording sessions. Precautions such as a back-up tape- or video-recorder, batteries, etc. are a must, as is flexibility in the time-tabling of the participants (sessions can easily extend beyond their allotted time). The positioning of microphones (and cameras if used) will have been addressed in the pilot, and the optimum chosen for the recording. Individuals taking part in the study should be shown all equipment when the purpose of the investigation is explained to them.

Verbal protocols step 4: augmenting the data   The user's commentary does not always give us a clear picture of just what it is he or she is doing. More often than not, there will be a need to record additional information about his or her actual behaviour. There are various means of doing this, but one of the key requirements is that the two sources of data (verbal and action) can be synchronized. One of the simplest techniques is to keep a time-stamped record of users' actions. This can simply be a set of time-based observations kept by the researcher. Alternatively, a video-camera can be set up so as to record both the user's actions and his or her comments – in which case synchronizing the two data sources is not a problem.

Each method has its merits: time-stamped notes require that the researcher remains alert and busy throughout the entire session – but the observations can be easily integrated with the verbal protocol. A computer-based log is an automated equivalent, but may be too elaborate – coding up every minor action the user initiates; while a video-recording may miss some of the key behaviours, unless it is very carefully set up. In the electronic mail example, the best method is probably note-taking, since the study would be conducted *in situ*, with the researcher moving from room to room.

Verbal protocols step 5: analysis of the data   The first stage in the analysis of verbal protocol data is to produce an accurate verbatim transcript of all utterances. This provides the initial transcript of the 'think aloud' protocol. The principle usually followed in further analysis is to reduce the transcript (analogous to 'distillation' of the information) in order to address those aspects of specific interest. Great care must be taken when reducing the amount of data between transcript versions. It is often useful to have a second opinion, say from a colleague, on the data reduction being carried out.

The data reduction process itself will often depend upon the overall goals of the investigation. The idea that you can distil a verbal protocol down to its essence is much simpler in principle than in practice. In many cases, a taxonomy directed by the research questions and the issues of major interest (for example, error types, hesitations and points of

Table 4.2 *Example of verbal protocol (raw data)*

Verbal protocol	System notes
'. . .	
and enter my number . . . er I wasn't aware of all the er the functions, I only wanted to get cash when I came up to it . . . the dispense, er well that's cash and I'm wanting	[Screen changes showing menu options] [moves finger towards 'dispense' function key, then presses key] dispense = cash screen changes to next . . .
$50, so that's – oh, hold on . . . but, oh – well, if I press OTHER . . . um . . .	user searches screen, uncertain? screen changes to next . . .
Right, so it's telling me to wait for my cash, . . . and oh it's giving me a receipt which I didn't ask for . . .'	[wait screen] [cash given . . .]

uncertainty) will determine the reduction of the raw data, as will the chosen form of data representation. The initial form of representation is usually the raw transcript augmented with notes concerning the users' actions. The reduced transcript can become little more than a set of key steps or rules that relate to a specific problem-solving strategy, or even a simple comparison of frequency counts that refer to use of elements of the system.

In Table 4.2 we provide an example of a verbal protocol which was elicited during an investigation of the usability of an automatic teller machine (ATM). The extract has been augmented with the researcher's notes. We can see from the protocol how hesitations and expressions of uncertainty can be written into the raw transcript; and how useful they can be as signals that the user is rather confused by the display. (In this case, because the user has been presented with rather more information than she had anticipated.) This is effectively the raw data and, as mentioned above, must then undergo reduction.

As with most popular techniques, a number of variations have developed as non-standard situations are encountered, and researchers seek to tailor the basic method. Two such variations are described below: 'retrospective verbal protocols' and 'co-discovery protocols'.

The retrospective verbal protocol

Where a task or interaction is subject to extreme time pressure or attention demands, where an environment is potentially dangerous, or where the nature of the task is essentially a verbal one, the use of retrospective verbal protocols can be considered. Clearly, these are situations in which a standard verbal protocol approach may well be impractical because of task demands, or where there is a high probability that production of a verbal protocol (at whatever level) will distort the very behaviour under investigation (Ericsson and Simon, 1984). The basic retrospective method is one where the user–system behaviour is fully recorded and then later inspected by the users who took part, commenting on specific occurrences and actions. It should be clear that this method is open to biases; namely, the possibility of post-task justification, the inability to recall reliably (or recognize) aspects dealt with at a specific moment, and the likelihood of elaboration about certain aspects. Despite these caveats, the technique can be useful for special cases, although more care needs to be taken in the interpretation of the verbal data. Finally, it is worth mentioning that interesting insights can often be gained by applying this retrospective approach using the recorded behaviour of another: for instance, in a situation where one experienced (specialist) user comments on the detailed behaviour of another.

Co-discovery

There has been much interest recently (for example, Hackman and Biers, 1992) in the potential of using verbal protocols as data where there are two users rather than one. The term 'co-discovery' is applied to a case where two individuals together undergo a similar experience, typically exploration of a product or system. The resulting information from two participants who will inevitably interact with one another (advising, commenting, sharing tasks, etc.) can provide much richer data than a single individual. The obvious advantage of this approach is that participants will (as instructed) 'think aloud' together, in, say, joint problem-solving. Questions such as whether the individuals know one another are important, as are the task characteristics. Co-discovery is typically applied in usability work, where a new or different solution is offered, perhaps in the form of a prototype. The use of novice (for example, student) and expert (for example, trainer) can also be powerful in producing data that reveal some aspects of the underlying nature of a specific task.

The main disadvantages of this approach tend to be unwillingness on the part of one of the two individuals to participate fully, and, second, the amount of apparently irrelevant (but actually very useful) data that result from non-task-orientated dialogue between users. The co-discovery technique gains much of its power because it is a 'natural' approach: people regularly tackle problems (or new systems) together.

As a hypothetical example of the application of co-discovery, consider the evaluation of a new video conferencing facility. Two users (probably experienced in telephone conferencing) could form a pair of evaluators. They would then be given a set task, such as setting up an electronic meeting with staff in other parts of their organization, and would jointly try to solve the problems generated by this activity. The advantage gained from this co-discovery technique would lie in the rich dialogue generated by the two participants as one offers advice, or makes requests of the other. The verbal data recorded will include valuable information on what is expected from such a facility, including assumptions about what functions are likely to be available, and what sequence of activities might be appropriate. As cooperative systems become more feasible, co-discovery techniques are finding increasing applications.

Advantages and disadvantages of verbal protocols

Although some of the advantages and disadvantages have already been touched upon in earlier sections, it is worth noting the main advantages and disadvantages of using verbal protocols. Clearly, there is an overlap here with question-asking protocols and their strengths and limitations.

The following advantages are normally associated with verbal protocol techniques. They offer a means of accessing mental processes that are not easily accessed in other ways. The process of actually collecting the verbal protocols from individuals can be straightforward, using simple, generally available, equipment. Third, the face validity of the technique is reasonably high, with the results easily appreciated by those not concerned with or aware of applied cognitive psychology. Fourth, protocols can provide accurate and very detailed information about many kinds of behaviour, not just cognitive behaviour, and its perceived importance to individuals. Finally, verbal protocols can capture much of the context of behaviour and are usually suited to field-based study – they do not require a laboratory setting.

The disadvantages of verbal protocols are that individuals differ greatly in their verbal skills, influencing the collection of verbal data. Second, language cannot always describe particular events: for example, when a process seems to rely upon a certain degree of imagery and its subsequent manipulation. Protocols can be subject to a number of biases – particularly when participants feel a need to rationalize their behaviour. The fourth limitation is that the data analysis phase can be very time-consuming, and increasingly open to researcher bias as decisions are taken about, say, the category into which a piece of verbal data ought to be placed. Finally, performance levels are not necessarily reflected in protocols: that is to say, they cannot be directly used to assess performance quality.

Concluding remarks: applications of question-asking and verbal protocols

One of the first applications of verbal protocols was in the area of process control, where human operators are often required to monitor and control very complex systems. In an attempt to reduce human error, researchers were keen to develop descriptive and predictive models of human control processes, and many adopted verbalization techniques of the type described here in order to define the task from the user's perspective (see Bainbridge, 1979). These control process models could then be employed in the redesign of the system interface.

Since then, the field of usability analysis has grown, in line with the proliferation of interactive computer-based systems and products. In most usability investigations, an interactive product or system is assessed in terms of effectiveness, efficiency and user satisfaction, as the evaluator seeks to describe the important cognitive aspects of the interaction. Both question-asking and verbal protocol techniques have been found to be of great value in these studies (see for example, Briggs, 1988; Vries and Johnson, 1992; Wright, 1992); although the two techniques can be differentiated with respect to the design phase within which a system or product is developed. Question-asking, for instance, is ideally suited to very early stages where the overall requirements are sought, and is also readily applied to later stages where the exact content of (on-line) help and tutorial information is to be constructed. Verbal protocols, on the other hand, are often applied to functional prototypes and their iterations which determine final designs.

Increasingly, these qualitative methods are playing a major role in the research and development of 'intelligent' systems (see, for example, Gammack and Young, 1985). Both knowledge elicitation and cognitive modelling are predicated upon an investigation of users' or experts' mental processes – and the techniques we have described here can tell us a great deal about processes such as reasoning, recall, planning and problem-solving (see, for example, Briggs, 1987, 1990; Johnson and Briggs, 1988).

This chapter has provided a basic overview of the question-asking and verbal protocol method, illustrating, step-by-step, how to make use of these techniques. The advantages and disadvantages of each have been discussed, with reference to real-world applications, and we have described those situations in which the methods can be employed.

It is quite likely that the coming years will witness an increased use of question-asking, verbal protocol techniques and their variants. This is seen, in part, as a product of the increasing automation being introduced into the workplace, and also as a function of the growth of usability engineering and human–computer interaction research. There is little doubt that as both the number and type of everyday interactive products increases, and the impact of these products upon out lives becomes greater, the demand for tools for the investigation and description of human interactions with machines can only grow.

References

Ainsworth, L.K. (1984) 'Are verbal protocols the answer or the question?', in E.D. Megaw (ed.), *Contemporary Ergonomics*. London: Taylor & Francis.

Bainbridge, L. (1979) 'Verbal reports as evidence of the process operator's knowledge', *International Journal of Man–Machine Studies*, 11: 411–36.

Bainbridge, L. (1990) 'Verbal protocol analysis', in J.R. Wilson and E.N. Corlett (eds), *Evaluation of Human Work: a Practical Ergonomics Methodology*. London: Taylor & Francis.

Briggs, P. (1987) 'Usability assessment for the office: methodological choices and their implications', in M. Frese, E. Ulich and W. Dzida (eds), *Psychological Issues of Human–Computer Interaction in the Workplace*. North Holland: Elsevier.

Briggs, P. (1988) 'What we know and what we need to know: the user model versus the user's model in human–computer interaction', *Behaviour and Information Technology*, 7 (4): 431–42.

Briggs, P. (1990) 'Do they know what they're doing? An evaluation of word-processor users' implicit and explicit task-relevant knowledge, and its role in self-directed learning', *International Journal of Man–Machine Studies*, 32: 385–98.

Carroll, J.M. and Campbell, R.L. (1986) 'Softening up hard science: reply to Newell and Card', *Human–Computer Interaction*, 2: 227–49.

Carroll, J.M. and Rosson, M.B. (1985) 'Usability specifications as a tool in iterative development', in H.R. Hartson (ed.), *Advances in Human–Computer Interaction. Vol 1*. Norwood, NJ: Ablex.

Ericsson, K.A. and Simon, H.A. (1984) *Protocol Analysis: Verbal Reports as Data*. Cambridge, MA: MIT Press.

Gammack, J.G. and Young, R.M. (1985) 'Psychological techniques for eliciting expert knowledge', in M.A. Bramer (ed.), *Research and Development in Expert Systems. Proceedings of the 4th Technical Conference of the BCS Specialist Group on Expert Systems*. Cambridge: Cambridge University Press.

Gould, J.D., Conti, J. and Hovanyecz, T. (1983) 'Composing letters with a simulated listening typewriter', *Communications of the ACM*, 28 (3): 295–308.

Grover, M.D. (1983) 'A pragmatic knowledge acquisition methodology', in *Proceedings of IJCAI-'83, International Joint Conference on Artificial Intelligence*.

Hackman, G.S. and Biers, D.W. (1992) 'Team usability testing: are two heads better than one?', in *Proceedings of the Human Factors Society 36th Annual Meeting*. Santa Monica, CA: HFS. pp. 1205–9.

Hoffman, R.R. (1987) 'The problem of extracting knowledge of experts from the perspective of experimental psychology', *AI Magazine*, 8: 53–66.

Johnson, G.I. and Briggs, P. (1988) 'Declarative knowledge elicitation: using concept-sorting to study structural aspects of user knowledge', in E.D. Megaw (ed.), *Contemporary Ergonomics 1988*. London: Taylor & Francis.

Kato, I. (1986) 'What "question-asking protocols" can say about the user interface', *International Journal of Man–Machine Studies*, 25: 659–73.

Kirwan, B. and Ainsworth, L.K. (eds) (1992) *A Guide to Task Analysis*. London: Taylor & Francis.

Miyake, N. and Norman, D.A. (1979) 'To ask a question, one must know enough to know what is not known', *Journal of Verbal Learning and Verbal Behaviour*, 18: 357–64.

Newell, A. and Card, S.K. (1985) 'The prospects for psychological science in human–computer interaction', *Human–Computer Interaction*, 1: 209–42.

Newell, A. and Card, S.K. (1986) 'Straightening out softening up: response to Carroll and Campbell', *Human–Computer Interaction*, 2: 251–67.

Shadbolt, N. and Burton, M. (1990) 'Knowledge elicitation', in J.R. Wilson and E.N. Corlett (eds), *Evaluation of Human Work: a Practical Ergonomics Methodology*. London: Taylor & Francis.

Vries, G. de and Johnson, G.I. (1992) 'Het gebruik van GOMS en de "limited information task" bij de evaluatie van een autoradio', *Tijdschrift voor Ergonomie*, Nederlandse Vereninging voor Ergonomie, December, 17 (6): 2–9.

Wright, P.C. and Monk, A. (1991) 'A cost-effective evaluation method for use by designers', *International Journal of Man–Machine Studies*, 35: 891–912.

Wright, R.B. (1992) 'Method bias and concurrent verbal protocol in software usability testing', in *Proceedings of the Human Factors Society 36th Annual Meeting*. Santa Monica, CA: HFS.

5

Repertory Grid Technique
in Constructive Interaction

John G. Gammack and Robert A. Stephens

Organizational inquiry often entails investigating the knowledge and viewpoints of individuals, and in this chapter we examine the use of the repertory grid as one qualitative method for eliciting constructions of knowledge from organizational members. After discussing some necessary philosophical background, we present the mechanics of the method itself, illustrated through two organizational case studies, and conclude by critically examining its methodological utility with respect to psychological inquiry in organizations.

Repertory grid focuses on the construction of meaning by individual participants in some context of interest, such as job evaluation or staff training. Originating as a clinical psychology test in therapeutic contexts, the technique has been developed more generally for use in a variety of settings. Repertory grid has been widely used in academic fields such as cognitive, clinical, educational and social psychology, and several theoretical extensions to the basic method have been proposed (see Beail, 1985; Neimeyer and Neimeyer, 1989; and Shaw, 1981, for collections of papers, and relevant journals such as *The International Journal of Personal Construct Psychology*). It has also been found useful in organizational research, and examples of its practical use are found in strategic management and decision-making (Dutton et al., 1989; Ginsberg, 1989; Hunter and Coggin, 1988), personnel management (Donaghue, 1992; Dunn et al., 1987; Furnham, 1990), information requirements analysis (Gutierrez, 1987), expert systems (Gammack, 1987; Shaw and Gaines, 1987), organizational behaviour (Arnold and Nicholson, 1991; Brook and Brook, 1989), recruitment (Anderson, 1990), business analysis (Hisrich and Jankowicz, 1990) and consumer relations (Smith and Harbisher, 1989). Many of these studies describe the qualitative use of the repertory grid as a technique to supplement or replace the interview, stressing its comparative efficiency and flexibility, and its greater potential for objective validity and reproducibility. Our use of the technique follows the constructivist philosophy of its originator, the psychologist George Kelly, and we begin our chapter by describing some necessary theoretical background.

Constructivism: some basic concepts

The repertory grid technique is derived from Kelly's (1955) Personal Construct Theory, and aims to identify the personally meaningful distinctions with which a view of the world is constructed. This implies that meaningful use of the technique requires its encapsulation within a constructivist philosophy. We argue that constructivism provides a fruitful theoretical framework for understanding and describing knowledge-use in human activity systems.

As one qualitative technique for investigating knowledge construction, we view the repertory grid as addressing more general issues of organizational inquiry. Although modelling organizational knowledge is conducted for a wide variety of purposes, our case studies concern the elicitation of organizational knowledge for information systems development. However, whether or not an information system development is the goal of the research, the process of identifying knowledge, opinions or beliefs is a form of psychological inquiry commonly found in organizational research. For such investigations, the repertory grid provides a powerful and flexible method, and, unusually for a psychological technique, is formulated within a theory which takes an explicit epistemological and ontological stance.

For complex domains, a methodology sensitive to the social and dialogical processes involved in constructing knowledge formulations is seen as appropriate (Gammack and Anderson, 1990). The repertory grid technique respects a constructivist ontology: rather than viewing knowledge as a disembodied commodity that can be removed from its context for independent analysis, the explicit construction of knowledge is seen as a process meaningful to the knowers involved in producing it. This has consequences for interpreters of symbolic knowledge structures. In organizational information systems, for example, it explains why users should participate in development, identifying the terms and concepts used naturally in everyday practice, and relating them closely to their work concerns.

Expanding on the issue of meaning, it is important to note that in formulating a knowledge structure for objective reference, meaning resides not in the structure itself, but in the interpretative processes of humans situated in a social domain of which that structure is a part. In any social milieu, this necessitates facilitating the intended interpretation of a semantic structure by ensuring that it is meaningful to the users. Practically, this implies a methodological emphasis on participation: for example, as an essential component in organizational IT developments (Floyd 1987), or in psychological studies employing cooperative research strategies (Heron, 1981). This emphasis helps reduce alienation of the user or 'subject' from the product of the inquiry.

Knowledge thus produced is to be considered formally not as either true or false, but as meaningful to its users in its context of use. Attention to situated practices changes the emphasis of the inquiry from a passive recording of 'true facts' (guaranteed by correspondence to the real world) to a qualitative act of construction with locally validated interpretation.

The theoretical framework of constructivism, which supports this change in emphasis, has an intellectual tradition established through the work of idealist philosophers to more contemporary thinkers such as John Dewey, Wilhelm Dilthey and Gregory Bateson. Constructivist ideas have also proved practically useful in areas as diverse as physics, biology, semiotics and law, as well as numerous cybernetic and systems applications in a variety of disciplines. In psychology, Piaget and George Kelly himself are notable representatives of this tradition.

This transdisciplinary diversity implies there is no single constructivist ontology, but that individual practice is informed by recognizably sympathetic assumptions. In an elegant introduction to radical constructivism, Glasersfeld (1984: 24) formulates some key assumptions as:

1   'All communication and all understanding are a matter of interpretive construction on the part of the experiencing subject.'
2   'The world which is constructed is an experiential world, that consists of experiences, and makes no claim whatsoever about "truth" in the sense of correspondence with an ontological reality.'
3   Structures are viable in an environment: reality 'limits what is possible'.

These ideas are essentially shared by all constructivists, although radical constructivism, the strong form advocated by Glasersfeld, makes ontological commitments which not all constructivists share. One key difference concerns the nature of reality. For Kelly, although people are free to construct their own ideas, there is none the less an objective reality which exists independently. For other constructivists, epitomized by Maturana (1988), such a reality is denied, and must remain a hypothetical construct appealed to rhetorically by the observer. In this sense Kelly and Maturana exemplify the differing ontological tendencies of philosophical realism and idealism, although they share the basic epistemological position that reality cannot be known directly; that reality is constructed and not directly revealed; and that we come to know reality through our processes of construing. Further clarification of these differences, with particular reference to Kelly, can be found in Feixas (1990).

It is not appropriate to tease out further differences in constructivist thinking in this chapter; instead, for the purposes of organizational inquiry, we would emphasize the following constructivist ideas:

1   Humans attribute meaning, it is not a simple property of the referent.
2   Meaning is negotiated through social action and dialogue.
3   Socially recognized knowledge constructions are adapted through interaction in a linguistic domain.

Knowledge construction and organizations

Another motivation for employing constructivist approaches becomes clear upon examining the nature of organizations in everyday action. Organizations are complex, social phenomena that can be understood in a variety of ways, and, as Morgan (1986) has made clear, much of this understanding is, in fact, based on metaphors such as the machine, brain, organism or political system. Very often the detached researcher is presented with an official story suggesting a functional or mechanical view where members perform procedural routines according to role and structure. The machine image provides a familiar and powerful metaphor for understanding and it is tempting for the researcher to accept this picture as foundational and proceed accordingly. But such a metaphor can be dangerously misleading, especially in qualitative investigations of organizational knowledge. The mechanical view is unable to account for most of the phenomena that would be of interest to the psychologist or organizational researcher. It is unable to account for organizational change; for the generation of problems, goals and objectives; or, indeed, for the generation of organizational structures, roles and boundaries themselves. Although such activities cannot be explained by a naïve mechanical view, this metaphor is still commonly adopted despite organizations essentially being constituted by the constructive processes of their members (see Lincoln, 1985). Tasks seeming mechanical to the outside observer actually result from knowledgeable choices, decisions, judgements and interpretations. Furthermore, since organizations 'are' people and people are meaning-attributers, it is insufficient to view them as automata with clearly limited and bounded functions, without self-will, and without private goals based on their own interpretation of their role in the organization. The orderly behaviour that suggests the organization to be mechanical is founded on such interpretative action: the machine image is accurately representational only at the level of metaphor, not of function.

Characterizing organizations instead by transformation, reproduction and mutual change directs the emphasis of inquiry towards the interpretative action of the individuals themselves and the systemic structural relations of the organization. Analysis conducted with this in mind identifies a more process-orientated view where people are observed applying skills, communicating, coordinating activity (in cooperation or conflict), and so on, all of which is seen to be self-determined, knowledge-based and purposive within the general organizational constraints.

Constructive interaction attitude and repertory grid method

The term constructive interaction (Miyake, 1986) was coined to describe situations in which pairs or groups produce a collective performance which is superior to that of any of the individuals involved. Through mutual evaluations and criticism of one another's perspectives, a new (shared) perspective can emerge enhanced by input from all parties. When different specialities are involved, a mutual learning and appreciation of others' assumptions can occur, increasing knowledge and identifying a common language in which various parties can find their understanding reflected.

By having intrinsically different perspectives on a problem, however, justification and explanations are naturally required, as well as straight knowledge transfers and clarifications. Constructive interaction is less a specific method than a methodological attitude, and has been used in numerous fields from peer-tutoring to problem-solving in human–computer interaction. (Some references and further details are given in Gammack and Anderson, 1990.)

The interpretation of the repertory grid is most meaningfully grounded in terms of Kelly's Personal Construct Theory, and, as a 'conversational technology', it also fits sensibly within the constructive interaction ethos. Kelly's work in clinical practice led him to adopt the principle of constructive alternativism, which allows for the interpretation of events to be revised, with therapeutic consequences in future dealings with the world. Kelly contrasted this principle with what he called accumulative fragmentalism, namely the idea that truth (and in particular psychological truth) is collected piece by piece and is not subject to higher-order reconstruction which may render findings trivial.

The fundamental postulate of Personal Construct Theory is that a person's thought processes are psychologically channelled by the ways in which events are anticipated. This is elaborated through 11 corollaries, prime among which is the construction corollary, which states that in order to anticipate events, a person construes or places an interpretation on their replication. The patterns which people invent in order to make sense of their world (whatever it may actually be) are called constructs, and Kelly suggests that, much as scientists might, individuals strive to improve these constructs to increase their repertory by altering them to provide better fits within larger systems.

Kelly, concerned with a person's social roles, devised a method (the Role Construct Repertory Test) for exploring a person's construct system according to terms and categories the subject spontaneously produces. Although other variations have been developed, here we describe the three stages of the basic repertory grid technique:

1   the elicitation of elements, identifying the entities in the area of construing to be investigated;
2   the elicitation of constructs, identifying the distinctions which can be applied amongst these elements; and
3   the construction of a matrix (grid) of elements and constructs.

In Kelly's original clinical work, exemplary elements are the names of the family and significant others, which may have been suggested by the clinician, rather than the client. Having identified a set of, say 20 or 30, the name of each element is written on a card and the elicitation of constructs begins.

The best-known method for eliciting the constructs is the minimum-context card or triadic method. This involves presenting three elements, asking the question 'In what way are two similar?' or 'How does one differ?' or 'What is the opposite of that characteristic?' There are no fixed rules and as many triads may be presented as the investigator deems necessary.

Using an illustrative example from Kelly (1970), the subject may say that both *mother* and *boss* always seemed to know the answers, but *father* hesitated, or said to seek out your own answers. This distinction produces two contrasting poles, which may be labelled for convenience as *knowledgeable* and *hesitant*. This distinction can probably be extended to the other people in the set, and, if constantly applied, does more than characterize the individuals concerned: it also provides an operational construct, giving a more extensive definition of a particular channel of thought than the words used to symbolize it.

The next step in the method is to enter the data for this construct in the grid. A matrix with elements along the top and constructs down the side is drawn up and the subject assigns a number to each cell representing how each element is regarded in terms of that construct. Typically, a five- or seven-point scale is used. By selecting another set of three cards, the cycle is repeated and the matrix is gradually built up, until it is large enough to give us a stable idea of how the person construes. Kelly's (1970) clinical experience suggests that around 20 to 30 constructs are generally required, but, as he notes, repertories used in everyday affairs are generally quite limited, especially among those who prefer to act rather than reflect, and in many practically orientated domains considerably fewer often suffice.

Having built up a grid in this way, analysis can begin. This analysis may take either or both of two forms: a statistical analysis involving the mathematical properties of the grid itself; and/or a more interpretative analysis involving the constructs and their labels and how the constructs abstract each element. Mathematical analysis makes it evident which constructs are effectively synonymous and the degree of variety or transformability among them, but even though mathematical analysis may identify apparently redundant constructs, subsequent interpretative analysis may reveal these to have distinctive semantic utility.

In the next section, we show the development and analysis of repertory grids through two practical case studies, the first of which emphasizes a more interpretative analysis of the grid labels, while the second illustrates one way in which the grid values themselves may be displayed as a focus for dialogue.

Applications of the technique

Our first study which illustrates the method concerns the quality control
of strip steel. Continuous inspection of strip steel is necessary to maintain
a high product-quality regime and to monitor production faults. The
organization employed four inspection teams (total 18 persons) working in
shift rotation, with a single member attending a remote video link
displaying both surfaces of the hot strip as it exited from the rolling-mills.
At the typically very fast rolling speeds, defects are only visible on the
video monitor for a split second. Distinguishing these from normal
markings or interference is a highly-skilled but tedious task, demanding
intense concentration. Teams normally share the burden of remote
inspection, with one member not expected to operate the cameras for
more than two or three hours.

In order to extend this inspection process to one of its other plants, the
company commissioned research to assess the potential for automatic
computer detection and classification of steel defects. Because each
inspection team had its own work practice and because levels of
experience varied, one research concern was to discover the degree of
uniformity of defect categories used by the inspectors and to establish
working definitions appropriate to the quality inspection task.

This objective implied that our research be sensitive to the inspectors'
own working experience and not merely reinforce categories imposed by
prior assumptions. The chosen method involved three stages:

1   an initial repertory grid exercise with each member of the four
    inspection teams;
2   constructively analysing and documenting the grid data;
3   participant review and critique to clarify the data and discuss
    ambiguities.

Although the repertory grid exercise is normally marked by its economy
in time and application, this particular study involved the added difficulty
of introducing into a verbal arena phenomena normally encountered only
visually, so our sessions generally took between one and two hours. As
the research had to conform to cyclical shift patterns, the complete study
covered a period of about three months, which, including subsequent
discussion sessions, required considerable effort from each inspector. In
many situations this investment could not be warranted, but as the
inspectors had been working with the experimental technology as it
evolved, they generally considered this an opportunity to exert an
influence on the overall development. In addition to the grid data,
concurrent informal discussion enriched our understanding. In particular,
inspectors commented on the relative information yielded by digitally
recorded images, and the elicited knowledge was used to produce a
comprehensive common catalogue of defects. Aiming to establish a
catalogue of categories familiar to all inspectors, we continually refined

this central research document until there was broad agreement over the descriptions, and areas of ambiguity and disagreement were fully recorded.

Having provided an overview of the research, we now examine in more detail how the repertory grid was used to investigate the inspectors' category schemes. In our example, it seemed reasonable to take the names of defects, although in the course of the investigation it became apparent that we might just as effectively have used events (such as mechanical process interruptions) as the elements. The elements were selected from samples and photographs of defective steel strip, identified by numbers throughout elicitation; only later were agreed names attributed. We found writing these names on individual 'post-it' notes to be particularly useful as they can be conveniently manipulated and incremented, and readily attached to various surfaces such as photographs and documents. The elements were chosen to be representative in consultation with the first inspector, and subsequently validated with the others. After identifying 30 elements, the participants chose a subset to work with, and results were recorded in a spread-sheet for convenience of analysis and graphical presentation. This also allowed individual inspectors' shared constructs to be compared.

Figure 5.1 shows part of one inspector's repertory grid with elements as columns and elicited constructs as rows. Thus, if a *bruise* defect is present on the strip, the image will display a gloss, rather than a matt appearance. As the grid is being constructed, checking the cell values indicates when elements are persistently grouped together and therefore the investigator may choose a triad from that group to force a distinction. For example, the three firecrack defects (E, G and H) had the same generic origin so some participants chose not to treat them as distinct elements; comparing this triad, however, produced the construct *matt* vs *gloss*. Conversely, if distinguishing a triad fails, the elements may be sufficiently similar to be combined.

We repeated this exercise with each inspector and generated a large set of constructs from which we could infer the contextual information associated with the defects. Using the grid as a focus for dialogue, we determined that the constructs largely fell into three categories: those concerning the origin of defects (process diagnosis); those concerned with appearance (ease of detection); and those concerning the progression of the defect (process control), from which we developed a diagnostic profile for each defect (detailed in Stephens, 1992). By using the element rankings from the cells in the grids, unique descriptions of each defect were documented and represented to the inspection teams for verification. Over a period of some weeks the document was continually revised according to inspectors' recommendations until a measure of stability and agreement was achieved.

In indexing the 30 visual images to our catalogue, *jet* and *fleck* scale defects proved to be particularly problematic. Although each could be

Elements

Constructs	Lamination	Scratch	RIS	Sliver	B/M firecrack	Fleck	Rad. firecrack	Firecrack	Spall	Pickup	Jet	Rub mark	Eruise	
Regular	4	1	1	4	1	2	1	1	1	1	3	1	1	Haphazard
Continuous	5	1	2	5	3	1	3	3	3	3	4	3	3	Periodic
Lipped	1	3	3	1	3	3	4	4	1	2	3	2	5	Smooth
Large mark	3	3	2	4	4	5	3	3	3	3	1	4	2	Small mark
Matt	4	2	1	3	1	1	4	4	5	4	1	5	5	Gloss
Narrow band	2	1	2	3	5	5	4	5	2	4	3	5	4	Wide band
	A	B	C	D	E	F	G	H	I	J	K	L	M	

Figure 5.1   *Part of a quality inspector's repertory grid*

classified as either a *roller* type of defect, or a *scale* type, there was little consensus among inspectors. The repertory grid technique has highlighted the fact that an element can support different interpretations, and, therefore, ambiguity, which we suggest is best practically resolved dialogically through constructive interaction. Practically, this took the form of using the document as the focal point of an ongoing dialogue for both raising and recording areas of disagreement. As the causes of some defects were a matter of speculation, it was important to preserve, rather than suppress, alternative views and explanations.

We had begun our investigation with the intention of gaining classificatory information about the perceived visual characteristics of steel defects. The process of identifying this characterization revealed that the task was not simply isolated visual inspection but part of a larger process diagnosis or quality management operation, evident from the relative paucity of constructs only concerned with appearance. Using Kelly's terms, a constellation of events occurs allowing a recognized defect to be anticipated. It was observed during the study that the names of defects symbolized these events, and, as we have noted, perhaps the events themselves could have constituted a suitable element set. Although identifying categories is done naturally by humans, the repertory grid forces verbal labels which may not have been previously reified, and this can prove difficult. The method was suitable, however, since assigning symbols to visual information and categorizing them for purposeful use was the point of the research. Our initial naïve view, endorsed by corporate perspectives, that the job essentially involved placing defect images into known categories, proved incompatible with how the inspectors themselves conceived their work, and the extant classification used for reporting defects was not vindicated. The strength of the repertory grid in allowing a construction in the subject's own language provided the basis for a more valid account, with implications for information system design.

Our second example of repertory grid technique concerns the classification of health concepts, and in particular the names of diseases and medical conditions. This was done as part of the knowledge elicitation for an expert system development in an insurance company (Gammack, 1992). Taking a list of about 90 diseases which commonly appear on a life insurance application form, our aim was to produce a principled classification structure to determine whether a medical risk was constituted. As 90 items were too many to list on a single screen in our expert system, we wished to discover classifications from which we could derive a taxonomy that could form the basis of a hierarchical menu-driven system.

The original classification provided by our expert underwriter from medical textbooks and insurance manuals divided the diseases along the lines of bodily functions, so our top-level classification consisted of 14 categories such as endocrine diseases, cardiovascular diseases, pulmonary diseases and so on. The seven or so diseases within each category were effectively divided into risky and non-risky types, so when the end-user of the system saw, for example, tonsillitis, he or she would choose the *ear, nose and throat* option from the top menu, and find that tonsillitis was generally a non-risky condition.

What we had not foreseen, however, was that, unlike the expert, our end-users would not have had sufficient medical training to know that tonsillitis fell into the ear, nose and throat category, and thus they would be unable to proceed beyond the first screen! The classification constructed along the lines of medical theory was not meaningful to this type of user, and instead we had to develop a different classification which could relate to the concerns of underwriters, and based on criteria which they could be expected to know from their own experience. This was done using the repertory grid, and provided a rather different angle on the same set of diseases.

Using another experienced (but not medically trained) underwriter as our expert, we chose three diseases at random, and this elicited the first construct, *treatable* vs *terminal*, along which dimension the 90 diseases were rated. Our second random triad elicited the construct *symptom indicative of something more serious* vs *limited risk*, and our third the distinction between *chronic* and *acute* diseases. Although this was still medical knowledge, it had been acquired incidentally through general experience, basic training, conversation with peers, and the media. After five triads, we had enough information to design a classification in terms of the constructs meaningful to underwriters. A similar exercise with another underwriter produced similar constructs, and, although no formal validation was required, informal discussion with each underwriter confirmed that the other's constructs and ratings made sense.

Figure 5.2 illustrates a Pathfinder associative network analysis (Schvaneveldt, 1990) of this (reduced) repertory grid data which concisely represents the underwriter's conceptual model of the concepts. The Pathfinder technique discovers the inter-item structure in proximity matrices. Taking each cell of a square matrix to contain the associative strength between a pair of items, the technique iteratively removes cells when there is a shorter path through the data, converging on a minimal spanning tree. This represents the strongest associations for each item in the data set, and user-adjustable parameters allow different metric assumptions to be applied. Thus if there is only a distant association between item A and C (a large valued cell), but it is possible to go in two short steps from item A to item C via item B, the direct link A–C will be dropped.

Links show nearest neighbours in the subject's conceptual space, with strength of association determined by the similarity on the repertory grid profiles. For this, only ordinal assumptions have been made about the data, and although links have numerical weights, these have been omitted from this figure. It is, however, evident that the 'non-life-threatening diseases' are associated with one another towards the top of the figure, while the 'serious diseases' are clustered towards the bottom of the figure. This is an effective way to present the construed similarities of elements in a domain, for further investigation or to inform the design of information systems. The figure, however, must be understood by reference to the context in which it was produced, and to the constructs which give coherence to the associations. When this figure was shown to a group of nurses, they laughed at its apparent incoherence according to known medical theory, but when told the context, they accepted that it made sense given the underwriter's concerns. This classification study identified the information which designers need to know to provide effective help screens, and allowed the explanations given on these screens to be cast in terms of the classifications that trainees need to learn and to which they can relate.

Following the same method, a second repertory grid using these 90 elements was conducted with an experienced nurse as subject, providing yet another categorization. This time the diseases were construed in terms of their implications for care. Constructs such as *out-patient* vs *hospitalization, round the clock* vs *occasional monitoring* (level of care) and *prescription* vs *high-street availability* (of drugs) were the relevant

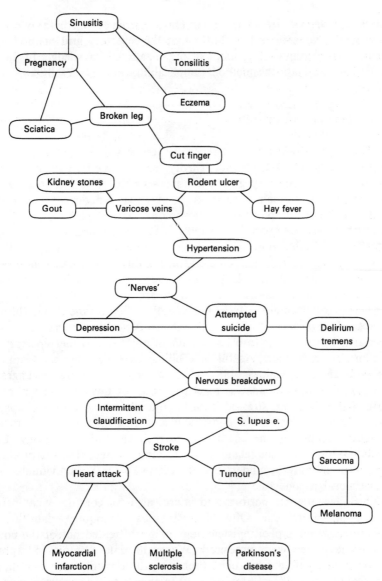

Figure 5.2 *Simplified Pathfinder network of an underwriter's medical concepts*

discriminations among diseases, and naturally provided a very different association pattern.

These studies show the use of the repertory grid in identifying the distinctions and concerns relevant to working life, and have obvious implications for the provision of information systems specified in the terms understood by their users. Our experience in these two (quite different) organizations has shown that the repertory grid method works well in discovering constructions of organizational knowledge. In the final section we evaluate the method's applicability more generally.

Conclusions and critique

Kelly's original role construct repertory test was developed in the clinical context of Personal Construct Theory, so the question arises: to what extent can the repertory grid technique sensibly be used outside Kelly's theory in other domains? Apart from our own experience, its continued and widespread application is testimony to its general utility, and researchers' use of quantitative analysis techniques and variant forms of construct elicitation suggests that the method is robust against violation of its theoretical assumptions. One reason for this is that much inquiry and formularization of knowledge is founded on identifying theoretical distinctions and classifications, and these are intrinsically delivered by the repertory grid technique. It is worth noting, for instance, that the more successful applications of expert systems typically concern the use of specialized distinctions to classify domain objects, and the repertory grid has proved particularly useful in eliciting these distinctions (Gammack, 1987; Shaw and Gaines, 1987). Indeed, many software packages are available to elicit and analyse repertory grids for this and other purposes.

We have, however, stressed from the outset the importance of applying the technique following the constructivist spirit in which it was originally designed. Applying the method constructively, and (following Kelly) assuming humans to be meaning-constructors, implies that the product of the research must be understood by reference to the individuals in the social world it concerns.

This view of the repertory grid is critical if we consider what psychological data represent. Often in psychological inquiry, data are not referenced to an explicit epistemology and are treated out of the context from which they were produced. When the data purport to represent knowledge constituted by social processes, the classifications of data may not be meaningful without explicit reference to that environment. A constructivist interpretation of the repertory grid recognizes this, in contrast to the accumulative fragmentalism common in psychology (but rejected by Kelly).

Another methodological concern in this chapter has been the promotion of individual autonomy through forming representations in language sensible to the participants involved. Heron (1981) has criticized standard research procedures on the grounds that they undermine the self-determination of their 'subjects', denying that very aspect we are interested in: the creative thinking that goes into 'making sense'. Unless the inquiry is firmly based in the experience of those it seeks to understand, knowledge becomes 'alienated' and therefore lacks validity. The value of the repertory grid, by not prescribing the content, is in offering a structure in which the inquiry can proceed in the subjects' own terms, while, in contrast, a purely quantitative analysis of disembodied numbers cannot address the sense-making process of knowledgeable subjects.

As a qualitative technique, the repertory grid is often compared with structured interviewing. Each has strengths and weaknesses, but the relative efficiency of the repertory grid is one commonly reported advantage. This is important in organizations where people's time is at a premium and it is important for the investigator to be perceived as professional in obtaining relevant information. The fact that the structure is not imposed as in a questionnaire but represents the subject's own construction makes it more ecologically valid, and in practice can reduce resistance to the inquiry.

In the remainder of this chapter we critically appraise the element, construct and analysis components of the repertory grid as a general research instrument. The steel inspection study showed how subjects identified, and for the first time explicitly reified, a phenomenon of their world which, having been explicated, could then be formally agreed in shared documentation. This explication uniquely pertains to the social world in which it was produced, and could not a priori have been prescribed by an experimenter. When the elements are provided by an experimenter, this can compromise subjects' freedom to choose elements meaningful to themselves, and requires the experimenter to assume that a subject's construal of the elements is in some way compatible with the reasons behind the choice of elements themselves. For example, a range of elements selected as representing medical theories of bodily systems may not be the best set for eliciting criteria for differentiating patient care. When elements are not properly owned by the subject, there is also the danger that the classifications will be inappropriate, superficial or even unknowledgeable. Elements supplied by management may elicit mere company line, rather than the distinctions used in practice. Furthermore, externally supplied elements may include obsolete items no longer relevant to current operational concerns. When the subject is billed as an expert the encounter becomes particularly value-laden and there may be a tacit and unrealistic expectation, condoned by both sides, that each element is sufficiently well known to be reliably assessed. As long as the subject is understood to be more knowledgeable, the investigator is in no position to gainsay the subject's version.

Without a detailed knowledge of the research context it will be initially difficult for the subject to provide a representative element set without discussion with and direction from the investigator. Equally, however, it is difficult for the investigator to ensure beforehand that a supplied set of elements is representative of the subject's real concerns. Indeed, since identifying appropriate elements is a critical part of the inquiry, there is a strong motivation for embedding the technique within a methodology of constructive interaction. Approaches to cooperative inquiry are outlined by Reason (1988), who advocates the establishment of a research partnership where all parties collaborate equally to establish topics and methods from the outset. Gammack (1988) suggests using interview and card sorts to ensure representativeness by identifying gaps and redundancies in element sets. These supplementary techniques aid in the choice of 'stimuli' at the outset. For instance, in one study concerning the classification of steam trains, a set of photographs was culled from a coffee-table book and arranged by the expert using a hierarchical card sort. This revealed that there were many 'heavy express passenger' trains and relatively few 'light freight', which produced an unbalanced tree structure. Questioning revealed that, while this reflected a real-world bias, it was also the case that express passenger trains were overrepresented in the sample, and there were only minor differences between those items. This led to the removal of several items before conducting the repertory grid proper. Even then, however, significant elements may still be missed, and there are the inevitable assumptions associated with generalization from samples, that is, that these elements are sufficient to capture the relevant properties of the domain, and that the distinctions that pertain to them apply more widely.

Kelly's notion of range of convenience applies here, namely the idea that constructs have a limited range to which they apply. Thus *weather* and *light* are outside the range of convenience of the construct *tall* vs *short* (Kelly, 1963: 69), which causes difficulties for quantitative analysis, as we discuss later. One practical way to minimize this is to ensure the homogeneity of elements, that is, the elements should identifiably belong to some coherent class. Apart from this restriction, one great advantage of the repertory grid is that the elements can be anything which is identifiable as a domain object, be it verbal token, visual image, sound, event or whatever.

Sometimes, not all the elements in a triad are equally representative, and one may epitomize a distinctive characteristic. When one element is salient compared to the other two, the relevant distinction may be exemplar/non-exemplar. The theoretical rationale for using triads is not merely to identify a binary distinction, but a construct which has greater descriptive generality. This generality is ensured by the requirement that two elements on the construct pole share some common likeness, which thereby distinguishes them from the contrast element. Because the method itself anticipates equal representativeness, weaker distinctions are likely to be contrived. To obviate this, the investigator should attempt to establish independently the utility of the distinction at the time of construct elicitation by asking for the person's view, and allowing him or her to replace elements in an unproductive triad.

The question arises, however: should the formulation of knowledge be in terms of triad-dependent distinctions at all? It may be that the most practical distinction is a simple binary split. A main concern of an art-buyer, for example, is the distinction between *fake* and *authentic*: discrete categories where the degree of the property is not applicable. In such cases it makes no sense to force a weaker, triad-dependent distinction, such as *greenish* vs *reddish* paintings.

Repertory grid technique's emphasis on the forcing of distinctions may result in missing important and even definitional characteristics of the elements. For instance, an important fact about all trains is that they run on tracks, but a repertory grid to distinguish trains from one another will never elicit this information. Relatedly, the method provides little guidance as to the degree of distinction required. Triads can be 'milked' to produce further distinctions with the proviso that subsequent distinctions may be weaker, or contrived. On the other hand, the further consideration required may produce stronger distinctions, perhaps more tacit and less verbally accessible.

Not all constructs are equal and the investigator must attempt to ascertain which are truly relevant. The corollaries of Kelly's PCT provide theoretical guidance here. For instance, the *organization corollary* notes that a person's construction system embraces ordinal relations between constructs such that one construct will subsume another, while the *commonality corollary* and the *individuality corollary* allow for different people to construe the same events in similar terms or in different ways respectively. Methodologically, our use of multiple repertory grids helped shared or public constructs to be identified, and simple computational techniques to detect correlations and other transformations relating constructs allow implicit organization to be discovered. In a repertory grid for eliciting classificatory knowledge of trains, for example (Gammack, 1987), the primary construct *freight* vs *passenger* subsumes highly correlated constructs concerning wheel-size, which, although mathematically equally discriminating, are semantically less salient than (if not actually contingent on) the primary distinction.

One general danger of the method of triads, especially for minor constructs, is that the construct elicited is too strongly determined by the particular triad. Although the ratings for the elements in the triad may be accurate with respect to the specific construct, a subject may not know enough about the other elements to rate them accurately, or even to say if the construct is particularly relevant, and this was observed with the less experienced subjects in both our case studies. Methodologically, this may be detected by a preponderance of mid-point values, and it is in any case advisable to use the grid conversationally as a focal point for qualitative investigation, rather than as a simple quantitative product.

This brings us to analysis of the repertory grid. Although the grid is numeric, it can be misleading to assume it has conventional metric properties. Scale mid-point values, for instance, may represent several different significations. A mid-point value may mean that the construct is irrelevant; that neither extreme applies; that both extremes apply; that an intermediate value genuinely applies; or that the subject simply does not know which value to assign to an element. For this reason, the researcher should ascertain which interpretation is appropriate, possibly using zero to signify irrelevance or symbols to reduce the temptation to overinterpret the numbers.

Two related aspects are the issues of equivalence and dimensionality. Quantitative techniques assume that all instances of a number in the grid can be treated as equivalent. But, if a construct is not particularly relevant to an element, then a value given to that element will have less force than the same value given to a highly relevant item (such as one in the original triad from which the construct was generated). Similarly, with weaker constructs, analysis techniques should use inter-construct correlation statistics to help distinguish important from contingent distinctions and reduce any redundancy in the dimensional space of the grid. The problem with reducing the mathematical dimensionality, however, is that it can lose important semantic information.

If it is further assumed that the original triad constitutes both extremes of the construct (reflected in the assignment of extreme values of the scale), then there is no guarantee that other elements in the set will not require still more extreme values to be assigned. Moreover, there is no indication as to how this range of values equates with the population at large. If one construct covers a broader spectrum than another, the ranges may not be commensurable. Finally, rating elements on a range implies, mathematically, that the construct embodies a dimension with at least ordinal properties. This may be misleading as a construct is essentially a semantic device, with no a priori requirement to conform to the limitations of metric space. For example, in Figure 5.1 there is no sensible mid-point on the construct *smooth* vs *lipped*, and while values below (or above) the mid-point may be relatively ordinal, the two halves of the scale do not constitute a single dimension.

Any quantitative analysis must be referenced against a qualitative appreciation of the data's meaning, and the technique is compromised if merely applied as a cookbook recipe for obtaining a data matrix which is then subjected to disembodied analysis. Users of the repertory grid technique who disregard its original constructivist intention and un-critically apply quantitative analyses may be making unjustifiable metric assumptions. Although quantitative analyses of the grid data may provide useful insights into domain relationships, we recommend instead that the matrix be used primarily as a conversation focus for complementary qualitative analysis involving in-depth interviews; exploration of definitions; relating elicited constructs to events and work practices, and more specifically identifying their range and foci of convenience. Such analysis should also aim to elaborate the semantic and organizational properties of the elicited grid with respect to the purpose of the inquiry.

The practical value of the repertory grid exercise lies in discovering a common language, with an associative structure, which in our first example gave form and content to our descriptions of a particular segment of organizational knowledge, and in the second example was used in the development of a knowledge-based system. The grid, diagrams and documentation gave a shape and terminology to the domain which could be mutually referenced, since it represented a common understanding in a recognizable way, while also providing the basis for building and documenting information systems. The cooperation involved in producing this intermediate representation thus reflects the understandings required by both participants in the research process.

Regardless of the grid and its analysis, there remains, however, the need to establish independently whether the distinctions elicited are of practical consequence in the domain of interest. This inevitably lies beyond the method itself which is why we have emphasized that it should be methodologically embodied within constructive inquiry. When repertory grid is conducted within this atmosphere it fulfils Kelly's original aspirations for a more scientific psychology: a terrain in which subjects can display the same imaginative and creative powers that investigators attribute to themselves.

Acknowledgement

We would like to thank Anne Moggridge for helpful comments on an earlier draft of this chapter.

References

Anderson, N.R. (1990) 'Repertory grid technique in employee selection', *Personnel Review*, 19 (3): 9–15.

Arnold, J. and Nicholson, N. (1991) 'Construing of self and others at work in the early years of corporate careers', *Journal of Organizational Behavior*, 12 (7): 621–39.

Beail, N. (ed.) (1985) *Repertory Grid Techniques and Personal Constructs: Applications in Clinical and Educational Settings*. London: Croom Helm.

Brook, J.A. and Brook, R.J. (1989) 'Exploring the meaning of work and nonwork', *Journal of Organizational Behavior*, 10 (2): 169–78.

Donaghue, C. (1992) 'Towards a model of set adviser effectiveness', *Journal of European Industrial Training*, 16 (1): 20–6.

Dunn, W.N., Pavlak, T.J. and Roberts, G.E. (1987) 'Cognitive performance appraisal – mapping managers' category structures using the grid technique', *Personnel Review*, 16 (3): 16–19.

Dutton, J.E., Walton, E.J. and Abrahamson, E. (1989) 'Important dimensions of strategic issues: separating the wheat from the chaff', *Journal of Management Studies*, 26 (4): 379–96.

Feixas, G. (1990) 'Personal construct theory and systemic therapies: parallel or convergent trends?', *Journal of Marital and Family Therapy*, 16 (1): 1–20.

Floyd, C. (1987) 'Outline of a paradigm change in software engineering', in G. Bjerknes, P. Ehn and M. Kyng (eds), *Computers and Democracy: A Scandinavian Challenge*. Aldershot: Avebury.

Furnham, A. (1990) 'A question of competency', *Personnel Management*, 22 (6): 37.

Gammack, J.G. (1987) 'Modelling expert knowledge using cognitively compatible structures', *Proceedings of the Third International Expert Systems Conference*. Oxford: Learned Information.

Gammack, J.G. (1988) 'Eliciting expert conceptual structure using converging techniques'. Unpublished PhD dissertation, University of Cambridge.

Gammack, J.G. (1992) 'Knowledge engineering issues in decision-support', in G. Wright and F.M.I. Bolger (eds), *Expertise in Decision Support*. New York: Plenum Press.

Gammack, J.G. and Anderson, A. (1990)'Constructive interaction in knowledge engineering', *Expert Systems*, 7 (1): 19–26.

Ginsberg, A. (1989) 'Construing the business portfolio: a cognitive model of diversification', *Journal of Management Studies*, 26 (4): 417–38.

Glasersfeld, E. von (1984) 'An introduction to radical constructivism', in P. Watzlawick (ed.), *The Invented Reality*. New York: Norton.

Gutierrez, O. (1987) 'Some aspects of information requirements analysis using a repertory grid technique', in R. Galliers (ed.), *Information Analysis: Selected Readings*. Singapore: Addison-Wesley.

Heron, J. (1981) 'Philosophical basis for a new paradigm', in P. Reason and J. Rowan (eds), *Human Inquiry: a Sourcebook of New Paradigm Research*. Chichester: Wiley.

Hisrich, R.D. and Jankowicz, A.D. (1990) 'Intuition in venture capital decisions: an exploratory study using a new technique', *Journal of Business Venturing*, 5 (1): 49–62.

Hunter, J.E. and Coggin, T.D. (1988) 'Analysts' judgement: the efficient market hypothesis versus a psychological theory of human judgement', *Organizational Behavior & Human Decision Processes*, 42 (3): 284–302.

Kelly, G.A. (1955) *The Psychology of Personal Constructs*. New York: Norton.

Kelly, G.A. (1963) *A Theory of Personality*. New York: Norton.

Kelly G.A. (1970) 'A brief introduction to Personal Construct Theory', in D. Bannister (ed.), *Perspectives in Personal Construct Theory*. London and New York: Academic Press.

Lincoln, Y.S. (ed.) (1985) *Organizational Theory and Inquiry: the Paradigm Revolution*. London: Sage.

Maturana, H. (1988) 'Reality: the search for objectivity or the quest for a compelling argument', *The Irish Journal of Psychology*, 9: 144–72.

Miyake, N. (1986) 'Constructive interaction and the iterative process of understanding', *Cognitive Science*, 10 (2): 151–77.

Morgan, G. (1986) *Images of Organization*. Beverley Hills, CA: Sage.

Neimeyer, R.A. and Neimeyer, G.J. (eds) (1989) *Advances in Personal Construct Theory*. Greenwich, CT: JAI Press.

Reason, P. (ed.) (1988) *Human Inquiry in Action: Developments in New Paradigm Research*. London: Sage.

Schvaneveldt, R.W. (ed.) (1990) *Pathfinder Associative Networks: Studies in Knowledge Organization*. Norwood, NJ: Ablex.

Shaw, M.L.G. (ed.) (1981) *Recent Advances in Personal Construct Technology*. London: Academic Press.

Shaw, M.L.G. and Gaines, B.R. (1987) 'An interactive knowledge-elicitation technique using personal construct technology', in A.L. Kidd (ed.), *Knowledge Acquisition for Expert Systems: a Practical Handbook*. New York: Plenum Press.

Smith, D. and Harbisher, A. (1989) 'Building societies as retail banks: the importance of customer service and corporate image', *International Journal of Bank Marketing*, 7 (1): 22–7.

Stephens, R. (1992) 'Defect categories employed in the quality inspection of hot strip steel'. Technical Report, Bristol Transputer Centre, University of the West of England, UK.

6

Discourse Analysis in an Occupational Context

Harriette Marshall

The analysis of discourse became established through the 1980s as an alternative perspective to the examination of psychological issues. Discourse analysis builds on developments in literary theory, linguistics and sociology, such as ethnomethodology, speech act theory and semiotics. These developments all emphasize the constructive and action-orientated nature of language and focus attention on language as a social practice in its own right. While there are now many examples of the use of discourse analysis on central concepts and subject areas in psychology including attitudes, attributions, memory, personality and self, there are relatively few examples in an occupational context. Previous research which has studied various areas of relevance to an occupational domain from a discourse analytic perspective includes the examination of psychological assessment in organizations (Hollway, 1984), gender and occupational opportunities (Wetherell et al., 1987) and representations of occupational identity (Marshall and Wetherell, 1989).

Recent research has defined discourse analysis in a variety of ways. Beyond the realm of psychology, both research into broad-based historical shifts in ways of speaking about individual pathology (Foucault, 1971) and the micro-examination of conversational exchanges (Stubbs, 1983) have been characterized as discourse analysis. The 'version' of discourse analysis that will be adopted in this chapter follows that of Potter and Wetherell (1987). Discourse analysis places the focus on language as used in social texts, both written and spoken. This therefore includes interview material, open-ended questionnaire responses, group discussions and policy documentation. Attention is given to the structure and organization of discourse with concern for the possible consequences of the use of particular versions or constructions in the text. In this chapter, the analysis concerns the linguistic resources used by midwives and health visitors as they talk about occupational role and good maternity practice.

Discourse analysis has a theoretical background which differs from other, more traditional approaches in psychology. Two key differences are outlined in this chapter as they have important implications for the aims of research in an occupational domain. One difference concerns the perspective taken towards language, and the other the unit for analysis.

First, with respect to language. Traditionally, psychologists, including occupational psychologists, have taken language as being a transparent medium which is thought to reflect reality unproblematically. This understanding of language can be seen in standard questionnaires where a pool of statements about a certain object or issue are compiled by the researcher. Participants are then requested to respond to each statement, either in the form of a 'yes' or 'no' response, or on a scale ranging from 'strongly agree' to 'strongly disagree'. The sum of the participant's responses are then used for classification, to place that individual into a category, as being a certain sort of person, for example an extrovert or introvert. The language used in the questionnaire statements is thus used as a means of getting at, or tapping, some underlying entity, in this example a particular personality trait. It is taken as being a useful pathway for the examination of some other psychological phenomena, and no more.

Alternatively, discourse analysts reject this realist assumption and make language the focus for study in its own right. Language is seen as playing an active constructive role. Discourse analysts make the argument that any person, policy or event can be described in many different ways and that speakers draw on varying characterizations of 'reality' according to what they are doing. For example, they may move from formulating a positive evaluation of a particular policy in the context of discussing their year's work with an employer, to talking about the same policy in negative terms as creating additional work and unnecessary stress, when talking about job dissatisfaction with a friend. A central concern of discourse analysis is the examination of variation, to see how and when variation emerges and what purpose it serves. In taking the perspective that language is constructive, discourse analysts argue that the linguistic resources available to a speaker set certain parameters on our understanding and action. By taking apart and denaturalizing the linguistic constructions used in a social text, it becomes possible to examine the parameters in terms of the possibilities and constraints set by one particular construction over another.

A second way in which the theoretical background of discourse analysis differs when compared to other methodological approaches concerns the unit for analysis. Most traditional methods are concerned with the individual subject. There are numerous examples in the history of occupational psychology of the examination of individual differences, whether in terms of motivation, job satisfaction, productivity or management potential. These studies draw on a range of methodologies, with questionnaires and interviews frequently playing a key role in this endeavour. The aim in each case is to categorize individuals, for example those with intrinsic as compared to extrinsic motivation, or those with management potential, as compared to those without. An essentialist perspective can be seen in the assumption that there is something located within the individual, a particular personality trait or package of traits, which is consistent over time and across situations, which causes the individual to act in a certain way. Thus the explanation for all sorts of social phenomena is sought within the individual. The researcher scrutinizes the individual subject in the attempt to measure certain characteristics and thus differentiate between individuals.

In contrast, discourse analysts work from the assumption that diversity and fragmentation is to be expected at an individual level, and that individuals will represent themselves in varying ways according to context. Thus, discourse analysts are concerned with regularities at the level of language in terms of recurring patterns in the constructions or repertoires used in social texts. So, then, the aim of discourse analysts is to examine the constructions and meanings of phenomena in society that are available and drawn on by people as they make sense of various aspects of their lives. The concern is at the level of shared meanings and conceptualizations available and used by participants to inform their work, as voiced in their accounts. Discourse analysis does not represent a form of subjectivism. Repertoires are conceptualized not as originating from the individual but as culturally and historically embedded and socially communicated. Thus, health carers' discussions of good health care are made possible by a pre-existing pool of linguistic resources which participants draw on to represent themselves and their ideas. Thus discourse analysis moves the unit of analysis away from the individual.

Working from this theoretical base means that discourse analysis looks somewhat different from traditional analyses. Given that the focus is on language in its own right, a first step in the analysis involves the identification of shared systems of meanings or constructions used in particular social texts. The term 'interpretative repertoires' is useful here. These have been defined as clusters of terms, descriptions and figures of speech and can be understood as the building blocks used to make constructions or versions of cognitive processes, actions, policies and other phenomena (Gilbert and Mulkay, 1984; Wetherell and Potter, 1988, 1992).

Discourse analysts are concerned not only with the identification and description of various repertoires as used in particular contexts, but also to examine the consequences of the use of that particular repertoire. In this sense, close attention has to be paid to the context of use. Discourse analysts argue for the importance of working with extended segments of discourse, rather than short decontextualized extracts, as with questionnaires. This concern with context allows any variation which emerges to be fully explored, and this plays a central part in the analysis. The process of discourse analysis is illustrated in this chapter through the description of a study of health carers' discussions of occupational role and good maternity care. An outline of the background to the study is provided in the following section.

Application example: good maternity care in Britain in the 1990s

There have been many changes in health care policy through the 1980s and 1990s in Britain. These changes include the ways in which the role of the health carer is defined. Whereas, previously, the role of health carers, including that of the midwife and health visitor, was said to entail being in a position of 'telling', conveying knowledge and advice to each client, now the emphasis is placed on 'listening', and engaging in a dialogue with the client (Iliffe, 1982; Lynam, 1992). Thus the conceptualization of good care has moved away from being unidirectional to being a two-way process of communication between carer and client.

Similarly, there have been changes in the way good practice is characterized. Reciprocity or reciprocal care is now emphasized where health carers find out and respond to the individual client's needs, choices and values (UKCC, 1986). The importance of empathic care is also stated, defined as communicating concern, responding to client needs and acting from a base of mutual understanding, cooperation and exchange. These broad prescriptions of good care share the representation of the relationship between carer and client as acting in partnership.

These policy changes have been justified by research. Reciprocal care is said to lead to greater client satisfaction at the time of care and subsequently to result in a more positive maternal experience (Foster and Mayall, 1990; Morgan et al., 1984). In terms of health education, a dialogue or partnership style is said to be more effective where the health carer works from an understanding of the client's priorities and circumstances. Alternatively, where a 'top down' style is adopted, this is said to be likely to result in alienation of the client and a subsequent rejection of advice (Naidoo, 1986).

These characteristics of good care have received increasing attention in the research literature. One main concern has been to develop measures for differentiating between individual health carers in terms of empathy (La Monica, 1981), or the empathic personality (Sparling and Jones, 1977), through to the identification of positive attitudes to client- or patient-centred care (Todman and Jauncey, 1987). In this respect, the concern with measurement of these personality traits shares the same assumptions and aims found within other areas of occupational psychology, as set out earlier. The following outline of a discourse analytic approach will question these assumptions and aims.

Gathering the data

Given that the aim of a discourse analytic approach is to examine the structure and organization of language as used in social texts, various texts could have been selected in exploring repertoires of good maternity care. Potential texts for this study included policy documentation, educational and teaching materials as used on health training courses, or the discussions of health workers in a group setting or with an interviewer. In this study, individual interviews with health workers were chosen for two reasons. First, the research question was concerned with how health workers make sense of their work. Therefore, the examination was directed at the interpretative repertoires available and made use of by health workers with consideration for the relationship of these repertoires with recent discussions of good practice articulated at policy level. Second, on pragmatic grounds, arranging times for group discussions proved difficult given the demands on health workers' time, therefore individual interviews provided a satisfactory alternative means of collecting accounts.

While interviews are useful in allowing the researcher to examine the same issues with each interviewee, there are certain limitations in terms of the material gathered. It can be argued that participants may offer only a limited version of accounts in an interview setting. Research considerations relating to the nature of the interaction between the interviewer and interviewee, including power inequalities in the relationship, are relevant here as in any interviewing context. Useful discussions of the importance of theorizing power in the research process, are provided by Bhavnani (1990) and Phoenix (1990), which provide more detailed considerations than can be given here. Ideally, interview transcripts can be combined with material gathered from other sources including naturalistic records, for example conversations with work colleagues or written material which relates to the research concerns. This then allows the researcher to build up a broader picture of accounting practices beyond that of the specific interaction that takes place in the interview.

The way interviews are carried out and used by discourse analysts bears close resemblance to King's description of the qualitative interview (Chapter 2, this volume). However, the discourse analytic perspective differs from the traditional approach to interviewing in two key respects which are emphasized here. First, using a traditional approach, the aim is to move from what is said in the interview to making inferences about the underlying attitudes or personality type of the interviewee, thus the attempt is to keep the interviewer as uninvolved as possible. In comparison, discourse analysts see the interview as a form of social interaction and the interviewer's contribution is taken to be important. Both interviewer and interviewee are seen as constructively drawing on a range of interpretative resources which are of interest in the subsequent analysis.

The second key difference to note in comparing a discourse analytic perspective with a traditional approach is that the interview is no longer seen as a means of measuring the genuine views of a participant but as a means of exploring the varied ways of making sense, or accounting practices, available to participants. The concern is at the level of language or discursive practices, rather than with the individual interviewee.

The interviews in this study comprised broad areas of questioning which included the changes in occupational role of midwives and health visitors, job satisfactions and dissatisfactions, and good maternity practice when working with different client groups including women from ethnic minority groups. (For a detailed account of this research, see Marshall, 1992.) Open-ended questions were used and all interviewees were asked the same questions, although they were not necessarily covered in the same order. The same areas of questioning were raised on different occasions during the interview, which was particularly useful for the analysis as it allowed for the examination of variability in use of different repertoires according to the particular concern being discussed.

In the study described here, 18 health carers, both midwives and health visitors, took part. All participants were taking courses to gain further health qualifications at a London university. They volunteered to take part in the study following a request during a lecture to be interviewed about the role and practice of health carers in Britain in the 1990s. All participants were assured of confidentiality and their permission to tape-record the interview was obtained prior to the interview. All the interviews were fully transcribed.

While 18 participants might seem a small sample size, it should be noted that small samples are quite adequate for allowing an in-depth exploration of discursive forms. A wide range of interpretative repertoires can emerge from a relatively small number of interviews and produce more valid information than hundreds of questionnaire or survey responses. Indeed, there are examples of discourse analytic research which has examined one text, with the aim of illustrating how certain effects can be achieved in discourse (for example, Potter et al., 1984; Woolgar, 1980).

The analysis of the transcripts

There are a number of steps involved in carrying out any discourse analytic research. First, the aim is to read and reread the transcripts and pick out recurrent patterns in the organization and content of the texts, here referred to as 'interpretative repertoires'. Therefore, a first step is to isolate any examples where there appear to be either similarities in what is being said, or differences or variation. In this study, a preliminary task entailed taking out any extracts where participants talked about good care, or their role as health carers. This process was repeated several times; each time extracts were placed under broad headings such as 'acting in partnership', 'telling clients what practices to adopt' or 'communicating with clients'. Unlike a traditional or realist approach to the analysis of interviews, consistency in response was not taken to indicate evidence of some underlying reality, such as the presence of a particular personality trait. Here consistency, whether within a particular interview or across different interviews, was used as a pointer to the use of a particular repertoire. At this stage in the analysis, attention to and examination of variation was in some respects more important as it aids consideration of the range of repertoires being used, according to context. All extracts were then examined with consideration for the ways in which they were being used, and then, later, attention was given to the possible consequences of the use of the various repertoires. One main concern was to examine the relationship between repertoires, for example whether one served to complement or undermine another.

Due to lack of space, and because it would be inappropriate in terms of the goals of this volume, the following section does not present a complete discourse analysis, which would present the broad range of interpretative repertoires used in the interviews with detailed consideration for their use and consequences. Instead, an outline is given of two repertoires that were used by the health carers. The importance of context, variability and the consequences of the use of the repertoires are highlighted.

In terms of presentation, each extract is labelled in terms of whether a midwife or health visitor is speaking, followed by participant number. The use of ellipses (. . .) indicates that there is material omitted from the extract. Given the emphasis that discourse analysts place on working with contextualized utterances, indication is given of the interviewer's question or comment preceding or during the extract. Relatively long segments of text are included to allow the reader to assess the researcher's interpretative conclusions. This means that the extracts presented in a discourse analysis tend to be longer than those included in traditional analyses.

Defining good care: the client-centred care repertoire

In terms of the discussions of good maternity care, there was shared agreement, voiced by both midwives and health visitors, that this was characterized by reciprocity, sensitivity and empathy. In general terms, this can be referred to as a *client-centred care* repertoire. There was explicit reference to the desirability of a two-way model of care where the carer worked from an understanding of the client's point of view and offered care in response to the individual client's wishes. This was said to be good practice, as the following extracts illustrate.

Interviewer: How would you define good maternity care?
Health Visitor 8 p2: I think that we've seen a change throughout nursing and caring from the idea that the nurse, or the health visitor knows best, to an emphasis on finding out from the individual client, what they think, what they want. Sort of a two-way process, listening and empathizing with the client, and then responding to what they have said. It's thought now to be very important to be sensitive and try to understand health needs from the client's point of view, because otherwise they can end up feeling in no better a situation, or even worse. I mean if you just provide the care you think they require, and go in to someone's home and think you already know what they need, then the care you offer can be inappropriate and you won't be meeting individual need.

> *Midwife 8 p3*: I think, to try and view everyone as an individual, and try and realize her value as a person, and I suppose, it's changed . . . now when they go into the labour ward it's lovely, because it's so much more relaxed. They seem to let the mother take her own pace and that sort of thing. So I think the perception of how we do care has changed so much, and we didn't used to realize that the mother wanted to be a partner, and I think again we have to be careful cos' she doesn't always, sometimes she wants to put herself in our hands. So I think good care is trying to be sensitive to the wishes and the needs of the mother.

Direct reference is given to empathy, sensitivity and meeting individual need as criteria which now define good care. In the second extract, there is mention of the way in which characterizations of good care have changed in a progressive way so that entering the labour ward is now 'lovely' and 'so much more relaxed'. Explanation and justification is given as to why care which works from the basis of finding out client needs is beneficial. Here it is suggested, in line with policy and research, that if no attempt is made to understand the client's point of view, then the care offered can be inappropriate and unsatisfactory, leaving the client 'in no better a situation or even worse'. While reciprocity is not directly referred to here, it can be argued that the discussion of caring being a two-way process complements the concept of reciprocity as quality care. In the second extract, the mother is explicitly characterized as being 'partner' to the midwife. In comparison, poor or inadequate care is characterized as being where the carer takes the position of 'the expert' and informs the client about good practice.

> *Health Visitor 9 p7*: I mean you won't get anywhere, with my clients anyway, if you're going to go in and say, 'Do this, do that.' You just haven't got a chance. You could see them. I mean if I was to try and do that you could imagine, you could just see the shutters going over their eyes. If I was to say 'You're doing that wrong, do this, do that,' they'd just say 'Who is she?'

Here it is suggested that if a health carer takes the approach of 'knowing best', it is likely to result in alienation, with the client rejecting information and failing to form any relationship with the carer.

If the aim of this study had been to differentiate between individuals with a positive as compared to a negative approach to reciprocity, empathy or client-centred care, the above extracts would initially appear to pose few problems. Indeed, if a questionnaire had been compiled of statements about the desirability of reciprocal care, it would be expected that these health carers would register a positive response. However, when closer attention is given to the context of the interview, these preliminary conclusions are challenged.

In discussing the changing nature of occupational role, there were many examples where dissatisfactions were voiced. These ranged from lack of recognition for the status of their role, conflicting demands from hospital management and other members of the health team, through to pressures posed by increasing caseloads. The following extract is one illustration of where occupational dissatisfactions are discussed.

> *Interviewer*: Do you have any dissatisfactions with your work as a midwife?
> *Health Visitor 8 p1*: Pressure of work, everything being measured in terms of results, too much paperwork . . . Sometimes when you just start to feel that you're getting somewhere with a client, you find that there's not enough time to follow things up, and you have to just put that case aside and move onto the next.
> *Interviewer*: Can you do anything about that?
> *Health Visitor*: Well it depends. Sometimes it's possible to go back to that client at a slightly later stage and check out how they are coping. At other times the feeling that there isn't enough time. Time is pressing and I find I have to, just have to get through the basics and leave, which isn't really very satisfactory for either myself or the client.
> *Interviewer*: Can you think of an example?
> *Health Visitor*: Well, like, we're always hearing about how we should listen to the client. Not just go in and think we know it all and tell them what to do, because then they can still end up feeling we've been no help. So we know that we should communicate, you know, listen and not just be sympathetic, but listen to what they want, what they find difficult, try and see their point of view and respond to that. But sometimes it's like, there just isn't time and it's not so much a case of listening, but just going in and doing checks, and reporting that you've made a visit. There's very little communicating does go on, more just trying to say to the client what you think they should do.

In this extract there is a clear discrepancy between the characterization of good practice in the abstract and actual practice. Mention is given to establishing communication, sympathizing and listening as good practice – 'we're always hearing about how we should listen to the client' – but situational constraints are also given which mitigate against this ideal and where 'There's very little communicating does go on, more just trying to say to the client what you think they should do.' This extract provides one example of where, when discussions of good care are considered in context, it is clear that the same health carer draws on conflicting discussions of maternity care. Clear reference is made to the desirability of reciprocal care and acting in partnership with the client in a similar way as set out in the client-centred care repertoire. Yet within the same interview, this is undermined by a characterization of practice where caseload pressure results in 'just going in and doing checks and reporting that you've made a visit'. Reciprocity and empathy as good practice are compromised here.

The importance of context can also be demonstrated by examining the discussions of the health carer's role in relation to other staff. Instances were related where midwives' attempts to work in partnership with mothers in their care was undermined by the hospital environment and problems of understaffing, or where practices adopted by other members of staff undermined that of the midwife.

Midwife 7 p5: I think the role of midwife is crucial, and carries with it so much responsibility. But in recent years we have seen frequent attempts to just categorize us as nurses, there to help the doctors. But that's not how it should be. We are there, in the hospitals, in our own right, and we stand in a particular position to the women in our care. For me, one of the most satisfying parts of the job is about trying to ensure that I build a relationship with each woman in my care. But that is what is also dissatisfying because we are often rushed and there isn't time to build up a relationship, let alone have a proper conversation. Increasingly, we are understaffed on the ward and we can't turn round and say, 'No, we can't admit this woman, wait until tomorrow.' We don't have control of the environment in which we work, like, the system in the hospital isn't like that, and I don't know how we can do anything about that. And, then, when we do respond to our client's wishes, and she says she wants to walk around and not lie on the bed, or she wants to squat, I've been in the situation where the obstetrician walks in and says, 'What's she doing, get her onto the bed.' And whether that's because it doesn't fit in with his ideas about having a baby, or because he thinks there isn't space on the ward to move around, you just end up feeling undermined.

A number of important points concerning the changing role of midwives, are raised in the extract above. There is discussion of the ways in which the attempts to offer reciprocal care and 'build a relationship with each woman' are not realized. This can be seen as another example where variability in the discussions of good care emerge. The extract illustrates that there are situations where the aims and priorities that the individual carer considers appropriate cannot be considered separately from the context of working with other health staff, and the hospital as an institution. Further, explicit mention is given to the experience of working in a context where the individual is not in control of the working environment and practices adopted within that environment.

This is important when considering the aims of occupational research. As in most organizations, health carers do not work in a purely individual capacity but alongside others, including those in a higher-status position to themselves. If research is concerned with the examination of health carers' perspectives on their occupational role, then this understanding has to extend beyond the attempt to identify the presence or absence of a personality trait, or attitude to a particular health practice. When the full context of health carers' discussions of their role and good care is included in the analysis, it can be seen that there is a complex discussion which goes beyond a simple form of agreement or disagreement as to the desirability of client-centred care.

Methodologically, the two examples above offer support for discourse analysts' arguments about the importance of context. A restricted response to the statements as demanded by traditional questionnaires would have veiled any variation in response. Participants would have had to give one response of agreement or disagreement to statements concerning reciprocity, empathy or client-centred care. No possibility of providing further qualifications or justifications of response would be allowed. It can be suggested that while, in this study, health carers frequently made use of the client-centred care repertoire to define good care, they varied in their use of this repertoire and undermined or drew on alternative formulations according to contextual considerations. The decontextualized nature of statements used on a questionnaire would have provided a limited and abstracted understanding of occupational role and good practice. It is important to note here that while, above, I have concentrated on examining extended extracts from two interviews to illustrate variability, this was not unusual but found throughout the interviews.

Theoretically, this is one step in the argument for the need to move away from the examination of the individual as the unit for analysis. Seeking consistency in terms of personality types and adopting methods which restrict variation results in a distorted picture. Instead, it is argued that the focus should shift to examine regularities at the level of language. The following section moves on to consideration of a second repertoire used in discussing occupational role and practice identified in the interviews.

Defining good care: the cultural diversity repertoire

Health carers' discussions of the ways in which their role and good practice has changed included consideration of working with clients from ethnic minority groups. A further repertoire called *cultural diversity* was frequently used throughout the interviews. This repertoire presents an argument for the importance of recognizing and responding to the needs of clients from ethnic minority groups. The repertoire includes consideration of the ways in which health carers consider that their training has provided only a limited understanding of cultural diversity, as the following extract illustrates:

Interviewer: Do you think health visitors are responding to the needs of a multi-cultural Britain?
Health Visitor 8 p3: That's difficult to answer, but I suspect the answer is no. There is some attempt to make sure that in health visitors' training there is information about different ethnic minority groups, but not a lot. I know some things about different foods and their nutritional value, and a little about different customs, you know, around the birth.
Interviewer: What more could be done?
Health Visitor: Well I think that there could be more information on courses about what foods different ethnic minority groups eat, and about their values and where to expect that they will adopt different practices from ours. More information, I think that would help. Like, I had a case recently where I was working with a Vietnamese family, and the mother had two young children and had just had another baby. I found that I simply didn't know much about Vietnamese culture, what they eat, what their family life is like, and so I was at a loss as to what information to give them when I visited.

Health Visitor 7 p8: I think more could be done. There are times when I find I am working with a client and I just don't know about their customs. Like, for example, with some Asian families, they have all sorts of customs when the child is young and I'm familiar with some but not all of the customs. It makes it hard because I don't always know what to tell them. I've done some reading about this, about customs in India, so now at least I know when I am given a new family to visit, and I know that it is an Asian family, I know what information to give to the mother.

Midwife 6 p4: Well what I have learnt about Asian culture is that the women are very close to their mothers-in-law and usually prefer them to be present at the birth. Often they are not comfortable with their husbands there. It's really seen as a woman's thing, and not done for the husbands to play much of a part.

The cultural diversity repertoire is used here to put forward the suggestion that information about different cultural groups could be usefully incorporated into health training courses. Good care is equated with being knowledgeable about cultural differences. In the first extract, the health visitor says she is not well informed about Vietnamese families, and consequently 'was at loss as to what information to give them when I visited'. Similarly, in the second extract, the health visitor characterizes her work as 'hard' when she doesn't know what to tell her client. In the third extract, the midwife discusses what she knows about Asian preferences concerning female company at the birth.

There are two important points to note concerning this cultural diversity repertoire. First, it sets certain parameters on the meaning of 'culture'. It is assumed that knowing a client's ethnic group tells the carer what practices and values that client will adopt. Thus, culture is not seen as dynamic and changing but static. No consideration is given to the ways in which the adoption and adaptation of cultural practices is shaped by an interrelationship of factors such as social class, geographical situation or education. Instead 'Asian culture' is taken to be unitary and it is assumed that a set of practices corresponding to ethnic group will be manifested in similar ways regardless of cultural context. In this respect, homogeneity within culture is assumed and it is taken for granted that certain practices or beliefs map on to cultural grouping in a one-to-one fashion. The suggestion that health education should provide 'more information' about cultural differences is problematic given that there is no one 'Asian' culture in the same way that there is no one 'European' culture. It can be suggested that there are detrimental consequences where a health carer draws on this cultural diversity repertoire to inform practice, assuming that knowing about different cultural practices tells the carer what care is appropriate for the client.

A second important point concerns the relationship of this cultural diversity repertoire to that of client-centred care. The key unit here is taken to be ethnic or cultural group. Thus, knowing a client's ethnic group overrides consideration of finding out about the individual client's choices, wishes or values. What is not mentioned here is any notion of 'acting in partnership' with the client, or of working from a base of understanding and responding to each individual client. Instead, caring is characterized as 'telling' the client what to do. In this sense, this repertoire provides a contradictory formulation of good care from that of client-centred care.

The analysis above does not present a description of all the repertoires drawn on by the health carers in talking about their work, nor all the occupational considerations they discussed. Given that there is no one discourse analytic method, the above description of the two repertoires cannot be said to be typical of a discourse analysis, but is instead one example which aims to illustrate some of the differences between discourse analysis and other, more traditional methodological approaches. The journal *Discourse & Society* (published by Sage) is a useful source to which to turn to gain a sense of the many different ways of carrying out discourse analytic research. In this chapter, attention has been directed at the importance given to context, variability and the ways in which the repertoires set certain parameters on the ways of making sense of 'good care'.

Evaluation of the method

Discourse analysis allows for a number of challenges to be made to both theoretical and practical implications derived from research which uses more traditional methodological approaches. Occupational psychologists have played a major role in developing personality measures for use in selection and appraisal procedures in a range of organizational contexts. However, such measures are limited in working with one personality trait at a time, and in terms of restriction of response. Using discourse analysis as shown in this chapter, when variability is allowed to emerge, and made a focus in its own right, it can be seen that there is complexity and diversity in the discussions of role and practice. Health carers represent occupational role and practice in varying ways, according to context. This provides support for the argument to move the focus away from the attempt to develop measures which aim to fit individuals to occupational posts, and towards consideration of the different repertoires of good care available and used by health carers.

In moving away from using the individual as the unit of analysis to consideration of regularities at the level of language, it becomes possible to examine the ways in which different repertoires limit the understanding of occupational role and practice. This has practical use for any attempt to initiate policy changes in an organization. The repertoires described in this study can be seen to set certain parameters on the conceptualization of good practice which contrasts with the ideals as set out in policy documentation. The analysis in this chapter points to the need to ensure that any changes in policy are fully articulated at every level in an organization. Further, attempts should be made to ensure that policy aims do not remain as abstracted ideals but are built into training structures in such a way as to allow health carers to explore fully their practical application in a range of domains.

There were several difficulties in using discourse analysis in this study. First, given the importance of the examination of context here, it was essential to transcribe all the interview material fully. This was a lengthy and a slow process. Second, it is a time-consuming task identifying the repertoires in any social texts. The researcher has to engage in a critical reading, attempting to 'stand back' from the text and question the assumptions being made. This is easier said than done, because the researcher draws on a similar pool of linguistic resources as the participants in the 'making sense' and representational process. Some of the interpretative resources used in this study are very familiar and appeared 'obvious' to the researcher, as, most likely, they seemed to the participants. Consequently, the process of denaturalizing these constructions and considering the parameters they set was not a simple task.

A related consideration emerged in relation to the use of interviews. There were instances during the analysis where potentially interesting segments from the interviews proved ambiguous and could not be included because the health carers had assumed that what they were saying was straightforward and did not need further qualification. This points to the importance of the interviewer playing an active role, ensuring that various issues are fully voiced at the time of the interview and that it is not assumed that the researcher knows what is meant.

Further, the importance that discourse places on the organization of language as related to specific contexts means that the researcher works with extended segments of talk. The aim is to present to the reader illustrative examples of the various repertoires used in the texts with a detailed interpretation which links the analysis to features in the extracts. Given that word limits are set for most academic publications, including this book, it was a difficult task selecting representative extracts to illustrate the various repertoires and their interrelationship sufficient to allow the reader to examine the move from the accounts to the analytic conclusions.

Additionally, this consideration of word length raises general issues relating to the publication of discourse research papers. Given that discourse analysts work from a somewhat different theoretical base as compared to much traditional psychological research, it is usually necessary to give a fairly detailed outline of the theoretical base of the research. However, limited word lengths do not allow for the presentation of several repertoires identified in the texts as well as a theoretical justification. One solution is to choose to submit the paper to one of the growing number of journals which offer flexibility in word length and encourage the submission of qualitative and textual analyses. Alternatively, it is possible to take a selective approach in the presentation of a paper so that certain aspects of the analysis are used to make key analytic arguments in a similar way as attempted here. This allows for a discourse analytic paper to be submitted to a journal whose guide-lines suggest a willingness to consider a range of approaches, although setting a limited word length. To date, both these options have proved satisfactory in relation to ensuring that this research is communicated both to specialized readerships in the domain of health care, midwifery and health visiting, and to a more general audience in terms of social constructionism, feminist theory and methods.

While these issues should be considered by any researcher using a discourse analytic approach, they are not necessarily disadvantages, but could instead be used to argue for the strengths of discourse analysis in exposing the workings of the analysis. Despite these disadvantages or difficulties, it can be argued that the emphasis that discourse analysis places on the examination of context, variation and consequence results in a powerful analysis which poses a number of challenges to alternative methods.

Acknowledgement

I would like to thank the midwives and health visitors who took part in this project, the research for which was supported by the ESRC.

References

Bhavnani, K.K. (1990) 'What's power got to do with it? Empowerment and social research', in I. Parker and J. Shotter (eds), *Deconstructing Social Psychology*. London: Routledge.

Foster, M.C. and Mayall, B. (1990) 'Health visitors as educators', *Journal of Advanced Nursing*, 15: 286–92.

Foucault, M. (1971) *Madness and Civilization: a History of Insanity in the Age of Reason*. London: Tavistock.

Gilbert, G.N. and Mulkay, M. (1984) *Opening Pandora's Box: a Sociological Analysis of Scientists' Discourse*. Cambridge: Cambridge University Press.

Hollway, W. (1984) 'Fitting work: psychological assessment in organizations', in J. Henriques, W. Hollway, C. Urwin, C. Venn and V. Walkerdine (eds), *Changing the Subject: Psychology, Social Regulation and Subjectivity*. London: Methuen.

Iliffe, S. (1982) 'The place of birth', *Maternal and Child Health*, 7: 9–17.

La Monica, E.L. (1981) 'Construct validity of an empathy instrument', *Research in Nursing and Health*, 4: 389–400.

Lynam, M.J. (1992) 'Towards the goal of providing culturally sensitive care: principles upon which to build nursing curricula', *Journal of Advanced Nursing*, 17: 149–57.

Marshall, H. (1992) 'Talking about good maternity care in a multi-cultural context: a discourse analysis of the accounts of midwives and health visitors', in P. Nicolson and J. Ussher (eds), *The Psychology of Women's Health and Health Care*. London: Macmillan.

Marshall, H. and Wetherell, M. (1989) 'Talking about career and gender identities: a discourse analysis perspective', in D. Baker and S. Skevington (eds), *The Social Identity of Women*. London and Beverly Hills, CA: Sage.

Morgan, B.M., Bulpitt, C.J., Clifton, P. and Lewis, P.J. (1984) 'The consumers' attitude to obstetric care', *British Journal of Obstetrics and Gynaecology*, 91: 624–8.

Naidoo, J. (1986) 'Limits to individualism', in S. Rodmell and A. Watt (eds), *Politics of Health Education: Raising the Issues*. London: Routledge & Kegan Paul.

Phoenix, A. (1990) 'Social research in the context of feminist psychology', in E. Burman (ed.), *Feminists and Psychological Practice*. London and Beverly Hills, CA: Sage.

Potter, J. and Wetherell, M. (1987) *Discourse and Social Psychology*. London: Sage.

Potter, J., Stringer, P. and Wetherell, M. (1984) *Social Texts and Context: Literature and Social Psychology*. London: Routledge.

Sparling, S.L. and Jones, S.L. (1977) 'Setting: a contextual variable associated with empathy', *Journal of Psychiatric and Mental Health Services*, 15: 9–12.

Stubbs, M. (1983) *Discourse Analysis: the Sociolinguistic Analysis of Natural Language*. Oxford: Blackwell.

Todman, J.B. and Jauncey, L. (1987) 'Student and qualified midwives' attitudes to aspects of obstetrics practice', *Journal of Advanced Nursing*, 12: 49–55.

United Kingdom Central Council for Nursing, Midwifery and Health Visiting (1986) *Project 2000: a New Preparation for Practice*. London: UKCC.

Wetherell, M. and Potter, J. (1988) 'Narrative characters and accounting for violence', in J. Shotter and K. Gergen (eds), *Texts of Identity*. London: Sage.

Wetherell, M. and Potter, J. (1992) *Mapping the Language of Racism*. Hemel Hempstead: Harvester Wheatsheaf.

Wetherell, M., Stiven, H. and Potter, J. (1987) 'Unequal egalitarianism: a preliminary study of discourses concerning gender and employment opportunities', *British Journal of Social Psychology*, 26: 59–71.

Woolgar, S. (1980) 'Discovery: logic and sequence in a scientific text', in K.D. Knorr-Cetina and M. Mulkay (eds), *The Social Process of Scientific Investigation*. Dordrecht: Reidel.

7

Participant Observation

David Waddington

The eminent American investigative social researcher Jack Douglas maintains that 'when one's concern is the experience of people, the way that they think, feel and act, the most truthful, reliable, complete and simple way of getting that information is to share their experience' (1976: 112). This is precisely the outlook subscribed to by proponents and practitioners of participant observation, the method I describe and evaluate in this chapter. The contents of the chapter are based on insights drawn from my own doctoral study of the 1981 Ansells brewery strike – a bitter five-month conflict involving opposition to redundancies and revised working practices which eventually resulted in the permanent closure of the brewery and the dismissal of the entire 1,000-strong workforce.

From January to June 1981, I spent most of my waking hours as a participant observer of the strike. Basic details of my methodology are outlined elsewhere (Waddington, 1987), but in this chapter I set out a fuller and more candid account of my approach than I have ever previously divulged. As Shaffir and Stebbins point out,

> Social science textbooks on methodology usually provide an idealized conceptualization of how social research ought to be designed and executed. Only infrequently, however, do sociologists (and field researchers in particular) report how their research actually was done. As most field researchers actually would admit, the so-called rules and canons of fieldwork frequently are bent and twisted to accommodate the particular demands and requirements of the fieldwork situation and the personal characteristics of the researcher. (1991: 22)

Here I intend to refer to my own experience of the strike, both as a practical illustration of participant observation, and as a demonstration of the type of hard-headed pragmatism and extemporization which is inevitably required when conducting fieldwork of this nature. I begin by outlining the essential features of the method, defining the type of circumstances to which it is best suited, the particular skills required of the practitioner, and the techniques by which data are accessed, recorded and analysed. I then indicate how far and how successfully these skills and principles were applied in my study, before using this experience as a basis for evaluating the method.

troduction to the method

According to Taylor and Bogdan (1984: 15), participant observation 'involves social interaction between the researcher and informants in the milieu of the latter', the idea being to enable the observer to study firsthand the day-to-day experience and behaviour of subjects in particular situations, and, if necessary, to talk to them about their feelings and interpretations.

The extent to which participant observers immerse themselves in the activities of the people they are studying may vary from one project to the next. Burgess (1984) discusses four possible research identities:

1   the *complete participant*, who operates covertly, concealing any intention to observe the setting;
2   the *participant-as-observer*, who forms relationships and participates in activities but makes no secret of an intention to observe events;
3   the *observer-as-participant*, who maintains only superficial contacts with the people being studied (e.g. by asking them occasional questions); and
4   the *complete observer*, who merely stands back and 'eavesdrops' on the proceedings.

The overall strategy is *inductive* rather than deductive: the participant observer uses his or her initial observations as the starting-point from which to formulate single or multiple hypotheses. These hypotheses may subsequently be discarded or refined to take account of any unanticipated or contradictory observations which may emerge (Kidder and Judd, 1987).

According to Jörgensen (1989), participant observation is best suited to research projects which emphasize the importance of human meanings, interpretations and interactions; where the phenomenon under investigation is generally obscured from public view; where it is controversial; and where it is little understood and it may therefore be assumed that an 'insider' perspective would enhance our existing knowledge. Jörgensen maintains that the method is likely to prove most successful when: the *researcher* is confident of obtaining reasonable access; the research *problem* is observable and capable of being addressed by qualitative data; and the research *setting* is sufficiently limited in size and location for it to be effectively observed. Finally, Jörgensen emphasizes that participant observation is seldom as rewarding and exciting as one might imagine, often involving fear, apprehension and, ultimately, disenchantment.

Entering the field

Research settings inevitably vary in the extent to which they are open or closed off to public scrutiny, and sometimes incorporate private or 'backstage' regions (Goffman, 1959) which researchers may be especially keen to investigate. Such variables obviously have a bearing on the amount of preliminary negotiation required to gain access, and how far the participant observer must be prepared to conceal or declare his or her true objectives and identity. Most textbooks highlight the importance, at this initial stage, of creativity, common sense and interpersonal skills.

As Taylor and Bogdan explain, 'Getting into a setting involves a process of managing your identity; projecting an image of yourself that will maximize your chances of gaining access. . . . You want to convince gatekeepers that you are a non-threatening person who will not harm their organization in any way' (1984: 20). These authors advocate an initial approach which guarantees confidentiality and privacy, emphasizes that the researcher's interests are not confined to any one particular setting or group of people, and gives a 'truthful, but vague and imprecise' summary of the research procedures and objectives to reduce the risk of eliciting defensive or self-conscious behaviour.

Conduct in the field

Once the researcher has gained access, he or she must concentrate on maintaining a positive and non-threatening self-image. According to Fetterman (1991: 89), the researcher should try to remain 'courteous, polite and respectful', avoiding unwarranted or uninvited displays of friendliness and familiarity. Taylor and Bogdan (1984) recommend that fieldworkers should try to emphasize whatever features they may have in common with their respondents; that they should take care to show sufficient interest in people's views, avoid being arrogant, and do favours or try to help people whenever possible. Taylor and Bogdan further insist that fieldworkers must 'pay homage' to the routines of the persons with whom they come into contact – by not requiring them to depart from their usual schedules or contexts of interaction.

Recording data

Due to the importance attached to direct observation as the principal source of data, participant observers are often anxious about the possibility of failing to be in the right place at the right time, or of having to cope with and make sense of a seemingly incessant stream of activity (Gans, 1982). For this reason, experienced fieldworkers often recommend an initial period of acclimatization during which note-taking is suspended. Since note-taking is the principal means of recording data, participant observers place a heavy priority on comprehensiveness and self-discipline, stressing that it is common for observers to devote up to six hours of writing up for every hour spent in the field. According to Taylor and Bogdan, this process

> should include descriptions of people, events and conversations as well as the observer's actions, feelings and hunches or working hypotheses. The sequence

and duration of events and conversations are noted as precisely as possible. The fabric of the setting is described in detail. In short, the field notes represent an attempt to record on paper everything that can possibly be recalled about the observation. A good rule to remember is that *if it is not written down, it never happened.* (1984: 53, emphasis in original)

Although participant observation is chiefly concerned, as its name suggests, with the observation and recording of human activity, most practitioners of the method adhere to the principle of 'triangulation' – the use of more than one source or method of data collection (Denzin, 1978). Thus fieldworkers regularly rely on other forms of information, such as documentation (for example, diaries, minutes, letters and memoranda), mass media coverage and discussions with respondents, which may vary in formality from casual conversations to tape-recorded interviews and routinized surveys (Jörgensen, 1989).

When used sensibly, such devices are often complementary, resulting in a fuller and more revealing portrait of the situation and people involved. This is evident in Handy's (1991) study of occupational stress among psychiatric nurses. Handy spent six months as a participant observer, 'shadowing' nurses as they went about their shift work. In addition, he tape-recorded interviews with all nurses on the two units in which he was especially interested, analysed their written comments in patients' case notes, and asked each nurse to keep activity schedules, documenting their actions in the course of a single week. Consequently, 'This research strategy enabled the strengths and weaknesses of the different techniques to be counterbalanced and a more complex picture of organizational life developed' (Handy, 1991: 821).

Analysing data

As already indicated, participant observation involves an essentially inductive approach. This means that data analysis is seldom a one-shot process. Rather,

The analysis of qualitative data is dialectical. Data are dissembled into elements and components; these materials are examined for patterns and relationships, sometimes in connection to ideas derived from literature, existing theories, or hunches that have emerged during fieldwork or perhaps simply commonsense suspicions. With an idea in hand, the data are reassembled, providing an interpretation or explanation of a question or particular problem; this synthesis is then evaluated and critically examined; it may be accepted or rejected entirely or with modifications; and, not uncommonly, this process then is repeated to test further the emergent theoretical conception, expand its generality, or otherwise examine its usefulness. (Jörgensen, 1989: 110–11)

Whilst this may seem an incredibly taxing and complicated process, it nevertheless ensures that the research problem becomes progressively more focused and susceptible to explanation – often in terms and concepts spontaneously introduced by the subjects themselves (Hammersley and Atkinson, 1983). Oremland's (1988) five-year participant observation study of the relationships between eight school-aged boys with haemophilia, their parents and siblings, constitutes an excellent illustration of how this approach may be used to good effect, and helps to refute the accusation that such research is necessarily 'unrigorous' or 'unsystematic'.

Leaving the field

Conducting fieldwork may well prove an extremely absorbing and time-consuming activity, making it difficult for the researcher to determine when to break off from further study. Ultimately, the decision to withdraw or depart from the field is likely to rest on a combination of practical imperatives (for example, time or research funds running out) or the fact that *theoretical saturation* (the point at which no major new insights are being gained) has occurred (Glaser and Strauss, 1967).

As authors like Taylor and Bogdan point out, leaving the field may often prove painful: 'It means breaking attachments and sometimes even offending those one has studied, leaving them feeling betrayed and used' (1984: 67). Sensations of joy and relief may be intermingled with feelings of sadness and regret (Jörgensen, 1989: 118–19). Textbooks advise the researcher to 'ease out' or 'drift off' without terminating relationships too abruptly. Any negative impact on informants may be lessened by maintaining contact and keeping them informed about any publications arising from the research (Taylor and Bogdan, 1984: 68).

Applying the method: the Ansells brewery strike

How far were the basic skills and principles of participant observation utilized in my study of the Ansells strike? I should begin by acknowledging that my study is by no means unique, and that participant observation has frequently been used within occupational psychology, organizational studies and industrial relations (see Rose, 1991). Most participant observation studies of strikes have involved the researcher or researchers as complete observers or observers-as-participants.

For example, Batstone et al.'s (1978) study of the shopfloor organization of strikes was based on the systematic observation of shop stewards' daily interaction with their members, involving the recording of, among other things, the different systems of argument used for or against industrial action. Two further studies (Hartley et al., 1983; Lane and Roberts, 1971) involved researchers unobtrusively attending strike committee meetings. In each case, the researchers also administered a questionnaire survey. In a rare example of complete participation, Fantasia (1983) worked in a steel-casting foundry for 10 months, a position which enabled him to observe the mobilization of two wildcat strikes. In contrast to these studies, I spent the duration of the Ansells strike occupying the role of participant-as-observer.

The five-month strike was precipitated when management disciplined a group of production workers for allegedly engaging in action calculated to disrupt the smooth running of a four-day working week which Ansells had recently imposed due to slack consumer demand. Three weeks into the strike, management delivered an ultimatum that, unless the employees agreed to accept a package of redundancies and revised working practices as the basis for an immediate return to work, they would be dismissed for breach of contract and the brewery would be permanently closed. Far from intimidating the workers, management's threat merely hardened their determination to win. A long battle of attrition followed, involving the 'secondary picketing' of other production units belonging to Ansells parent company, Allied Breweries. Ultimately, the strike was defeated and the brewery stayed shut. The seemingly half-hearted support provided to the strikers by their union, the Transport and General Workers' Union (TGWU), provoked accusations of cowardice and betrayal by the disillusioned brewery men.

Fortunately for me, Ansells brewery was located a mere two miles away from Aston University, where I was conducting postgraduate research at the time. In the strike's early stages, picketing was confined to the brewery. These factors were obviously advantageous and encouraged me to try to gain access. My first, nerve-wracking encounter with Ansells pickets occurred when the strike was only a few days old. Finding myself overawed by the prospect of introducing myself to the group of six pickets and two police constables who were standing outside the brewery's front entrance, I opted for the intermediate step of phoning my wife in search of moral support. I need never have panicked. Much to my eventual relief, I found that not only these pickets, but a larger group of their colleagues who were picketing the main delivery gate, were overwhelmingly receptive of my stated intention of exploring the 'feelings and experience of workers who were out on strike'.

The pickets none the less advised me that I should seek the official endorsement of the strike committee before progressing any further with my study. I therefore arranged to see the branch chairperson, his secretary and treasurer, together with six senior shop stewards, and repeated my broad objectives. The officials explained to me that, while they were generally happy to lend their cooperation, they were only prepared to do so on condition that I promise not to 'interfere' in any activities or pass on information to other interested parties, such as management or the local press. Once I accepted these conditions, the branch secretary immediately wrote out a letter, formally approving my involvement, and encouraging all members to support me wherever possible.

At the outset of the strike, I had no preconceived research strategy, other than a vaguely defined intention to administer some sort of attitude survey to a representative sample of the workforce. On entering the field, I quickly realized that such a preformulated approach would be incapable of probing the rich but often transitory layers of meanings underlying the strikers' actions. I soon found myself mesmerized by the ceaselessly unfolding activities of the strike and the corresponding attempts to interpret them. On the day I first arrived, most strikers I talked to confidently predicted that the dispute would be settled within a week. Ansells then threatened to close the brewery and, suddenly, every picket I met was adamant that management was out to smash their trade union organization and that the strike would drag on for months. I therefore realized that, in order fully to understand the strikers' beliefs and motives, it was imperative that I immerse myself in the distinctive culture of the participants and witness first-hand the manufacture and transmission of their ideas.

Consequently, I spent most of my research activity attending picket lines, mass meetings and planning discussions, and accompanying the strikers on flying picketing and intelligence-gathering manoeuvres. The objectives of such missions were to trace the suppliers of 'scab beer' or deter the delivery of essential brewing ingredients like sugar and carbon dioxide. Due to the long distances travelled, it was sometimes necessary to sleep rough on hostel floors or the back seats of cars, or spend whole nights walking rainswept streets.

In my everyday dealings with the strikers, I consciously projected an image of myself as an earnest, sympathetic, if slightly naïve, student who was grateful for the opportunity to learn from their experience. I set out to gain the strikers' affection and respect by spending long hours on the picket line, often in the foulest weather imaginable, participating in such mundane, off-duty activities as gambling, drinking in pubs, sharing jokes and tall stories, and accompanying them into situations involving elements of physical or legal risk.

The fact that I am a working-class male with a pronounced northern accent undoubtedly influenced the strikers' willingness to accept me into their ranks. Rightly or wrongly, I assumed it necessary for me to demonstrate more personal commitment to the dispute than the majority of actual strikers in order to ensure their continuing trust and support. This was vividly underlined when one picket refused to be conscripted for flying picket duties in Romford on the grounds that he was not prepared to be separated from his 6-month-old baby daughter. I ruefully reflected that my own baby was a month younger at the time, but did not hesitate to volunteer for the mission. The picket organizers quickly recognized this attitude, and frequently exploited it, knowing full well that they could always depend on me to 'make the numbers look respectable' when volunteers were scarce.

Much of the data I collected were derived from direct observation or the contents of informal interviews. I knew of no ready formula to indicate the type of informant I should preferably talk to, or where I should ideally locate myself to observe the most 'important' action. I merely settled in one location sufficiently long enough to engage in long conversations with separate gangs of pickets, or to watch a particular episode of activity run its course, before moving on to where I knew, or suspected, that the next important round of activity was imminent.

My note-taking usually occurred in the lulls between major bouts of activity. Pickets soon grew accustomed to this practice and, in due course, helped to maintain its accuracy by cross-checking my recollection of events against their own (a form of voluntary triangulation). Far from resenting or objecting to this activity, many pickets seemed to regard my interest as a form of flattery and looked forward to reading the final chronicle. My notes most typically took the form of scribbled down words or phrases or, less commonly, verbatim quotes, which I expanded when entering them into my log book at the end of the day.

I supplemented this basic approach by collecting all forms of documentation issued during the strike (for example, letters, strike bulletins, propaganda leaflets), and selected local and national media coverage (including radio bulletins which my wife recorded on my behalf). I deliberately avoided any contact with management during the strike to offset any risk of jeopardizing my relationship with the strikers. I also decided not to let full-time TGWU officials know of my involvement until the strike was over because I was afraid they might consider me a meddler and instruct their members not to cooperate. Subsequently, however, I conducted interviews with representatives of Ansells management and the TGWU. As a result of these meetings, I amassed huge quantities of documentary material (for example, formal correspondence and minutes of union–management meetings spanning two decades), statistical information and off-the-record insights relating to the strike.

By immersing myself so deeply in the strike, I found it easy to comprehend how the workers interpreted their situation, and how their collective definitions of reality had been shaped by their own subjective history. It was fascinating to observe, for example, how management's ultimatum to the strikers was collectively understood in terms of a shared cognitive schema – the *BL script* – which characterized their behaviour as an imitation of the strategy used by Sir Michael Edwardes to undermine trade union power at BL Cars (see Willman, 1987). According to this definition, the strike represented an all-or-nothing struggle for the survival of the trade union organization:

> Ansells management is clearly trying to be the Michael Edwardes of our industry, both in job reductions and the destruction of union organization. Our fight to keep Ansells open is not just a question of saving jobs. For us it is a matter of trying to stop our employers going through our trade union organization like a dose of salts. WHAT IS HAPPENING TO US CAN AND WILL HAPPEN TO ANYONE. (Trade union correspondence)

Similarly, I saw how the strikers contemptuously dismissed the threatened closure of the brewery on the basis of a pair of 'closure scripts' which referred to analogous situations where management had administered similar threats but subsequently climbed down. The strikers' confidence in their eventual success rested on a recent record of strike victories and proven commitment to cherished trade union values. During our conversations, Ansells workers regularly referred to their participation in the infamous Fox and Goose Affair of 1975 to 1977 as proof of their unyielding tenacity. Here the steadfast refusal of Ansells draymen to comply with a TUC directive to lift their blacking of supplies to a West Midlands public house resulted in the TGWU's suspension of them from Congress. Far from embarrassing the Ansells workers, the Fox and Goose Affair was mythically retained as evidence of their supreme solidarity.

By linking the everyday slogans, comments and anecdotes of the strike to material deriving from newspaper archives, company and trade union documents, letters and richly detailed minutes of trade union–management meetings, I was able to develop a longitudinal-processual analysis (Pettigrew, 1979). This demonstrated how the contemporary beliefs, values and attitudes of the workforce, and the mutual feelings of animosity and distrust between employees and management, were shaped by a sequence of historical events stretching back over 20 years.

Hartley et al. point out that there have been many studies of separate strikes, each containing a wealth of narrative detail: 'This detail, however, is often purely descriptive and partisan, with impressions and anecdotes (often very interesting) abounding in place of hard data and rigorous analysis' (1983: 11). I believe that my own study succeeded in avoiding these tendencies. Once I had collected all my data, I immediately delved into potentially relevant areas of social scientific literature (social psychology, sociology, political science, etc.), much of which I was previously unfamiliar with, in order to unearth a sufficient range of explanatory concepts to build my social-cognitive analysis of the entire dispute (see Waddington, 1986, 1987, for further details).

The termination of my fieldwork was something I had no control over; rather it was induced by the formal ending of the strike and all related picketing activity. My withdrawal from the field was a sobering experience. For several days afterwards I was affected by the feelings of bitterness and despondency which inevitably accompany a strike defeat. Long after such feelings had subsided, I continued to miss the companionship of the strikers and often worried about what might have become of them. Worse still were the recurring feelings of guilt I suffered – based on the knowledge that I was one of the few people to come out of the strike with something tangible to show for the considerable anguish and hardship it entailed.

Evaluating the method

Such was the character of my research. Later in this section, I argue that no other methodology could have given me such a penetrating insight into the cognitions and emotions of striking employees. It would be stupid to pretend, however, that any form of research undertaken in such a politically sensitive and emotionally charged environment could ever be expected to proceed entirely straightforwardly and unproblematically. My own research gave rise to a number of practical and ethical problems which require close examination.

It is evident from the wider literature that participant observers often find themselves confronted by ethical dilemmas involving such hard choices as whether or not to inform the authorities about illegal and potentially dangerous activities. For example, Powdermaker (1966) describes the dilemma which confronted her when she stumbled across a white American lynch mob in hot pursuit of an intended black victim. With little time to think, Powdermaker decided neither to protest personally nor to inform the law. It was only because the hapless fugitive somehow managed to flee across the border that she was spared the dire consequences of her decision and finally able to breathe a sigh of relief.

I, too, was confronted by an ethical dilemma of this broad type, though certainly not its magnitude. My dilemma arose in the third month of the strike – shortly after the local press had started to concentrate on numerous allegations of sabotage, assault, intimidation and vandalism that were being levelled against the strikers. I can say, on the basis of personal observation and reliable hearsay, that at least some of these accusations were valid. The implications of such tactics were melo-dramatically underlined by a *Birmingham Post* editorial of 19 March 1981 which appealed to Ansells strikers to 'remember that parents of, say, a child killed by a runaway brakeless lorry would be disinclined to listen to a recital of "facts as we see them" or participate in a "meaningful debate on the issues"'. Thereafter, I found myself struggling to decide whether my personal commitment not to interfere with the 'natural course' of events should override what might be regarded as my moral obligation to complain about life-threatening activities or, where necessary, report them to the police.

Mercifully, the negative publicity associated with these activities discouraged their further use and thus rescued me from a dilemma I was finding practically impossible to resolve. None the less, this example emphasizes Taylor and Bogdan's assertion that 'one is not absolved of moral and ethical responsibility for one's actions or inactions merely because one is conducting research. To act or fail to act *is* to make an ethical and political choice' (1984: 71). They further point out that 'People who cannot tolerate some moral ambiguity should not do fieldwork or at least have the good sense to know when to get out of certain situations' (Taylor and Bogdan, 1984: 74).

I can count myself extremely fortunate that the Ansells strike took place very close to my own academic institution and involved a group of people to whom I could easily relate. Circumstances might well have proven less conducive for, as Haralambos and Holborn, explain:

In personal terms such research may be highly inconvenient and demanding. The researcher may be required to move house, to live in an area they would not otherwise choose and to mix with people they would rather avoid. They may find it necessary to engage in activities they dislike to fit in with the group and they may even face personal danger. (1990: 745)

This final possibility is highlighted by Thompson (1967), who was beaten up by members of a Hell's Angels' chapter for refusing to pay them cash for the privilege of observing their activities. There were numerous times during the strike when I could easily have been arrested during picket-line mêlées, or when my personal safety was jeopardized. Once, as we mounted an all-night picket of Ind Coope's Romford brewery, undisciplined groups of Metropolitan police officers repeatedly drove past our small picket line, taunting us to respond to their challenge of a fight, and promising us – falsely, as it transpired – that they would return to 'get us' before daybreak.

On another occasion, I was almost beaten up by Ansells pickets who suspected me of working for the Special Branch! This improbable development was the direct result of a *Daily Mail* article of 21 April 1981 which established that the Special Branch had been brought in to investigate 'an extreme Left-Wing terror campaign against pub managers and their families', allegedly perpetrated by 'Trotskyist hard men' who had recently infiltrated the strike.

This represented a scurrilous attempt to attribute the strike violence to the influence of two Workers' Power activists (a slight, bespectacled man and a silver-haired woman) who had been distributing leaflets urging the strikers to form 'defence squads' against the police. Nevertheless, some strikers took the *Mail's* disclosure seriously and, shortly after the article appeared, I was seized and interrogated by three burly draymen who knew me only as a stranger. It was only after I had received a blow to the ear that two familiar pickets returned from the local fast-food restaurant to vouch for my identity and spare me from further injury.

The fact that participant observation involves a relatively intimate approach invites the obvious possibility that the researcher's presence may have an impact on the reality he or she is observing. One common criticism of participant observation is that people are likely to react to the researcher being present by engaging in untypical or extreme forms of behaviour. My own experience suggests that any exhibitionistic or unusual forms of behaviour excited by the researcher's arrival tend progressively to disappear the longer he or she remains part of the research setting.

That said, I found it extremely difficult to maintain a passive role in such a politically volatile and dynamic environment. This difficulty is best illustrated by the outcome of a week spent picketing the large Ind Coope brewery in Romford, Essex – a sobering episode in which we tried, unsuccessfully, to obstruct the delivery of essential supplies. Nevertheless, when we returned to Birmingham, my erstwhile colleagues grossly exaggerated our achievements, having already appealed to me not to say anything which might contradict their story and thereby undermine rank-and-file morale.

Afterwards, I rationalized my part in this 'conspiracy' by convincing myself that it was the least disruptive of all the available options. Much closer to the truth was the fact that I very much wanted the Ansells workers to succeed in their action, and that it was inconceivable that I would have said or done anything to weaken their commitment. In taking me for someone who was relatively detached from the strike, pickets often asked me for my prognosis of the outcome. Privately, I considered it extremely unlikely that the strikers could effectively resist such a powerful and well-prepared adversary as their multinational parent company; but this view was something I never publicly conceded.

While I have no accurate way of establishing how far my impressions of events may have been refracted by my sympathetic attitude towards the Ansells strikers, I can point to numerous instances where my analysis of their tactics and behaviour could be construed as critical or unflattering. Indeed, one of my major theoretical assertions (Waddington, 1987) was that the strikers 'used their history badly' – overestimating their strength by failing to see how important contextual factors, notably the declining demand for beer and the presence of over-capacity at another of Allied Breweries' production units, made the straightforward repetition of previously successful tactics (striking as a first resort and calling management's bluff) extremely unwise.

During the course of my postgraduate studies, it was put to me by more established colleagues that I should regard my Ansells research as merely an exploratory or 'pilot' study: that it would be 'courting disaster' as far as the outcome of my PhD was concerned to rely exclusively on such a soft methodology; and that I should perhaps 'hedge my bets' by carrying out a laboratory simulation of a strike. Looking back, I can see how I wrongly allowed myself to be intimidated by a prevailing orthodoxy which required me to justify my method against positivist assumptions of what constituted 'good' academic research.

I now realize that I should have argued more assertively that some degree of researcher bias is not only inevitable in studies of social conflict, but can also prove extremely *beneficial* to the study; and that, whilst a researcher's presence is bound to have an impact on his or her data, it is preferable to address the possible effects head on than to merely pretend – as positivists do – that research can be carried out in a social vacuum.

For all my former diffidence, I have never had much difficulty emphasizing that the benefits to be gained from adopting a participant observation approach to an appropriate research issue will far outweigh any practical or ethical problems likely to be encountered. One of the most advantageous reasons for using this approach is that it promotes the development of confidence and trust between the researcher and his or her respondents – all the more so if the latter have reason to assume that the former is sympathetic towards them! I doubt very much whether the Ansells strikers would have been prepared to confide in me to the extent they did, or allowed me to enter the 'backstage' regions of the strike, had they not been given adequate time to appraise my character thoroughly.

Participant observation also helps to reduce the likelihood of being deceived by one's respondents. During my research, I was able to assess the consistency of people's statements, moods and behaviour at different times and in contrasting situations, eliminating the possibility of being fooled by initial appearances. I was also in a position to witness sudden or progressive changes in people's definitions and emotions – something I could never have appreciated had I used a more conventional, one-off method.

One critic of prestructured psychological measures makes the point that they 'may be providing a more partial and inaccurate sample of experience than is necessary. Furthermore, none of them pay much attention to how the experience is constructed over time and to explaining why the experience has those particular contents. Who constructs the constructs?' (Armistead, 1974: 120). There is no doubt that my chosen methodology afforded me an excellent opportunity to observe the creation and exchange of key social ideas. This is best illustrated by the build-up to a crucial mass meeting of 14 February 1981.

During this period, I observed the way that shop stewards systematically mingled among the pickets in order to innoculate them against the potentially damaging views of full-time TGWU officials who were preparing to tell them that it would be futile to prolong the strike. One steward after another reassuringly explained to his members that the TGWU were desperately looking for a strike victory in order to reverse a recent trend of humiliating defeats at the hands of local employers. District and regional officials were preparing to risk the union's remaining credibility by 'fully backing' the strike, but first they had to convince themselves that the Ansells men had sufficient determination to last out what might well prove a long and bitter struggle. For this reason, the TGWU officials were planning to convey an extremely pessimistic (though entirely bogus) impression of the strikers' chances at the forthcoming mass meeting.

As a 'member' of the picket line, I observed how one shop steward impressed the following message on his members:

> We've got to show them that we're solid. If we do that, we'll have the full weight of the 'T and G' behind us. So, we want none of this 'orderly meeting' stuff. Say what you want and open your bloody mouths. Raise the roof off. (Quoted in Waddington, 1987: 86)

Thanks in no small measure to this preliminary activity, the members voted, virtually unanimously, in favour of continuing the strike. This meant that, notwithstanding their genuine misgivings about prolonging the dispute, the TGWU's full-time representatives were politically obliged to pledge their organization's financial and moral support.

By joining the brewery workers on strike, I found myself capable of empathizing with many of their cognitions and emotions. While it was clearly impossible for me to share the full extent of their material hardship and psychological anxiety, I none the less experienced a wide spectrum of mental states ranging from temporary euphoria to exasperation and despair. I see no need to apologize about the so-called softness and subjectivity of my approach; rather I take an immense pride in the 'thickness' of my data and analysis (Denzin, 1989), maintaining that no other methodology could have given me such an authentic insight into the strikers' subjective experience.

Conclusions

In this chapter I have used my own study of the 1981 Ansells brewery strike to examine some of the main features of participant observation, the principal methodology used in field research. We have seen how this method of investigation involves the researcher immersing him- or herself within a distinctive culture or social setting in order to study at first hand the actions and experiences of its members.

The particular skills and abilities required of the participant observer are very different to those required in most other forms of psychological research. The majority of conventional psychological methodologies emphasize proficiency in sampling techniques, experimental design and statistics. Participant observation, however, places a priority on such personal qualities as an open and inquiring mind, tenacity and determination, and a chameleon-like capacity to adapt to different types of people and situations. As Van Maanen points out, 'Fieldwork is an always emerging task. It involves both tension and surprise. There are no easy or preformulated answers to the dilemmas of fieldwork since one cannot know what one is getting into until one gets into it' (1982: 138). Thus the ideal fieldworker is someone who is blessed with a thick enough skin and an ability to depend consistently on their own initiative.

There is a second reason why the researcher's personal attributes are likely to be important. I have already indicated that certain of my status characteristics (notably my gender and class location) appeared to make it easier for me to gain access and develop an easy rapport with the strikers. Had this been a strike primarily involving, say, Asian women – as was the case at Grunwick (see Dromey and Taylor, 1978) – my progress may not have been so smooth. This emphasizes the crucial point that fieldworkers should remain aware of the various ways that structural variables like age, gender, class and ethnicity can influence the research process and affect the 'reality perspectives' of the observer and respondents alike (Easterday et al., 1982; Gurney, 1991; Warren, 1988).

It stands to reason that there will be particular research projects which require certain observer status characteristics in preference to others. I have also made the point in this chapter that participant observation is ideally suited to some situations (notably those requiring the observer to explore meanings, interpretations and motives) and is likely to be less effective in others.

When conducting my Ansells research in 1981, I tried to delude myself and others into believing that I was capable of remaining like a fly on the wall: unaffected by emotions, and having little or no impact on the people I was observing. Similarly, when writing up my research I carefully avoided any significant discussion of my personal feelings and loyalties, fearing that this might provoke charges of subjectivity and emotionality and detract from the perceived validity of my analysis. Now I have acquired the confidence to concede that, whilst participant observation is less tidy and more complicated than I formerly pretended, it is one of the surest ways I know of getting directly to the heart of human experience. As Van Maanen so cogently informs us: 'Fieldwork means both involvement and detachment, both loyalty and betrayal, both openness and secrecy, and, most likely, both love and hate. Somewhere in the space between these always personalized stances toward those one studies, ethnographies get written' (1982: 139).

References

Armistead, N. (1974) 'Experience in everyday life', in N. Armistead (ed.), *Reconstructing Social Psychology*. Harmondsworth: Penguin.

Batstone, E., Boraston, I. and Frenkel, S. (1978) *The Social Organization of Strikes*. Oxford: Basil Blackwell.

Burgess, R. (1984) *In the Field: an Introduction to Field Research*. London: George Allen & Unwin.

Denzin, N.K. (1978) *The Research Act* (2nd edn). New York: McGraw-Hill.

Denzin, N.K. (1989) *Interpretive Interactionism (Applied Social Research Methods Series, Vol. 16)*. Newbury Park, CA: Sage.

Douglas, J. (1976) *Investigative Social Research*. Beverley Hills, CA: Sage.

Dromey, J. and Taylor, G. (1978) *Grunwick: the Workers' Story*. London: Lawrence & Wishart.

Easterday, L., Papademas, D., Schorr, L. and Valentine, C. (1982) 'The making of a female researcher: role problems in fieldwork', in R. G. Burgess (ed.), *Field Research: a Sourcebook and Field Manual*. London: George Allen & Unwin.

Fantasia, R. (1983) 'The wildcat strike and industrial relations', *Industrial Relations Journal*, 14: 74–86.

Fetterman, D.M. (1991) 'A walk through the wilderness: learning to find your way', in W.B. Shaffir and R.A. Stebbins (eds), *Experiencing Fieldwork: an Inside View of Qualitative Research*. Newbury Park, CA: Sage.

Gans, H. (1982) 'The participant observer as human being: observations on the personal aspects of fieldwork', in R. G. Burgess (ed.), *Field Research: a Sourcebook and Field Manual*. London: George Allen & Unwin.

Glaser, B. and Strauss, A.L. (1967) *The Discovery of Grounded Theory: Strategies for Qualitative Research*. Chicago: Aldine.

Goffman, E. (1959) *The Presentation of Self in Everyday Life*. Garden City, NY: Doubleday.

Gurney, J.N. (1991) 'Female researchers in male-dominated settings: implications for short-term versus long-term research', in W.B. Shaffir and R.A. Stebbins (eds), *Experiencing Fieldwork: an Inside View of Qualitative Research*. Newbury Park, CA: Sage.

Hammersley, M. and Atkinson, P. (1983) *Ethnography Principles in Practice*. London: Routledge.

Handy, J.A. (1991) 'The social context of occupational stress in a caring profession', *Social Science and Medicine*, 32 (7): 819–30.

Haralambos, M. and Holborn, M. (1990) *Sociology: Themes and Perspectives* (3rd edn). London: Unwin Hyman.

Hartley, J.F., Kelly, J.E. and Nicholson, N. (1983) *Steel Strike: a Case Study in Industrial Relations*. London: Batsford.

Jörgensen, D.L. (1989) *Participant Observation: a Methodology for Human Studies*. Newbury Park, CA: Sage.

Kidder, L.H. and Judd, C.M. (1987) *Research Methods in Social Relations* (5th edn). New York: CBS Publishing Japan Limited.

Lane, T. and Roberts, K. (1971) *Strike at Pilkingtons*. London: Fontana.

Oremland, E.K. (1988) 'Work dynamics in family care of hemophilic children', *Social Science and Medicine*, 26 (4): 467–75.

Pettigrew, A.M. (1979) 'On studying organizational cultures', *Administrative Science Quarterly*, 24: 570–81.

Powdermaker, H. (1966) *Stranger and Friend: the Way of an Anthropologist*. New York: Nelson.

Rose, H. (1991) 'Case studies', in G. Allan and C. Skinner (eds), *Handbook for Research Students in the Social Sciences*. London: Falmer.

Shaffir, W.B. and Stebbins, R.A. (eds) (1991) *Experiencing Fieldwork: an Inside View of Qualitative Research*. Newbury Park, CA: Sage.

Taylor, S.J. and Bogdan, R. (1984) *Introduction to Qualitative Research Methods: the Search for Meanings* (2nd edn). New York: Wiley.

Thompson, H.S. (1967) *Hell's Angels*. New York: Random House.

Van Maanen, J. (1982) 'Fieldwork on the beat', in J. Van Maanen, J.M. Dabbs and R.R. Faulkner (eds), *Varieties of Qualitative Research*. Beverly Hills, CA: Sage.

Waddington, D.P. (1986) 'The Ansells brewery dispute: A social-cognitive approach to the study of strikes', *Journal of Occupational Psychology*, 59 (3): 231–46.

Waddington, D.P. (1987) *Trouble Brewing: a Social Psychological Analysis of the Ansells Brewery Dispute*. Aldershot: Gower.

Warren, C.A.B. (1988) *Gender Issues in Field Research*. London: Sage.

Willman, P. (1987) 'Industrial relations issues in advanced manufacturing technology', in T.D. Wall, C.W. Clegg and N.J. Kemp (eds), *The Human Side of Advanced Manufacturing Technology*. London: Wiley.

8

Group Methods of Organizational Analysis

Chris Steyaert and René Bouwen

Studying group contexts, wherein people meet, talk and work, is probably the most natural method for gathering knowledge about social events and human interaction, especially in an organizational context. Throughout human history and in all places and circumstances people have gathered in groups to discuss what is going on and how to make sense out of it. The local village community, the United Nations taskforce on a special mission in the field, the project team in an engineering project – all meet to be informed. Meeting as a group is in all these cases the first step by which the social community keeps track of what is going on, and for all those involved it is the unique context in which meaning can be made out of the ongoing events. Members of small groups are 'natural' social research actors in that they are constructing, deconstructing and reconstructing the meaning of social realities. Although groups are natural contexts for study and have been a main research theme in social psychology and organizational behaviour (Levine and Moreland, 1990), it is surprising that the study *through* groups is less well known and used. This chapter revalues the group method as a research vehicle.

Our concept of social research includes not only contexts created by the researcher in an interview or by introducing questionnaires, but all contexts where social actors meet to 'reconsider' the social reality they are building together. We will distinguish throughout this chapter between (1) group contexts created explicitly by the researcher for 'exploratory' purposes, (2) work group contexts which intend to 'generate' insight and new action, and (3) 'intervention' contexts where the group is mainly an instrument for intervention. These three forms are illustrative of the more subtle nuances and combinations of all kinds of group forms where social knowledge is generated and distributed.

A social constructionist perspective on group contexts

Before entering into the description of different small group contexts for social research, we want to make explicit the social science paradigm we support. The choice of a research method, especially in the social sciences, is always steered by the epistemological assumptions of the researchers. It is therefore desirable to be explicit about those assumptions, because they will guide the conceptualization of problem issues, the concrete operationalizations of the research approaches and the states of the conclusions.

From our research experiences in two different but related fields, 'conflict in work settings' (Bouwen and Salipante, 1990; Salipante and Bouwen, 1990) and 'organizational innovation and entrepreneurship' (Bouwen and Steyaert, 1990) we discovered the potential contribution of a 'social constructionist' approach (Gergen, 1985) for framing social research efforts. In those research projects we discovered that one cannot talk about 'the' conflict of 'the' innovation as if there is a single social reality which can be defined in an unequivocal way. There are as many perspectives to a problem as there are actors. Actors define the issue by relating their definition to other definitions. There will never be a complete overlap among perspectives nor a definite understanding. There is a continuously ongoing negotiation relationship among the actors and in that sense the social reality is 'continuously in-the-making'.

Although Allport stated: 'The way a man defines his situation constitutes for him its reality' (1955: 84), the full consequences of this idea were only recently drawn into organizational theory by Karl Weick (1979). The social constructionist approach holds that organizations are not objective entities but socially constructed phenomena (Berger and Luckmann, 1967). People meet in groups in organizations to negotiate and renegotiate social realities. Studying organizations leads to the study of groups as the natural contexts (Srivastva et al., 1977).

The organization, therefore, is no longer considered as a 'given reality' which has to be discovered by using increasingly sophisticated instruments of measurement: this is the so-called functionalist view on social reality (Burrell and Morgan, 1979). An organization is not even the collection of the cognitive maps of the actors involved which exist as a kind of master software in people's minds. That would match a cognitive approach, also very popular nowadays in system analysis and experimental psychology, and gradually becoming dominant in organizational psychology. Rather, the organization is a continuously ongoing negotiation process where people interact and influence each other to define social reality jointly. Group members negotiate what constitutes 'the working organization' here and now. Structures, systems and other arrangements are considered to be the outcomes of agreements about the social reality. In all organizational contexts where there is some accepted interdependency, the social ordering is negotiated through symbolic processes, in which an actor interacts and sometimes competes with others for acceptance of their descriptions of the social reality and for the translation of these descriptions into action (Hosking and Morley, 1991).

Since social constructionism emphasizes the relational qualities and the multiplicities of social realities, we find it an adequate theory to guide qualitative research in a group context.

Three group contexts for studying organizations

Different ways of using the group method

A very large variety of group contexts can be studied as a vehicle for generating data and interpretations about organizations on different levels. Some groups are created especially for research or intervention purposes. The researcher is then a major constituent of the group context. Other group contexts are 'natural' in the sense that they exist as work-groups, teams or committees, which are part of the natural organizational environment. Thus we can distinguish between 'natural' and 'created' group contexts. However, this distinction is not discrete, but should be seen on a 'continuum', where a researcher has more or less influence on the 'staging' of the group context.

A second dimension for distinguishing group contexts is the purpose of the convenor or the researcher. Is this purpose just the mere *exploration and description* of ideas? Is the purpose the *generation* of ideas by creating a stimulating interaction? Or is the group meeting intentionally set up to *intervene* in the experienced social reality? We can distinguish an increasing influence of the coordinator or organizer of the group situation under study and also an increasing embeddedness in an existing organizational reality.

Combining both dimensions (natural/created and purpose), six generic group forms are distinguished which can be used for data collection and subsequent analysis and interpretation. Group interviews ([1] in Table 8.1) are often considered as the most characteristic form for data collection.[1] They have a long tradition in marketing research and in opinion survey. Even more often, this kind of group will be an existing or previously formed group (6) in the organization, In group experiments or simulations (2), the conditions are handled intentionally, and in the work-team study (5) a committee or group of representatives is formed to develop alternatives for action. In organization development projects, intervention work is often done within group contexts. The capacities for interaction and creativity are used to a fuller extent when the group context is used to generate new behaviour or new alternatives for action. Team-building efforts (4) seek to enhance the functioning of existing groups. In task forces (3), the group is created explicitly as an intervention device to decide upon and implement the intended changes.

This distinction of group forms is not exhaustive and there are many overlapping forms, but specification of group characteristics is important

Table 8.1 *Different types of group method*

Group setting/ purpose of research	Natural	Created
Exploration	Work-groups/Group observations (6)	Group interviews/Focus groups (1)
Generation	Work-team study/Group meetings (5)	Group simulations/Group experiments/Role plays (2)
Intervention	Team-building/Action research (4)	Project group/Taskforce analysis (3)

to typify the role of the researcher, the involvement of the group members and the kind of interaction that is going to emerge. Taking all these aspects into account is essential in processing the data and in making interpretations.

Previous work

With this scheme, it is possible to integrate methodological literature from different origins. Literature on group methods is scarce. Even one of the classics of the group method, the group interview, is poorly referenced or thinly discussed in handbooks on qualitative methodology (Marshall and Rossman, 1989; Patton, 1980; Strauss and Corbin, 1990; Yin, 1989). Furthermore, there has been a preference for the use of groups as a means of data gathering in applied contexts, such as marketing, personnel selection, training, group therapy, organizational development, applied social research, rather than for theoretical purposes.

Among the created group contexts, group interviews and focus groups (1) are the best known. Traditionally they have been very popular in marketing and consumer psychology, where consumers comment in a small group on a certain product or service (Templeton, 1987; Wells, 1974). Morgan (1991) has written a very useful and comprehensive monograph on focus groups as a qualitative research method. Greenbaum (1988) and Krueger (1988) have produced practical handbooks while Stewart and Shamdasani (1990) have placed the use and interpretation of focus groups within their theoretical contexts. Also, in applied social research, groups are used to facilitate the conduct of research and for 'brainstorming' about social and organizational problems (e.g. 'round tables' among personnel directors concerning unemployment). Moore (1987) has explained how these group techniques can be applied. In organizational psychology, group discussions are associated with the human relations and organizational development schools (Argyris and Schön, 1978; Locatelli and West, 1990). Examples of using group discussions for assessing organizational culture can be found in the research work of Calori and Sarnin (1991), Rentsch (1990) and Tucker et al. (1990). However, they have been evaluated negatively in terms of organizational culture research by Locatelli and West (1990) to the benefit of the Twenty Statements Test (see Chapter 3).

Creating groups for data collection in theory-testing for organizational understanding is done in very different ways: experiments, simulations, role plays (2). In handbooks of experimental research, group experiments are rarely discussed. In organizational psychology, experiments have been used in the laboratory and the field, and as organizational simulations. Following Sackett and Larson (1990),[2] experimentation has become one of the most used methodologies in the field of industrial and organizational psychology. Methodological considerations can be found in Fromkin and Streufert (1976) and Sackett and Larson (1990), an example of organizational experiments in Litwin and Stringer (1968), and of organizational simulations in Rabbie and Van Oostrum (1984) and even in the early Weick (1968). Although the difference between group and organizational experiment/simulation is rather vague, typical group experiments (see the classical Hawthorne experiments) are again lacking. Mostly, behaviour is measured at the individual (not the group) level in a simulated organizational environment (for example, Latham and Steele, 1983). Group simulations and role-playing have been used in the applied context for gaining human understanding, for example role-playing in conflict-handling (Hare, 1985), in training organizational consultants (Bouwen, 1984), and in educational and training situations (Eiben and Milliren, 1976). In the personnel context, group simulations and discussions are used during selection procedures and especially in assessment centres (Blanksby and Iles, 1990), where groups are used to generate data on individual candidates (for example, during group tasks or leaderless group discussions).

The gaining of information through groups for intervention activities has been used in team-building (Dyer, 1987; Steyaert, 1992) and in organizational development programmes (Lundberg, 1990; Neilsen, 1984). For learning purposes in particular (individual *and* organizational), the group (both the created [3] and the natural [4]) has been accorded a prominent place (Srivastva et al., 1977). But also within the context of action research, groups form the context where insights and new possibilities are generated on the collective level, as has been broadly explored in the 'appreciative inquiry' approach (Cooperrider and Srivastva, 1987).

Finally, the observation of groups for exploring (6) and generating (5) concepts and models of organizational processes has been used in organizational ethnography (Rosen, 1991), although groups do not have a privileged position compared to other kinds of observation contexts. This form is, in our view, the least known and applied, and is one of the three forms we discuss in more detail.

A social constructionist approach to the group method

In this chapter we concentrate on three types of group method: the classical form of group interview; the study of meetings for generating theory; and the intervention project group or task force, where the emphasis is on the interaction process itself. These three types can be viewed as representative of the broad scope of applications.

How does a social constructionist view facilitate data collection and data-processing in these three types of group method? First, the group interview or group discussion gives the opportunity to hear different accounts or voices at the 'same' time on the 'same' phenomenon or problem. Individuals are asked to tell their stories concerning the problem highlighted by the researcher. Each story can be aligned to or expand the story of another participant or can contrast a previous story. The aim is to catch in a condensed way the range of different voices. The group situation makes the differences and similarities between the different participants, and also the dynamics between the perspectives on a problem, directly visible.

Second, the observation of 'natural' group meetings goes one step further. It is comparable to the group interview in the way that organizational members give their view on the subject of the meeting. So the natural mix of differences can be 'caught' there as well. But the researcher also comes in contact with the evolution of the different voices as they develop and emerge in a living social context, expressing the construction and deconstruction of shared meaning (Gray et al., 1985).

Third, the group intervention context explores the organizational change dynamics. The group is answering the questions: where are we now, where do we want to go, and how do we bridge this gap? The 'natural' interplay between the different voices is questioned, and the intervention aims at revitalizing the organizational dialogue that has become impeded or fixated (Bouwen, 1993).

Now we proceed to a more concrete level of description of these three types of group method. For us, using each of these different methods has been a tentative learning process, a process of discovery. There is no single form of using a specific method, since it is a creative and context-bounded application. The methods will be presented by telling the research story. In each story, we will document both *why* it was useful to use the group method and *how* the method was used. As the group method is not presented as a singular and isolated research technique, the reader should feel free to draw on the insights from other chapters in this book. For the group interview, one can benefit from comparing with Chapter 2 (the qualitative research interview); for the project-group study, Chapters 5, 7 and 12; for the group-intervention study, Chapter 13 will be fruitful.

Three research stories with the group method

The group interview: the context of small and medium enterprises (SMEs)

In answering the question why group interviews?, it is important to distinguish the group interview from the individual interview, and to describe why we started a three-year research project with the former method. In answering the question how to do group interviews, we discuss the following stages: preparation, application, analysis and integration of the group interview. Examples refer to group interviews carried out during a three-year research project on 'Consulting for growth and innovation in SMEs'.[3]

Why group interviews?   The general aim of this study is to understand the quality of the relationship between consultants and SME-leaders in the light of the possibilities of consulting firms and the needs of the SMEs. The research project has three parts. The group interviews were carried out during the first part of the study, to explore the general accounts of SME-leaders and consultants as to the quality of their cooperation. Furthermore, the group interviews could help us: to get a first impression of the field (together with some other exploratory individual interviews); to collect some general themes to aid in constructing questionnaires for the next research stage; and to confront the participants with some of our first thoughts (hypotheses if you will) which we brought to the research project. There was also a more pragmatic reason since two different representatives of the supply-side proposed that one of the researchers organized a meeting: in one case with SME-leaders, in the other with consultants.

In understanding the use of focus groups, one should realize the different dynamics of the group interview compared to the individual interview. In an individual interview, the private and personal account is at stake, whilst in a group interview the accounts immediately have a public character. Although in the two-person interview (conversation) the person is making a public or 'provoked account' (Czarniawska-Joerges, 1992) as well as telling his or her story to the researcher, in a group setting the participants are giving their story to 'relatives', that is, significant others (for example, business leaders can be competitors/colleagues, so their stories will be different from those told to a journalist, a researcher, their partners, etc.). This process will 'colour' the story and make it more related or more contrasted to the others', or certain statements will be amended until accepted by the group or sustained. Second, and as well as, and maybe more than, the interviewer, the group process steers the interview process (rhythm, alternation between participants, depth, group-think, dominant and silent participants, etc.). Third, since more than one person participates, it is usually said that group interviews should at least have some structure. Although, for the individual interview, the structure question is central (see Chapter 2), we think group interviews can also have an open and in-depth character. We invited the participants during the opening sequence to tell their stories instead of 'answering questions' (see Mishler, 1986, for interviews as 'story-telling'). Realizing these differences already gives an important direction to the question 'how to prepare for and how to conduct a group interview'.

Preparing the group interview   Two points are important: determining the size of the group and the number of interviewers (the 'who' level) and the preparation of the content (the 'what' level).

First, the general size of the group can be between six and 10 persons. This norm is used in marketing research (Morgan, 1991). Since we were interested in extended personal stories, a smaller number was more adequate and realistic.[4] If possible, the participation of two researchers in the group interview will prevent a lot of problems, although it introduces fresh dilemmas: for example, how familiar are you with each other and with each other's interview style? We carried out the group interviews with two senior and two junior researchers. We wanted to have a joint research effort in which juniors could learn from seniors and in which both research teams (with different academic backgrounds) could learn to know each other in a concrete research setting.

Second, preparation on the content level on how open/structured the group interview will be. In our case, a list of guiding topics was prepared by one of the researchers, more as a security for the junior researchers to fall back on than as a set of fixed questions we had to go through. We preferred an open research situation, in which all participants could tell their documented and critical story. For an overview of types of questions, we refer to Spradley (1979) in his discussion of the (individual) ethnographic interview (see also Chapter 2).

Conducting the group interview   Here we discuss the flow of the group interaction (the 'how' level). Two roles were distinguished and divided among the two dyads of researchers. One dyad focused on the content level, the other on the procedural and process level. The first used the list of topics to invite participation. An example of such a topic is 'the short-term versus long-term outcome of the consultancy', which resulted in the following question: 'Are achievements by the consultant necessary in the short term?' Closed and tentative questions should generally be avoided. For example, the question: 'Don't you think it is important for the cooperation between SME and consultant that a relationship of confidence exists?' introduces a fundamental idea which frames the participants' comments as well as focusing them on 'the profile' of what the researchers seem to expect. Here the researcher wants to control and work more with 'his or her' data instead of being open to the 'data' the participants bring to the encounter. We would expect such a closed question at the end of the group interview or reformulate it as an open question: 'What are important features of the relationship between SME and consultant?'.

The second dyad made interventions in order to stimulate and steer the process and interaction between participants by asking structural and process 'questions'. These questions are not on a content level, but the researchers try at the same time to structure the ongoing dialogue and to stimulate the interviewees in telling their story, their opinion, their ideas. Concrete examples of structural questions are: 'asking for clarification and illustration', 'reformulating the account of a person' or 'contrasting two opinions and inviting other participants to comment on these' or 'adding a third opinion', 'reminding of the time schedule', etc.

Through structural questions, the interviewer steers the interaction by focusing on the ongoing communication patterns; he or she is following the discussion with the following questions in the back of his or her mind. Is it clear to the others or to myself what a person says? Are participants more or less equally active in the conversation? Are we respecting the available time? Are participants diverging too much or 'jumping around'? Experience and skills concerning 'conducting meetings' and 'time management' can be very helpful here to the group facilitator.

Through process questions, the interviewer focuses on the involvement and personal ease of the participants. This requires that the interviewer is an active listener and makes interviewees feel at ease, with the aim of building trust and creating an open climate. One should not forget that this group interview can be often the first one interviewees are involved in: they feel uncertain about what is going to happen and whether their contribution will be appreciated.

In the beginning of or even before the group discussion, the interviewer can 'test the water' and see how people 'feel' about the group interview. Interviewers often start by asking everybody to introduce themselves as a kind of 'ice-breaker'. Furthermore, the beginning of an interview is an ideal point to clarify one's own role and to illustrate how one is going to conduct the interview, for instance: 'I see my role as to give everybody an equal chance to participate in this discussion. Sometimes I will interrupt persons when I feel that other persons remain too much on the background.'

During the interview, the moderator can be confronted with some 'typical' situations such as the following:

- One person is dominating the discussion and giving his or her reaction on every single thing the others say. Here a process intervention can be needed by confronting the participant while not loosing his or her involvement: 'I appreciate very much your ideas and reaction, but I would suggest that we listen first to the other participants and, afterwards, I will ask you to give your reactions.'
- Everybody is speaking at the same time. Here a structural intervention can be used by remaking a short 'contract' with the participants on

how to run the discussion: 'I see that everybody has a lot to say on this topic, but I think that we should go around in a more systematic way.'

- Sometimes the group discussion can 'flag' and reach a dead end. How can one then reinvigorate the group? This can be the moment to bring in a new content topic or theme. By a structural intervention, the interviewer can make a summary of what has been said so far, and test if persons find it necessary to continue this 'chapter' or if they agree to address a new one. The advantage is that participants are involved as well in how the interview is conducted. A process intervention can also be useful: 'I see that we are a bit out of inspiration, maybe it is useful to take a small break.' Here the moderator focuses on the involvement of the participants.

- One person remains quiet during the interview, and gives no comments unless the facilitator asks this explicitly. How can one encourage this person without making him or her feel even more uncomfortable? Through a process intervention, the interviewer can repeat his or her appreciation for every opinion even if this is very equal to or very different from the opinions of others. Here it is important not to ask directly for participation but to keep some space open so that the quiet participant can decide if he or she wants to intervene.

In general, it is important that an interviewer is able to manage his or her own action space,[5] and keep it open enough so that he or she can be flexible in making content, structural and process interventions. Finding the right balance requires a learning process from the group interviewer which should be adapted to the specific group process as well. It is important not to talk too much during the group interview (as in the individual interview), but when the moderator sees/feels the discussion is going in the 'wrong' direction, he or she must not hesitate to make a facilitating intervention. Then it is as important to 'do something' as to clarify 'why one is doing this or that'. If participants understand the perspective behind the interviewer's concrete interventions, there is more chance that they will 'follow' him or her in steering the group interaction.

Analysis of the group interview   The interviews were tape-recorded and afterwards transcribed into a copy of more than 60 pages (for each interview). Permission for tape-recording was asked from all participants. There was no video-taping, since our intention was to explore general themes, and not to undertake an in-depth analysis of this group process.

The analysis took two forms. First, a classic 'content analysis' was carried out by one of the researchers (see, for example, Strauss and Corbin, 1990), leading to the first typology of possible relationships between SMEs and consultants. Second, the analysis of the group interview was seen in the light of the other data already collected and was obtained by integrating it into the larger project.

A first evaluation   The group interview is similar to the individual interview in many ways. It can have multiple formats and the principles of good questioning are much the same (for example, the type of questions, the danger of closed questioning; see Chapter 2 etc.).

However, the following elements can be considered as distinctive. First of all, the key interaction is not between the interviewer and interviewee, but between the participants. Also other (social) processes are involved. One concerns the public character of the stories participants bring in. Another concerns the group processes which steer the general outcome of the interview. This requires insights into group dynamics and the ability to facilitate the process rather than the content.

Finally, one of the main outcomes of the group interviews, which only became clear afterwards, was that within the research team, which consisted of two dyads of researchers from different universities and from different academic backgrounds, a joint research experience was created. This made discussion of our own research process possible and helped us to understand our different perspectives. Indeed, as a research team, we meet and discuss now in order to research (or learn from) our own research process. A joint discussion is never far away, and indeed necessary to evolve towards a shared concept of research.

The project group study: the context of innovation

Through the next story, we want to describe and document the use of observation and analysis of group meetings and group discussions in their 'natural context'. On the one hand, the distinctive contribution of the group study will be illustrated in relation to the larger organization case study which consisted of the use of interviews, questionnaires, the study of documents and feedback sessions as well. On the other, we will describe more practically how we learned to use this application of the group method. The 'materials' case study from which examples will be given was part of a three-year research project with the general aim of understanding the organizational processes underlying the implementation of innovation. It is one of seven longitudinal case studies which were set up for this research project. The researcher attended 18 project meetings as a participant observer. Besides the observation and analysis of this long sequence of group meetings, 28 interviews, an organizational climate survey, 100 pages of documents and a two-day feedback session were all part of the 'data collection'.

Why group study?   Besides the epistemological considerations for using a project group study, more pragmatic reasons were involved. In the context of innovation, where project groups are the focus of the innovative activities, group observation becomes advantageous compared to other methods for understanding how organizations innovate differently. Our aim was not to study project groups as such, but to understand how the organizational innovation process develops by observing group meetings. As teamwork becomes more and more crucial for the well-functioning and effectiveness of all kinds of firms (Woodman and Sherwood, 1988), increasing numbers of researchers will be confronted with studying groups at work *with the aim of describing and understanding the whole organization*. Although for the other cases, data were gathered through different methods (interviews, observations of meetings and study of documents), the use of the 'group meeting' method was much more important in the 'materials' case. This was not a clear option beforehand, but as we followed the innovation project *in vivo*, the project itself was developed through these meetings, which became more frequently used as a forum for direct interaction between the different participants in the project. At the time the researcher came in, he started a series of introductory interviews in order to explore the general context and evolution of both the organization and the innovation project. In this way, he became involved in studying an organization development project that followed a total quality (TQ) and a material resource management (MRM) programme. Efforts to install an MRM programme by a project leader using an existing system did not succeed. MRM and the earlier TQ programmes met a lot of resistance. Finally, after an off-site meeting of the production staff, led by the manufacturing manager, a series of weekly meetings started to diagnose and discuss the organization problems being experienced. The researcher then shifted from doing interviews towards participating as an observer in the meetings. By this, the researcher was more closely involved with the ongoing interactions, but, at the same time, he became more visible to the organizational members as well. There was no direct influence from the researcher on the meetings, since he never gave his opinion, nor made any comments. Indirectly, he reminded other participants that they could distance themselves from the intensive and chaotic discussions and ask themselves what was going on. It is an illusion to believe that one can be 'absent' as a participant observer. Furthermore, it would not have been possible to follow the evolution of the project through interviews or otherwise. For many participants, the interview would have been a difficult exercise in 'sense-making' since it was not always easy to say what had happened in these meetings, and would have been a significant activity in the course of the project; actually, the meeting was 'the' place where new sense-making in the group was undertaken week after week, as a kind of continuous story, interrupted but 'to be continued'.

We now focus on the different 'steps' in using this method: preparing and attending meetings, coming back to the research team, analysing meetings, and integrating with other methods. The distinction between data collection and data analysis will be made for didactic reasons, but they are strongly connected during the research process.

Preparing and following the group meetings   The preparation of and the participation in one actual meeting is not very demanding. During the meeting the researcher took notes both of what was said and by whom. He also made non-verbal observations (who came in late, silences, laughs, etc.). There was no tape-recording as the amount of data would have become too vast.

This research activity can be seen as an evolutionary task. The important step for the researcher at this stage is to get integrated and accepted in the social system of a firm and the particular project group. It takes some time before you as a researcher get invited spontaneously to the next meeting, get a copy of the notes and summaries of the participants, or get a phone call from the secretary to inform you that the meeting has been postponed (it happened once that the observer was present but that the group was not!). It is not easy to get accepted, but step by step people get used to the idea of the presence of a stranger, and also on certain occasions people discuss the role of the researcher. In the firm the researcher even got a nickname.[6] (The development of field relationships has been more fully described by Jörgensen, 1989.)

Coming back to the research team   We would call the period after the participation in the meeting more important than the participation itself. On returning to the research team, the first thing the researcher did was check his notes, completing and rewriting them. Second, the researcher discussed with colleagues what he had been up to, asking the very general question of what had happened there, in the context of the research question. This discussion of first impressions and ideas already constitutes an initial interpretation of the data.

Besides this informal reception of the returning researcher, the research team[7] itself had its weekly meetings through which the innovation project was steered. This is one of the main ways of making this kind of group study fruitful, or at least surviving it. Pettigrew (1990) has emphasized teamwork in longitudinal field research. The role and influence of the research team for the observant researcher is valid on many levels:

1   *Support*: the researcher follows the emotional life of this group in evolution. Furthermore, the researcher does not see where this invest-ment is leading him or her. Is there going to be a valuable outcome for the research? This creates a lot of uncertainty (should I go on with this or not?) which can be shared through coming back into the research team.

2   *Distancing* (Rosen, 1991): the team gives researchers another reality, which helps them to distance themselves from their participation. This is not only important emotionally: there is also a change of

perspective, which is necessary for interpreting the data. Following Pettigrew (1990), teamwork helps the researchers balance detachment and involvement in the field. It also inhibits any tendency to overidentify with particular interpretations or interests when analysing the data.

3 *Consensual validation*: in analysing and discussing the 'materials' case together, different perspectives and interpretations are added to the interpretations which the researcher originated.

Analysis of the meeting discussions Analysis is carried out in four related steps. The first is writing the story as explained. The story is a mix of 'actual sayings', descriptions of (inter)actions, and interpretations (everybody giving their opinion). This story is written after the concept analysis and the construction of meaning configurations (step two) in order to document a more general interpretation of this meeting, for example the interaction between group and group leader.

In the second step, concepts are formulated using the method of grounded theory (Glaser and Strauss, 1967; Turner, 1983). In practice, this means that the field notes (or interview transcripts) are analysed part by part. A part of the text is taken and 'interpreted' by deriving a concept, for instance 'recycling problem definition', 'continuous evaluation' or 'the facilitating role of the project manager'. This results in a long list of concepts which are related to each other and integrated in so-called meaning configurations.

In the third step, the outcomes of the group study are compared to and integrated with the outcomes of the interviews and the study of documents. Here, the research team works towards an integrated case study (see Bouwen et al., 1992; Bouwen and Fry, 1991). The research team uses a more 'holistic' interpretative style which can, however, be documented in more detailed parts of the analysis. Coming to an understanding of this complex sequence of events involves a circular consideration of both the whole and its parts (see Brown et al., 1989).

The fourth step consists of going back to the firm. Based on this set of analyses, an extensive report was written to present our descriptions and interpretations of the organization development project and was transmitted to all members of the project team. Furthermore, the supervisor and the researcher participated in a two-day residential seminar with the project team, where they gave an introductory presentation based on the report. This had a double aim. First, it was seen as a further step of analysis, based on co-inquiry. As researchers we have many questions like: Do they recognize our interpretations? Are they meaningful to them? Can they use them? What interpretations do they have? Can we agree on some interpretations? Here as a researcher you validate your findings with the direct participants, but it is also an exercise in communicating your findings and in exploring their usefulness. Second, this was a (well-elaborated) feedback exercise, which this group had been doing many times ('what have we been doing?'), and which helped it in finding the future path. Here we come close to the group intervention study, which will be discussed as a third type of the group method.

A first evaluation   Using the group method within the 'materials' case has been very fruitful. First, it gave the opportunity to do a longitudinal study *in vivo* based on a partial integration of the researcher in the social system of the firm. The richness and depth of understanding would not have been reached on the basis of interviews alone (as we have noticed in other cases). Second, it gave the opportunity to study the interaction of multiple parties at one and the same moment, and to focus on the dynamics of organizing: one can literally see the organization-in-the-making. Third, the researcher could observe persons in different situations, not only in the interview situation. It gave the opportunity to focus on the relation between what people do and what people say they do; also, the researcher could 'see' how people make sense of situations (in interviews) based on the meetings in which the researcher had participated.

This kind of group research method is quite complex and asks a lot of maturity of the researcher. First, it is a kind of selective form of organizational ethnography, making use of focused observant participation (see Czarniawska-Joerges, 1992). The researcher only goes now and then to the organization to participate in what can be regarded as 'significant moments' for the research problem. Although this can be seen as a minimal form of organizational ethnography, it asks for the same qualities as the organizational ethnographer (see Chapter 7). The researcher needs to build up a trust relationship and to define and redefine his or her role as the process goes on. Second, the researcher needs to be able to integrate different research methods into one overall case study. Third, he or she needs to have the courage to invest in a long-term affiliation with a particular firm with an uncertain and open end. The 'success' of this research investment is largely dependent on the learning process the researcher is going through during the study.

Group intervention: the implementation of team units

The third approach we want to discuss in using groups to collect organizational behaviour data concerns intervention contexts, where the primary purpose of the researcher and the participants is to get a view of where they stand and where they are heading. It is not the place here to discuss organizational development principles (Neilsen, 1984), but some concept of what social science can do to help an organization to set up such an organizational review and development process is necessary to frame the specific group meeting approach we are illustrating here. Group meetings, besides interviews, constitute a vital element of the possible intervention strategies. Examples refer to the Company Extruco, where a project involving the implementation of team units was started up as part of a general quality improvement process.

Why group intervention?   The researcher/consultant was invited to look into the implementation problems one year after the quality improvement programme was started up. Meetings with the general manager and the department heads, interviews with middle and lower management and seminars with several of these groups constituted a programme to re-align the ongoing change efforts as agreed among the researcher/consultant and the general manager. The group meeting on which we want to concentrate further here took place at the beginning of the project after a first contact with the general manager. An extended 'steering committee' of representatives of staff and managers across all levels and departments ($n = 16$) was held to assess the key elements of the implementation problem. The general manager did not participate to encourage an open expression of ideas and a free choice in building commitment to new action proposals.

The choice for a group meeting as a general starting-point for the intervention programme was made for several reasons. A steering group of flexible composition was already in existence, different levels and different functional specialisms could be combined and a direct link between collecting data and drawing consequences for action could be built.

The choice for a group method was very explicit here. Instead of having interviews with key persons and feeding the data back in a feedback session, this group meeting drastically shortens the data feedback cycle. It also connects data-processing at the content level with creating involvement at the social-relational level.

Conducting the group meeting   The meeting started with an introduction by the facilitator, siting it within the change project and previous contacts and discussing the group composition and the leading discussion question: 'What have we been doing up to now?' A co-worker was taking notes; no tape-recording was agreed upon so as to leave the ownership of what was said and decided as much as possible to the group meeting. The meeting was run in a training room in the plant next to the production hall.

The facilitator asked the participants to take time out to reflect and formulate ideas, putting these on paper if they wanted. Then there was an opportunity to go around and listen to each other's comments. People were invited to ask questions for clarification, but not to discuss or to make objections: 'Just try to understand what the other is saying.' Each participant in turn brought his or her views. Participants spent 90 minutes going around the group and listening to each other.

After this data collection inventory, the facilitator made a brief summary, not exhaustive but to illustrate the diversity of images about the change project in the group. He then raised the question: 'What is the highest priority action now to make further progress?' There was a nearly unanimous reaction: 'We have to reduce all the different change efforts to the same common denominator. At the moment we are going in different directions and we neutralize each other's efforts.' But this common concern was immediately followed by very divergent action proposals. So the attention was focused on 'how' we were going to do this instead of 'what' we should do now. Some action steps were then taken (meetings, a seminar etc.) to work on the development of shared meaning and consensual validation on the state of the project and the future lines of development.

The role of the researcher is mainly the role of a process facilitator of the communication process: providing space and attention among the group members to express diverse ideas, to listen and to understand similarities as well as differences. The main aim is to stimulate a session of collective sense-making and collective renegotiation of meanings around the so-called 'introduction of the team concept' project.

Data analysis   One way of representing the diversity of ideas in the described situation is to construct meaning configurations for the different parties involved. In this study we used a 'kaleidoscope of frames of meaning' (Bouwen, 1993). Briefly stated, four frames of meaning were distinguished for each party: a substantial frame, a relational frame, a procedural/structural frame and a political/interest frame. For each significant party (top management, middle management, staff services, operators), one can fill in the kaleidoscope of meanings to describe similarities and differences among the parties.

From a theoretical viewpoint, one can illustrate using this analysis how conflicting ideas among the significant stakeholders in this situation can be laid out into differences of frames. In practice, it offers an instrument to name the differences and to work on developing shared meanings. For each stakeholder, a configuration of meanings can be derived. For example, the meaning configuration of the Manager in the Extruco case connects failure in reaching the expected outcome with a lack of control; he intends to take cost measures, which further reduces the results of the team concept change. The staff people, using an organizational inference map, see a lack of involvement and consider training and support to the team leaders as a possible action strategy.

A second step is a comparative analysis of the different meaning configurations. How do the different parties relate their meanings to each other? Do they polarize the differences, do they eliminate or separate the differences, or can they alternate and adapt in exchanging their views?

A first evaluation   Clearly, the way of collecting, analysing and feeding back the data is strongly linked to the intervention purposes of the project. The aim is to work on the diversity of the perspectives of the ongoing innovation project. It is in fact an effort to facilitate the social negotiation in implementing new ways of thinking and working. The research is doing just that: drawing a picture of the experiences, revealing overlaps and differences to extend the field of shared meaning. This is indeed the task of an organization in innovation.

The group method in this case has several advantages over individual interviews or other data collection methods. In the first place, the feedback cycle is shortened. This makes communication among the different parties very direct and builds connections between data and action. Through the mutual presence of the different parties, one can directly observe the dynamics among their different viewpoints. This is made explicit in the second step of analysis.

The preparation of the meeting is very important. This supposes a proper contracting of the different parties. The role of the facilitator has to be clear and the process has to be steered so that an open expression and relating of viewpoints to each other can be facilitated.

The data collection and analysis can be used for theoretical purposes to build theories about organizational change. In the course of a consulting project, this group practice is very common and the challenge is to develop the proper concepts to work on the data reduction and data communication.

Finally, the role of the researcher/consultant is that of a process consultant in proposing the meeting, the group composition, the leading question and in facilitating the expression of views and the subsequent interaction up to a point where the next feasible and accepted action step can be agreed.

Comparing and contrasting the three cases

In Table 8.2, the group interview, the project group study and the group intervention type are compared and contrasted.

We have distinguished three types based on three research goals: exploration of a problem, generation of a theory and intervention in a concrete situation. From a social constructionist perspective, these three types allow the possibility of considering the multiplicity of perspectives, but with different accents. They are rooted in different methodological backgrounds, since the group interview goes back to content analysis, the project group study has affinity with grounded theory, while group intervention is related to intervention theory and action research. Although the context of use is not restricted to one area, in the past this has actually been the case.

In the group interview, the main data are loosely coupled ideas/ opinions, emerging from questions and given research themes. Through content analysis, several themes and exploratory insights emerge. Mostly the relationship between data collection and analysis is separated, although sometimes a new group interview is conducted in order to

Table 8.2   *Comparison between three types of the group method*

	Group interview	Project group	Group intervention
Goal of the research	Exploration of the problem or phenomenon	Theory generation	Intervention in the context
Social constructionist focus	Different voices on the same subject	Interplay between the voices	Change of the interplay between the voices
Background	Content and theme analysis	Grounded theory	Intervention theory/ action research
Context of use	Marketing and consumer studies	Social interaction and communication, conflict	Organizational change
Data generation	Loosely coupled opinions/ideas	Theme-orientated perspectives	Change-orientated interactions
Analysis	Emerging themes	Concepts and meaning configurations	Generation of new possibilities
Main point	Content	Process	Context
Role of the group	Stimulating ideas	Representing variety of perspectives on the problem	Joint action and co-learning vehicle
Role of the researcher	Discussion leader	Observant participant	Process consultant
Data collection/ analysis relationship	Mostly separated	Co-inquiry	By the participants/ Selective

confront the group members with the findings from the previous groups. In the project group study, the data resemble mostly theme-orientated perspectives, which are based on grounded theory principles processed as grounded concepts and integrated in meaning configurations. Data collection and analysis are interwoven. Moreover, the participants not only generate data, but are involved in interpreting these as well. In the group intervention study, the data focus on change-orientated interactions, which are analysed and discussed by the participants in the light of generating new possible actions. Data generation is highly selective here, mostly in conjunction with what participants find relevant and in line with the stimulations and questions of the researcher and the purpose of the project.

The group functions as the main arena of research for studying the larger organizations, but the role of the group can again be accentuated differently. In the group interview, the group is there to stimulate ideas, and it is expected that the group process itself, as opposed to the cumulation of individual interviews, will stimulate the quantity and the quality of the ideas. For the project group study, the group represents the variety of perspectives on the theme as this evolves throughout the development of the project. The group here gives the possibility of seeing the different parties and logics within a firm 'at work'. In the case of the group intervention, the group functions as a vehicle for joint action and co-learning. Most generally, the three types can be characterized differently, as content-, process- and context-orientated respectively, since in the group interview the main outcome is the ideas and their diversity; in the project group study, the focus is on the process of interaction; and in the group intervention, the organizational context in which the group is functioning is dominant. The role of the researcher asks for research competencies besides skills in group functioning and group dynamics. This requires process skills respectively for leading the group discussion, for building up a long-term integration as a participant observer, and for guiding the intervention and change process.

Although Table 8.2 gives an overview of the core features of the three types of group method, Table 8.3 presents a list of the main strengths and liabilities of these three types as they emerge from the three accounts of research approaches.

Conclusion: emerging choices

In choosing and using the group method, it is important to consider three main interrelated choices. First, the group method, as it has been demonstrated here in practice, was not used in isolation but was embedded in the development of a larger research project, where other methods were used as well. The emergent question here, therefore, is what other methods should be added? Without going into the discussion on triangulation, our stories revealed that the research questions as well as the practical possibilities guided us in the continuous 'designing' of the research trajectory, and in implementing the group as a research vehicle. However, if organizations are increasingly seen as networks of social interaction, the choice of working in group contexts will become more and more self-evident.

The second choice considers the purpose for which you are going to use the group method. Two contexts are explored: do you prefer to work with existing groups or to create your own groups? And for what purpose do you want to use the group method: for a general exploration, for generating new concepts and models, or for stimulating new action and intervention?

Table 8.3 *Comparison of strengths and weaknesses between three types of the group method*

	Group interview	Project group	Group intervention
Strengths	Different opinions at the same time Dynamics between different perspectives Easy to organize	Research *in vivo* and on a longitudinal base Depth of understanding Interaction between perspectives is accessible as well as their 'natural' evolution	Change of the perspectives is accessible Connection between data and action Relevant and useful research
Weaknesses	Less control over the outcome since the impact of the group (process) is quite high Difficult to guide Easier with two 'interviewers'	Difficult to analyse Long-term investment Need for support and distancing Easier when the researcher is part of a team	Active involvement of the 'researcher' Contracting with the different parties Need for process consultation skills

The final choice concerns your role as 'researcher'. Several distinctive competencies in using both qualitative research and the group method have been mentioned. This raises special concerns for the education and training of the social science researcher. The choice can indeed be made between 'inquiry from the inside' and 'inquiry from the outside' (Evered and Louis, 1981). Do you opt for an experiential involvement, for an open and unstructured research scenario (no fixed set of data, no a priori categories in analysis, multiple levels of interpretation and integration), and do you have the intention to understand a particular situation? In particular, the question concerns the choice between the complex and holistic site of social interaction *in vivo* and the simplified and fragmented focus on isolated individuals – isolated from others (as in interviews, questionnaires) and from their context (as in experiments, simulations).

The creativity of the researcher using qualitative methods is crucial in the whole of the research project and especially critical in the analysis phase to obtain some added value. Quantitative analysis works with weighting precoded categories. Qualitative research, in essence, is the creative development of concepts which can capture the richness of the data collected. In group meetings this richness is very high, and therefore for some people and some purposes they are maybe too complex and chaotic. But is it not precisely in group life that the natural complexity and diversity of social life is revealed? The challenge for social science is to develop approaches which can catch instantly the ongoing complex interaction while the social reality is being negotiated and renegotiated. Maybe then the social scientist can finally live up to the very pressing and demanding needs of present-day society, in a variety of contexts all over the world, to contribute substantially to urgent social tasks in conflictual environments.

Notes

1 Although the group interview and the focus group are regarded here as exploratory, this should not imply, as Morgan suggests, that they require supplementation or validation with quantitative techniques, but that they have a full potential on their own 'both as a self-contained means of data collection and as one of several components in a larger research programme' (1991: 24).

2 After reviewing the articles from *Personnel Psychology, Journal of Applied Psychology* and *Organizational Behavior and Human Decision Processes* for three years.

3 This research project was started in the beginning of 1992 and continued until 1994.

4 We had invited six persons in both cases, but in both situations one person was not able to come at the last minute.

5 In training graduate students for doing group interviews (by simulating them and role-playing), one of the first problems they meet is that they miss the action space to 'lead' the interview. They are so caught by the event itself that they find it hard to realize if the interview is going in the right direction, and what they can do in order to steer it. A frequently heard complaint is then 'the speed! the speed with which these participants talk and alternate with each other'.

6 The researcher, whose first name was Jan, was nicknamed 'Jan Matterne' after the famous writer of popular Flemish television serials based on observation of everyday situations (for example, a group of colleagues in a government agency) or more dramatic scenarios (for example, court trials).

7 The research team consisted of the supervisor and two other researchers besides the researcher who was doing the 'materials' case.

References

Allport, F.H. (1955) *Theories of Perception and the Concept of Structure*. New York: Wiley.

Argyris, C. and Schön, D.A. (1978) *Organizational Learning: a Theory of Action Perspective*. Reading, MA: Addison-Wesley.

Berger, P. and Luckmann, T. (1967) *The Social Construction of Reality*. New York: Anchor.

Blanksby, M. and Iles, P. (1990) 'Recent developments in assessment centre theory, practice and operation', *Personnel Review*, 19 (6): 33–44.

Bouwen, R. (1984) 'Een overzichtsschema van interventies in groepen', in *Leren en Leven met Groepen*, 1307: 1–18.

Bouwen, R. (1993) 'Organizational innovation as a social construction: managing meaning in multiple realities', in S.M. Lindenberg and H. Schreuder (eds), *Interdisciplinary Perspectives on Organization Studies*. Oxford: Pergamon.

Bouwen, R. and Fry, R. (1991) 'Organizational innovation and learning: four patterns of dialogue between the dominant logic and the new logic', *International Studies in Management and Organization*, 21 (4): 37–51.

Bouwen, R. and Salipante, P. (1990) 'The behavioural analysis of grievances: episodes, actions and outcomes', *Employee Relations*, 12 (4): 27–32.

Bouwen, R. and Steyaert, C. (1990) 'Construing organizational texture in young entrepreneurial firms', *Journal of Management Studies*, 27 (6): 637–49.

Bouwen, R., de Visch, J. and Steyaert, C. (1992) 'Innovation projects in organizations: complementing the dominant logic through organizational learning', in D. Hosking and N. Anderson (eds), *Organizational Change and Innovation*. London: Routledge.

Brown, L.M., Tappen, M.B., Gilligan, C., Miller, B.A. and Argyris, D.E. (1989) 'Reading for self and moral voice: a method for interpreting narratives of real-life moral conflict and choice', in M.J. Packer and R.B. Addison (eds), *Entering the Circle: Hermeneutic Investigation in Psychology*. Albany: State University of New York Press.

Burrell, G. and Morgan, G. (1979) *Sociological Paradigms and Organizational Analysis*. London: Heinemann.

Calori, R. and Sarnin, P. (1991) 'Corporate culture and economic performance: a French study', *Organization Studies*, 12 (1): 49–74.

Cooperrider, D.L. and Srivastva, S. (1987) 'Appreciative inquiry in organizational life', *Research in Organizational Change and Development*, 1: 129–69.

Czarniawska-Joerges, B. (1992) *Exploring Complex Organizations*. Newbury Park, CA: Sage.

Dyer, W.G. (1987) *Team Building: Issues and Alternatives*. Reading, MA: Addison-Wesley.

Eiben, R. and Milliren, A. (1976) *Educational Change: a Humanistic Approach*. La Jolla, CA: University Associates.

Evered, R. and Louis, M.R. (1981) 'Alternative perspectives in the organizational sciences: "inquiry from the inside" and "inquiry from the outside"', *Academy of Management Review*, 6 (3): 385–95.

Fromkin, H.L. and Streufert, S. (1976) 'Laboratory Experimentation', in M.D. Dunnette (ed.), *Handbook of Industrial and Organizational Psychology*. Chicago: Rand McNally.

Gergen, K.J. (1985) 'The social constructionist movement in modern psychology', *American Psychologist*, March: 266–75.

Glaser, B. and Strauss, A.L. (1967) *The Discovery of Grounded Theory: Strategies for Qualitative Research*. Chicago: Aldine.

Gray, B., Bougon, M. and Donnellon, A. (1985) 'Organizations as constructions and deconstructions of meaning', *Journal of Management*, 11 (2): 77–92.

Greenbaum, T.T. (1988) *The Practical Handbook and Guide to Focus Group Research*. Lexington, MA: Lexington Books.

Hare, A.P. (1985) *Social Interaction as Drama*. Beverly Hills, CA: Sage.

Hosking, D.M. and Morley, I.E. (1991) *A Social Psychology of Organizing: People, Processes and Contexts*. New York: Harvester Wheatsheaf.

Jörgensen, D.L. (1989) *Participant Observation: a Methodology for Human Studies*. Newbury Park, CA: Sage.

Krueger, M.A. (1988) *Focus Groups: a Practical Guide for Applied Research*. Newbury Park, CA: Sage.

Latham, G.P. and Steele, T.P. (1983) 'The motivational effects of participation versus goal-setting on performance', *Academy of Management Journal*, 26: 406–17.

Levine, J.M. and Moreland, R.L. (1990) 'Progress in small group research', *Annual Review of Psychology*, 41: 585–634.

Litwin, G.H. and Stringer, R.A., Jr (1968) *Motivation and Organizational Climate*. Boston, MA: Division of Research, Harvard Business School.

Locatelli, V. and West, M. (1990) 'On elephants and blind researchers: methods for accessing culture in organizations'. Working paper, Department of Psychology, University of Sheffield.

Lundberg, C.C. (1990) 'Surfacing organizational culture', *Journal of Managerial Psychology*, 5 (4): 19–36.

Marshall, C. and Rossman, G. (1989) *Designing Qualitative Research*. Newbury Park, CA: Sage.

Mishler, E. (1986) *Research Interviewing: Context and Narrative*. Cambridge, MA: Harvard University Press.

Moore, C.M. (1987) *Group Techniques for Idea-Building*. (*Applied Social Research Methods Series, Vol. 9*). Newbury Park, CA: Sage.

Morgan, D.L. (1991) *Focus Groups as Qualitative Research* (*Qualitative Research Methods Series, Vol. 16*). Beverly Hills, CA: Sage.

Neilsen, E. (1984) *Becoming an OD Practitioner*. Englewoods Cliffs, NJ: Prentice Hall.

Patton, M.Q. (1980) *Qualitative Evaluation Methods*. Beverly Hills, CA: Sage.

Pettigrew, A.M. (1990) 'Longitudinal field research on change: theory and practice', *Organization Science*, 1 (3): 267–92.

Rabbie, J.M. and Van Oostrum, J. (1984) 'Environmental uncertainty, power and effectiveness in laboratory organizations', in G.M. Stephenson and J.H. Davis (eds), *Progress in Applied Social Psychology, Vol. 2*. Chichester: Wiley.

Rentsch, J. (1990) 'Climate and culture: interaction and qualitative differences in organizational meanings' *Journal of Applied Psychology*, 75: 668–81.

Rosen, M. (1991) 'Coming to terms with the field: understanding and doing organizational ethnography', *Journal of Management Studies*, 28: 1–24.

Sackett, P.R. and Larson, J.R. (1990) 'Research strategies and tactics in industrial and organizational psychology', in M.D. Dunnette and L.M. Hough (eds), *Handbook of Industrial and Organizational Psychology*. Palo Alto, CA: Consulting Psychologists Press, Inc.

Salipante, P. and Bouwen, R. (1990) 'The behavioral analysis of grievances: conflict, complexity and transformation', *Employee Relations*, 12 (3): 17–22.

Spradley, J.P. (1979) *The Ethnographic Interview*. New York: Rinehart & Winston.

Srivastva, S., Obert, S. and Neilson, E. (1977) 'Organizational analysis through group process: a theoretical perspective for organizational development', in C. Cooper (ed.), *Organization Development in the UK and USA*. New York: Macmillan.

Stewart, D.W. and Shamdasani, P.N. (1990) *Focus Groups. Theory and Practice*. (Applied Social Research Methods Series, Vol. 20). Newbury Park, CA: Sage.

Steyaert, C. (1992) 'Teambuilding bij Organisatie-ontwikkeling', in J. Gerrichhauzen (ed.), *Interventiestrategieën in Organisaties*. Heerlen: Open Universiteit.

Strauss, A. and Corbin, J. (1990) *Basics of Qualitative Research*. Newbury Park, CA: Sage.

Templeton, J.F. (1987) *Focus Groups: a Guide for Marketing and Advertising Professionals*. Chicago, IL: Probus.

Tucker, R.W., McCoy, W.J. and Evans, L.C. (1990) 'Can questionnaires objectively assess organizational culture?', *Journal of Managerial Psychology*, 5: 4–11.

Turner, B.A. (1983) 'The use of grounded theory for the qualitative analysis of organizational behavior', *Journal of Management Studies*, 20 (3): 332–48.

Weick, K. (1968) 'Laboratory organizations and unnoticed causes', *Administrative Science Quarterly*, 14: 294–303.

Weick, K. (1979) *The Social Psychology of Organizing*. Reading, MA: Addison-Wesley.

Wells, W.D. (1974) 'Group interviewing', in R. Ferber (ed.), *Handbook of Marketing Research*. New York: McGraw-Hill.

Woodman, R.W. and Sherwood, J.J. (1988) 'The role of team development in organizational effectiveness: a critical review', *Psychological Bulletin*, 88 (1): 166–86.

Yin, R.K. (1989) *Case Study Research: Design and Methods* (rev. edn). Beverly Hills, CA: Sage.

9

The Analysis of Company Documentation

Nick Forster

Objectives

This chapter has three objectives: to describe briefly the use of formal documentation in social scientific research; to describe the use of the hermeneutic method in the analysis of organizational documents; and to provide a step-by-step fieldwork description of the application of the method in an organization.

Introduction to the method

The analysis of documentary, administrative and archival sources has often been regarded as a method to be employed by historians, anthropologists and linguists, rather than by sociologists or psychologists. However, many of the founders of western social science relied heavily on this methodology. Marx and Engels made extensive use of the reports of factory inspectors in England in their pioneering studies of the English working classes (Engels, 1968; Marx and Engels, 1970 [1846]). Durkheim (1952) used official statistics on suicide and religion. Weber (1922) made extensive use of religious tracts and pamphlets in his work on the sociology of religion and the origins of capitalism in the Occident.

A number of European and American social scientists continued to make use of official and administrative documents in research in the 1930s, 1940s and 1950s. These included: studies of managers (Dalton, 1959); studies of organizational doctrines and policies (Clark 1958; Selznick, 1949); and research on organizational productivity (Haire, 1959; Katz et al., 1950). However, this method fell largely into disuse in the 1960s and 1970s. Where documents were used, they were usually included only for illustrative purposes (for example, Billig, 1978).

With one or two noticeable exceptions (for example, Atkinson, 1990; Krippendorf, 1980; discourse analysts such as Marshall Chapter 6, this volume; and in textual investigation in communication studies), few social scientists appear to be concerned about analysing *words*. They still rely heavily on positivist methods in analysing behavioural phenomena, be it individual actions (psychology), the social systems in which they take place (sociology) or the relationships between both domains (social psychology). Despite the growth in interest in qualitative methods since this time, little apparent use has been made of company documentation. This is somewhat surprising because it can cast light on many aspects of organizational life.

Organizational documentation comes in many forms: company annual reports; public relations (PR) material and press releases; accounts statements; corporate mission statements; policies on marketing strategy; formal charters and legal documents; policies on rules and procedures; human resource management (HRM) strategies; policy directives on training, career management, job mobility and relocation management; formal memos between different groups and departments; and informal and private correspondence between staff and correspondence between respondents and researchers. It is important that any researcher is aware of these different kinds of documentation and of the variety of functions which different kinds of documents can play in organizational life – from the 'wide audience' type memo through to the more personal or even covert correspondence between individuals or informal groupings.

These varied documentary records constitute a rich source of insights into different employee and group interpretations of organizational life, because they are one of the principal by-products of the interactions and communication of individuals and groups, at all levels, in organizations. In coverage, these data are often more comprehensive than the kind of material which a researcher who is new to an organization could obtain from either interviews or questionnaires. They are often contemporaneous records of events in organizations. This can help researchers to look more closely at historical processes and developments in organizations and can help in interpreting informants' 'rewriting' of history in later verbal accounts. It is also important to note that most company documentation is not PR material. Most of it is kept within company boundaries and even those documents which are explicitly PR in tone can tell researchers a great deal about the kind of 'image' and culture a company is trying to present internally, to its own employees, and externally, to customers or potential competitors.

By definition, this information is already collected and there is no need to devote unnecessary time and resources to collecting some types of data through other methods. Collecting it is an unobtrusive and largely non-reactive process. It does not initially involve active intervention in the form of interviews with key (and often extremely busy) personnel. It can also save time in research – by accessing detailed information on, for example, organizational structure, succession planning systems, career development policies, training programmes and so forth. This knowledge can, in turn, improve the quality of the kinds of questions which we can ask in other research designs. Last, and perhaps most importantly, company documents provide another means of triangulating data. This can help to counteract the biases of other methods and supplement other sources of information. They can be particularly useful in adding strength to consultancy interventions and in feedback reports to companies.

Company documents are *(con)textual paradigms* which are an integral part of other systems and structures in organizations. They share many of the attributes of paradigms described by Kuhn (1971), in the way that they define understandings of particular problems, prescribe appropriate behaviours and different ways of *getting things done* in organizations. They are not merely a preliminary to quantitative analysis, although they can be used for this purpose: they are important in their own right. They can be analysed as systems of understanding in the same way as other manifestations of behaviour (Saussure, 1974). And, as the case study later in the chapter shows, they can highlight different understandings and interpretations of life amongst different sub-groups within companies (see also Burgoyne Chapter 11, this volume).

Company documentation may be fragmentary and subjective. It may not be an authentic or accurate record of actual events and processes. It may be difficult to generalize about organizations using these kind of data. They may not be truly representative of life in a particular organization. They are invariably political and subjective. They may be used by information gate-keepers in organizations with ulterior motives. Such documents need to be carefully checked, interpreted and triangulated with other data sources. They should never be taken at 'face-value'. In other words, they *must* be regarded as information which is context-specific and as data which must be contextualized with other forms of research. They should, therefore, only be used with caution. It can also be time-consuming to access and analyse all the relevant material. This is perhaps the principal reason why it is not used more frequently in organizational research at present.

So, critics of this method may ask where is the rigour in this kind of analysis? Why should these types of data be equally or more acceptable than the outcomes of other methods? Are they merely a precursor to quantitative analysis? Are the findings valid? If they are, how can this be demonstrated? The position taken in this chapter is as follows: there is no clash between either the objectives or methodologies of qualitative or quantitative research. Each form has its own strengths and weaknesses. Which one we choose is determined by the questions we are seeking to answer. Both are useful for generating and verifying theory. There is a large body of literature which has questioned and reformulated traditional understandings of 'facts and values', 'objectivity and subjectivity' and the criteria we employ in attempting to understand people's life-worlds (see, for example, Filmer et al., 1972; Giorgi, 1970; Gurwitsch, 1964; Luckmann, 1978; Merleau-Ponty, 1962, 1964; Silverman, 1985; Zimmerman, 1974). They have argued that any science of social life must, in the last resort, be a *hermeneutic* one, which is concerned to make sense of the 'objects' of study as a 'text or text-analogue' (Schutz, 1964). Such a science is based on an immersion in the data and readings of meanings. This process is invariably confused, cloudy, often contradictory and always incomplete. Such an approach rejects 'verification' and 'prediction' in the sense that these are understood by positivists.

Description of the hermeneutic method

In this section, a *general (context-free) description* of the hermeneutic method as applied to organizational documentation is provided. The second part of the chapter is devoted to providing a case study example of how a researcher can access these types of data and make use of them. It is therefore a *field methodology* (that is specific to the context).

The analysis of company documentation takes as its starting-point Goffman's (1971) contention that all human interaction is based on meaning-laden, negotiated interaction involving self-presentation, secrecy, 'front', political gamesmanship and so forth. Furthermore, this behaviour is conditioned by the awareness individuals have of the situations in which they find themselves. So, the meanings which people attribute to these situations, rather than 'causal variables', become the basic units of research. 'Understanding' rather than 'hypothesis-testing' becomes the key methodological issue to be resolved. These meanings cannot be reduced to a number of discrete variables acting within and on individuals. The meaning of the situation is, in itself, a *sui generis* reality, which is not reducible to a few independent and dependent variables. This method also emphasizes an *emic* orientation – conceptualizing the organization from within – rather than an *etic* orientation – the view from the outside as a 'detached' observer, screening data through a preconstructed filter of questionnaire scales.

At the core of this methodology lies interpretation – to be more specific, *hermeneutic interpretation*. Hermeneutics is concerned with the study of historical texts, particularly sacred documents (from the Greek *hermeneutikos*, meaning, in this context, *the clarification of what is unclear*). The interpretation of these texts is governed by a *hermeneutic spiral*. The understanding of disparate (and often contradictory) texts evolves upwards through a spiral of understanding: analysing the meaning of individual texts, relating these to the totality of the life-worlds in which they originated, and then re-interpreting the separate texts anew (Radnitzky, 1970). This is, therefore, different from content analysis, with its particular emphasis on micro-textual methods (Krippendorf, 1980).

There are seven stages in the hermeneutic process (see Figure 9.1). The case study described later in the chapter illustrates this process within a broader field study context. The first stage involves a continuous back-and-forth process between the parts and the whole. At first, the researcher will have a vague and unclear understanding of the documents at hand. The initial task is to search for themes within each document and then within clusters of documents. This requires the researcher to become

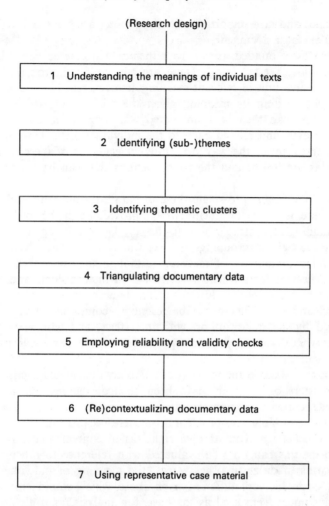

Figure 9.1 *The hermeneutic process*

empathically immersed in the available textual descriptions. At this stage, the focus of attention again is on *meanings* rather than *analysis*. Each document must be reviewed carefully and the 'taken-for-granted' assumptions and viewpoints of the author(s) of the document drawn out.

This requires an understanding of the texts in their own right. The biographical and psychological characteristics of the individuals who produced these is of secondary importance. What is important is to extend our understanding of textual themes and sub-themes. In the context of the research discussed in the case study, these included references to 'units of relevant meaning' such as culture, people management, communication and power relationships. It is important to note the actual number of times such units of relevant meaning occur since this will indicate significance and how important particular issues are perceived to be within the context of a document.

From this 'grounded knowledge', themes will emerge (see Glaser and Strauss, 1967; Wertz, 1983). These are elicited by rigorously examining each individual unit of relevant meaning, its occurrence in documents, and then understanding its meaning given the wider context(s) in which it exists. These can then be triangulated with our understanding of these other contexts, and related back to the individual texts. This requires the researcher to notice the way that different elements of these (con)textual life-worlds are linked and the contradictions that can be found amongst them.

The second stage is to relate these disparate themes with each other to see if there is a central theme which provides a higher-order level of understanding of contradictory sub-themes. The third stage develops from the second. Certain groupings of text will emerge which have an inner unity and commonality of meaning (although they may well contradict other clusters of texts which have their own internal logic and unity). It then becomes possible to cluster documents according to their own inner cohesion and logic. These can be tested by comparing them with texts produced by the same author, with interviews, and with texts by other authors who share different interpretations of the particular issues and problems discussed.

The fourth stage in the analysis of company documents is critical. Once these 'clusters of meaning' have been elicited, the researcher can then compare them with the research questions in which he or she is interested. A serious methodological problem arises here because whilst a segment of text may be analysed in its own right (as in content analysis), the true meaning of this can only be evaluated with reference to other texts and other forms of data. In other words, the meaning of individual textual segments can be very different from those which would emerge if the entire document were used as the basis for analysis, or if all the data at hand were employed. So, how can we ensure that the documents we use as our case material are representative of these varieties of meanings in organizations?

There are two ways of looking at this problem. The first is to recognize that it impossible to do full justice to the range and quantity of documents in any organization, unless this takes the form of a detailed case study. The best that we can hope to achieve is to provide selective accounts of segments or slices of organizational life in academic journals (although this criticism might be levelled equally at much of the quantitative output of social science journals). The corollary of this is a recognition that these data may be best employed in consultancy interventions or in feedback to organizations. If this is so, it is possible to use selective textual extracts purely for illustrative purposes, as is often the practice with interview data.

A second solution to these problems is to employ reliability and validity checks. This leads us to the fifth stage in the hermeneutic spiral. One reliability check is to train other researchers in the hermeneutic method in order to verify the findings. These researchers can confirm or disconfirm the general rigour of the study and check if the textual extracts employed by the researcher are representative of the document(s) of which they are a part and of other textual clusters. If there is significant disagreement between the two, then this indicates that the researcher has not controlled his or her presuppositions and subjective viewpoints or has not been rigorous in the application of the hermeneutic spiral.

If this is successful, the sixth stage is to recontextualize and retriangulate these data. Company documents do not exist in a vacuum. Whilst they may stand as sources of data in their own right, they can only ever be fully understood within broader organizational contexts and processes and with reference to other forms of data. The final step is to select which documents are to be sampled and used as the case materials in company reports, conference presentations and research publications. (The quotes illustrating the case study in this chapter represent less than 1 per cent of the material which was examined during the research.)

The hermeneutic spiral thus provides a framework with which to understand company documents – once they have been accessed. It describes the process of developing an inductive understanding of clusters of company documents through to a deductive understanding of the whole. It is not an exact methodology and there are still many difficulties to be ironed out in this process – particularly when differences of interpretation arise between a group of researchers studying the same texts. If company documents are used only in isolation, an agreed interpretation may arise from some sort of consensual validation or 'group-think' amongst the researchers concerned. If they are used in context and with appropriate reliability checks, this intersubjective agreement is unnecessary and the results are as reliable as the outcomes of other research methods. It is important that this higher-level order of understanding is reached because it also makes the process of selecting representative textual extracts in reports and publications a much tighter one.

Application of the method

There are five practical stages which are followed when using, accessing and utilizing company documents (see Figure 9.2). At the beginning of each stage, a number of operational questions are suggested and are illustrated in the case study below. However, these cannot be applied in a rigid and formalized way. This is inevitably a complex process. The questions need to be tailored and applied to the particular piece of work being undertaken. The hermeneutic process itself (described earlier) comprises stages 3 and 4.

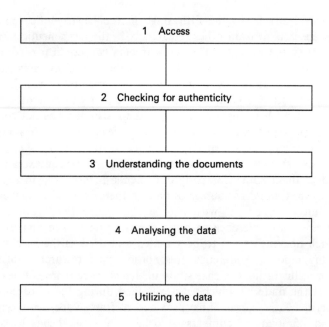

Figure 9.2   *Stages in accessing and analysing company documents*

Stage 1: Access

Does the researcher need to access company documents? What will this bring to the research? What documents are required? Where are these data to be obtained? Who are the principal 'gate-keepers' whom we need to access in order to obtain the data?

In 1988, a major retail company (referred to here as TC), which was expanding rapidly, was invited to collaborate in a study of career development, job mobility and relocation. The study embodied a systemic design which involved the analysis of three dimensions of these processes: organizational, individual and familial (Munton and Forster, 1990). The choice of documents was determined by the research questions we were trying to answer. For example, had we wanted to look at stress at work, it would have been appropriate to access as much documentation as possible on absenteeism and even employee medical records. In this particular study, we needed to access company documentation which would cast light on a variety of organizational planning issues: commitment to HRM, training, succession planning, career development policies, company culture(s), people management, and the management of employee job moves. This example focuses on one of these issues: the management of job moves.

It is important to get the backing of senior management in accessing this material. In this case, the Director of Personnel gave permission for most of the documents we wanted to examine to be released. However, two restrictions were placed on this access.[1] A junior personnel manager was appointed to help in locating the relevant documents – which were available in hard copy and disk format. These documents were accessed because they could provide a great deal of information on: formal company HRM policies, as viewed by senior executives within the company; the personnel function at the company's HQ; and personnel managers in the regions. These data were supplemented by a longitudinal questionnaire survey of 600 relocating staff; eight interviews with senior executives; 22 interviews with personnel managers; and 40 interviews with relocating employees and their partners.

Stage 2: Checking for authenticity

Are the data genuine? Are they from a primary or secondary source? Are they actually what they appear to be? Are they authentic copies of originals? Have they been tampered with or corrupted? Can authorship be validated? Are the documents dated and placed? Are they accurate records of the events or processes described? Are the authors of documents believable?

In most cases, these documents were from primary sources (that is, copies of originals or print-outs of computer files). In almost all cases, the documents discussed here were prepared by senior executives and HQ and regional personnel managers. Many of these were interviewed during the same period. So, both the accuracy of the documents and their authorship could be validated by the individuals who had produced them. There was no apparent evidence that any of these documents had been tampered with or corrupted before they were examined (indeed, there was no reason why the company should wish to do this). During interviews, the authors of the documents were invited to comment on them. They were asked if the document(s) were an accurate record of the events or processes which they had described. In all cases, they stated that these documents were objective accounts of issues and processes in the company, as they saw it (even though their views on particular topics might have changed over time). They also felt that these accorded with other information they possessed on the issues covered by the document(s). The implications of these 'well they would say that anyway wouldn't they' responses are discussed later.

Stage 3: Understanding the documents

How are the documents to be understood? How is this information to be triangulated with other sources of information? Does it add to this knowledge, confirm it or contradict it? What interpretations are to be placed on these outcomes?

One of the first set of documents which were analysed impinged directly upon relocation management. These were the company's formal HRM policies. TC was very keen to present itself as a modern and enlightened employer, with clear corporate goals and a shared mission.[2] This corporate self-image is most clearly illustrated in these extracts from the 1988 annual *Corporate Mission Statement*:

> (1) [TC] has a reputation as a carer for 'people', its staff and its customers. It is motivated by the desire for this reputation as much as a desire for profit growth.
> (2) [TC] is a place where the people enjoy working together, support each other, value each other, appreciate each other's views and problems, listen to each other and draw strength from the power of the group as a whole.
> (3) [TC] is a place where a clarity of purpose is shared by everyone. [TC] is a happy and successful community.

This perception of the company's culture was repeated in a series of guide-lines for interviewing new recruits to the company (*Staff Recruitment*, 1988):

> (1) It is the quality of the people recruited to [TC] that sets the company apart from its competitors. Few organizations in any sector can match the care and attention that [TC] pays to training and advancement, because at [TC] we believe that our people are important.
> (2) [TC] is recognized as one of the most enlightened and responsible employers in the retail industry.

The company also placed great emphasis on the quality of its management training, as this extract from a *Staff Development* document illustrates (March 1988).

> (1) The Staff Development Scheme has been designed to help employees develop the skills and knowledge necessary to pursue a successful management career with [TC]. *We offer training as and when staff need it to ensure that they perform to the best of their ability at all times.* (My emphasis)

The Senior Training Manager at the company's HQ also believed in this vision, as this extract from a training memo sent to the regions in June 1988 suggests:

> As you know, we have improved training tremendously over the last two years. I am proud to be part of those improvements and the company has realized that training is an important part of our overall business, in terms of the professionalism and standards of our management teams. We now have visible career paths and different training packages for different needs. We monitor training more effectively now. We know that we can count on you to continue this good work over the coming months and years.

However, the quote below, from a discussion document prepared by training managers in February 1988 *before the training memo above was issued*, shows unambiguous evidence of serious misgivings about the company's 'people-centred' culture and HRM management at this time:

> At this moment in time, we do not have either the time or the resources to train our managers properly. As you will be well aware, there is a company-wide problem of labour-turnover. We do not have any reliable information on why

this is happening – but we do know that many managers are under extreme work-pressures in this company. The consequence of this is that we are having to spend a disproportionate amount of time dealing with leavers and recruiting new managers, either internally or from outside. And, the bulk of training budget and our time is taken up in coping with people who have been recruited from outside [TC]. There is a growing feeling amongst established management staff that their training needs are not given a high enough priority by the company.

Many personnel officers in the regions did not share in the rosy executive vision of the company. The following comments in a letter from a regional personnel director to myself in 1989 highlight these concerns:

> There is a major discrepancy between formal company policy and the realities of life in [TC]. We get all these wonderful policy documents from HQ telling us what a great company we are and how well we treat out people. I suspect that most of these get binned, because we are having to deal with too many short-term problems such as labour turnover and management burn-out. We put these signs up all over the place saying 'the customer is king', 'smile and be happy in your work', but it's all image. If you have well-trained, motivated and committed managers who are performing well and happy in their work, you don't need all this 'hype'. Most of this is simply window dressing and does not even start to address the real problems facing this company.

What were the views of different management groups in the company about job mobility? Senior executives and divisional directors stated in interviews that their 'people-centred' policies carried over into guide-lines covering the management of job moves within the company. At the time of the survey in 1989, job mobility and relocation were facts of life for many employees in TC. Of a total management workforce of around 8,000, one in seven were relocating annually in 1988–9, at the height of the company's expansion programme. Some were relocating within 12 months of their previous move. Employee mobility was an essential lubricant in the organizational life of TC. In June 1988 a document on relocation assistance noted that:

> The effect of the new store opening programme and Head office expansion, *together with the requirement to recruit replacements for leavers*, makes it inevitable that the numbers on relocation will be maintained and are likely to grow. (My emphasis)

In spite of this, the Director of Personnel made clear to his personnel managers in a memo in 1988 that:

> *Mobility is not a condition of employment in [TC]. Management moves are organized solely on the basis of offer and acceptance.* Any suggestion or inference that a manager is under an obligation to accept a move is irresponsible, unprofessional and immoral. (Original emphasis)

He added later that:

> The relocation policy, including a detailed explanation of the various elements of the relocation package, *should be communicated to the manager concerned either by the Regional Personnel Manager or the General Store Manager prior to his accepting the move.* It must be made clear to the manager, that the

relocation policy sets out to do no more than provide assistance towards the move, and that the manager is responsible for the sale and purchase of the property. *No other guarantees, promise or hints should be given in this respect.* (My emphasis)

However, there was an awareness amongst staff in the regions that the company was experiencing considerable difficulties in its management of relocation. These extracts from an internal discussion document from a divisional personnel director to company HQ in 1989 (one year later) highlights some of these concerns:

(1) We are becoming concerned about the manner in which management moves are arranged and handled within store operations. Our concerns are concentrated in the following areas:

The frequency with which individual managers are asked to relocate
The manner in which managers are asked to move, sometimes against their wishes
The misleading impression and incorrect information that they are given about the extent of the company's relocation assistance.

(2) Managers who attempt to relocate have been given inadequate and misleading information [and] often encounter difficulties. . . . Some managers are misguided into accepting moves which, given their personal finances, are against their own interests and cost both them and the company a large amount of money. For the sake of brevity, no examples of these situations have been included in this report, but numerous case histories are available on record.

(3) The feedback received from many managers is to the effect that they have been pressurized into accepting a move which they did not initially feel inclined to take. They are given the impression that if they refuse, then their career will be damaged and they will not be given the opportunity to apply for other more personally suitable moves as and when they arise. Managers are made to feel that their loyalty is being questioned if they do not accept, and in short are under the impression that the company has the right to compel them to move.

But, in a document from a benefits and remunerations manager at HQ we find that no changes were to be made to the company's relocation policy (September 1989):

This paper does not recommend that any major changes should be made to the eligibility for relocation assistance or the range of items which are reimbursed. The information available from other companies shows that the relocation package is comparable with common practice . . . it is necessary that the relocation package is maintained to ensure the necessary degree of mobility amongst management staff.

Nowhere in this documentation was there any general discussion of the pressures being placed on managers to 'accept' job moves or any reference to the company's vision of itself as an enlightened employer with a strong commitment to 'putting its people first'.

How did this relate to other documentation? This showed that the Divisional Personnel Manager quoted above had a much more realistic understanding of the problems the company was facing at this time. Job changes caused many problems for staff. Employees had very mixed views about job moves within the company and the effects this had on their careers. Few believed that TC moved them solely in response to their career wishes. Many staff believed that job changes initiated by TC were largely in response to organizational change or restructuring and management labour turnover in the company (15 to 20 per cent per annum at that time). There was also widespread dissatisfaction with the way that these transitions were managed. Training was often not available or of little use when it was provided. It is also clear that there was considerable variation in the quality and levels of this support across the stores, as this training officer based in the Midlands observed in a discussion document circulated to regional personnel managers in April 1989:

> The management of job changes in [TC] is, frankly, a mess. We are over-promoting people at the moment and panicking because of the need to get trained personnel into new stores. We are also having to cope with a major problem of labour turnover. The result is that we are putting people into positions which they should not be put into. The only succession planning we do is to ask managers if they would like to start a new job 300 miles away next week. We fall into the trap of expecting too much from people and then we end up disciplining them because they are not doing the job properly. *The reality is that we often don't have either the time or resources to give people the right kind of support and training to do the job in the first place.* (My emphasis)

Other documents show that the company often used mobility, first, as a means of filling vacated posts caused by labour turnover, second, as a reward in the form of promotion, and, last, as a career development tool. Staff viewed job changes as being almost entirely a career step. It was therefore no surprise that job changes often did not have the beneficial outcomes that either the company or employees expected. There was inadequate communication about what the benefits and pitfalls were for employees who were 'encouraged' to move by the company. Other memos between personnel managers in the regions showed that, contrary to formal policy, transfers initiated by the company were often based on coercion rather than encouragement. Whilst *essential* to the effective functioning of TC at this time, they were increasingly unpopular types of moves for employees.

Relocation caused even greater problems for staff. We were unable to access any formal documentation prepared by regional personnel managers, but this interview quote from a senior personnel manager in the north-east highlights the concerns they had at this time (June 1989):

> The main problem we face is the lack of awareness that people have of the real problems which they can face. We don't give guidance or information on good housing areas or on the dangers and pitfalls of moving to high-cost housing areas. I actually asked for more information to be given and was actually quite astounded by the reply I got, which was pretty much what you have been told, that someone who accepts a move should have thought all this through and it's not [TC]'s problem. I am simply not prepared to accept that – if we are a

company that cares for people and yet when they have a problem we say 'tough that's their hard luck' – that just floors me!

When these data (and the findings of the questionnaire surveys) were brought to the attention of senior executives in the author's *Final Report* (Forster, 1990), a memo was circulated by the divisional directors to HQ and regional personnel managers. It concluded,

All our managers know that when they join [TC] they have to be mobile in order to advance in their careers. Obviously, that can involve some sacrifices in their personal lives. But, we have to take the view that if an employee decides to accept a job move then that decision must be left to them. We believe that the relocation package which we provide is very competitive and generous. We cannot justify changing current policies.[3]

Stage 4: Analysing the data

Did these documents distort or obscure the issues or processes being described? If so, what use could be made of them? How do we move from a literal to an interpretative understanding of these data? How do we relate selective (individual) interpretations of events to the objective reality of those events? What was the intended content of the data and what was their received content?

One of the clearest themes to emerge was the apparently incompatible interpretations of the same events and processes amongst three sub-groups within the company – senior executives, HQ personnel staff and regional personnel managers. The selected extracts presented earlier highlight clear differences between these groups. These, and the other documentation, clearly showed that different sub-cultures co-existed within the company which were having a dysfunctional effect on the organization as a whole. It should be stressed that the authors of the documents from the senior management group were not seeking consciously to deceive us, but to present an image of the company which they felt comfortable about and with which they could work. These documents were not produced deliberately to distort or obscure the events or processes being described, but their effect was to do precisely this.

Second, they highlight many of the problems and pitfalls which organizations can encounter when they try either to expand in size and/or to implement radical organizational and cultural change. TC confused change *intent* with change *implementation*. There was an assumption that merely by issuing mission statements and policy directives through personnel managers ways of doing things which had dominated the company's thinking for years would change in a relatively short period of time. These document extracts show that whilst many senior managers at TC's HQ and at divisional level believed that they were changing the company's working practices and culture (see p. 156), this was not actually being implemented further down the organizational hierarchy (see p. 157). Their individual interpretations of events in documents and interviews were clearly shaped by a *senior management sub-culture* which was extremely unresponsive to the messages which staff were trying (without success) to communicate up the organizational hierarchy (see p. 158). A wishful group-think emerged which was largely unresponsive to these concerns.

Another significant finding, as the documentation shows, was senior managers' failure to develop a shared cultural vision of what the company was trying to achieve as they implemented their ambitious change programme. This is critical in change implementation programmes in organizations (see, for example, Cummings and Huse, 1989). As a result, they were unable to change long-held behaviours and attitudes amongst different staff groups in the company which had been shaped by a hierarchical and authoritarian corporate culture in the 1970s and early 1980s.

Third, one of the main intentions of these documents was to change attitudes and behaviours in the company. However, the way that these were received by those responsible for implementing them was clearly very different (see pp. 158 and 159). Most managers and personnel officers did not have the time or resources to deal with them. In the regions, too many personnel officers were involved in reactive, short-term responses to high labour turnover and were trying to cope with inadequate training budgets. They were spending much of their time and energies engaged in 'fire-fighting' responses to the company's ambitious expansion programme, the high frequency of labour mobility between the regions and high levels of management labour turnover.

Fourth, these documents highlight the weak status of the personnel function in TC, in particular its lack of resources, its reactive responses to problems it was facing and the lack of influence it had on senior managers within the company (see p. 159). For TC to have succeeded in its ambitious expansion programme, there should have been much closer integration of strategic and HRM functions within the company. A growing body of knowledge suggests that the companies which will survive and thrive in the 1990s are those which have these organizational sub-systems closely integrated (see, for example, Storey, 1989; Wood and Peccei, 1991). The personnel function in TC has never achieved the status of a proactive HRM function, because it was never given the formal authority or resources to realize this position (see Forster, 1991, for a fuller discussion of these issues).

Fifth, these documentary extracts illustrate the logistical problems of effective HRM in large companies. Many of these refer to the lack of long-term HRM planning, a lack of resources to effectively train people, to deal with labour turnover and manage job relocation more effectively (see p. 159). One of the most visible signs of effective HRM in companies is the existence of a stable succession planning system (for example in companies like IBM and ICI). This enables personnel managers to plan career development effectively, budget for staff training programmes, plan effectively for recruitment and manage job mobility more efficiently. TC attempted to implement such a system. But, as the documentary extracts show, it never got off the ground. The scale and speed of the company expansion programme meant that all other aspects of its HRM policies suffered.

As a consequence, as the questionnaire data confirmed, many managers were overworked, highly stressed and under extreme pressures to meet sales and profit targets. Often, they did not get the career counselling or training they wanted. Training became fragmented within regions without overall planning and quality control. Many were pushed around between the stores like draught pieces because of new store openings and labour turnover. Many staff experienced personal difficulties with their job changes and family problems caused by lengthy and stressful relocations. These pressures forced good managers to leave the company and find alternative employment. The extreme competition between the regions prompted poaching of managers and an atmosphere of growing political competition over resources between divisional directors. These problems created a vicious circle within the company – one which it is still struggling to break out of.

Finally, the response of the company to the problems it encountered reflects the sub-cultures of senior executives, the HQ personnel function and personnel managers in the regions. My *Final Report*, which highlighted serious problems in TC's HRM policies, was largely ignored by TC's senior executives. Of the 40 detailed recommendations made to the company, only 14 limited changes were actually implemented by the HQ personnel function (see Appendix 1). This was issued to the regions as a policy directive. Their response was to ignore the directive, claiming lack of time or resources to implement it.

In many respects, this is a classical illustration of the short-term nature of planning in many British businesses in the 1980s. The extent of TC's problems (and their limited response to the findings of the research) has only come to the public's notice recently. For reasons of confidentiality, we cannot report fully on the extent of their difficulties but the company experienced a huge slump in profits two years ago and is struggling to regain its original market share. Two personnel directors have been sacked by the company since this time.

Stage 5: Utilizing the data

Can politically sensitive information be used in feedback to the collaborating companies? Who is this likely to benefit or harm? How can it be 'shaped' or disguised to protect the anonymity and interests of these organizations in publications?

Clearly, much of the information uncovered in this research project was, politically, extremely sensitive. But, to be of use, it had to be fed back to the collaborating company in the form of a usable *Final Report*.

Fairly tough decisions had to be made about who this was likely to benefit or harm. One way round this problem is to emphasize to a collaborating company that the findings of such reports are not simply those of a detached objective 'expert'. *It is rather an account of the company talking about itself, a vehicle which provided a large and hetero-geneous group of employees to talk openly and honestly about themselves, their careers and their company.* So, it can be emphasized that it would be unwise for the company in question not to listen to what its employees are telling it. Furthermore, the data are being presented to the company by an individual who has no vested political or partisan interest in it.

There are other obvious checks which should be followed.

First, obtaining the permission of the authors of documents to quote from them and ensuring that their identity is fully protected. This may require careful selection of documentary extracts – particularly if they are from a restricted circulation source.

Second, during interactive and collaborative projects, we will come across key members of staff who make additional contributions to the research. This is a central pay-off of qualitative research. They are often politically astute, are aware of a need for change and offer other forms of assistance (including providing documents not released by company gate-keepers). It can be helpful for them to offer comments on drafts of the report and suggest more effective and sensitive ways of feeding back the data to key personnel.

Third, often, there are specific individuals in organizations who are responsible for the problems which are identified in reports. One way round this is to depersonalize these issues by turning them into structural problems. For example, rather than saying '*senior executive X is completely oblivious to the problems faced by many regional personnel managers*', this can be stated as '*many personnel managers believe that there is poor upward communication between the regions and company HQ and not enough resources to achieve company objectives*'. Decisions about this have to be based on astute political judgement and consultation with key gate-keepers in the company. Inevitably, there are no hard and fast guide-lines which can be followed.

Finally, in terms of publications, there is one major issue to consider. This must be established at the outset of the research. Will the collaborating company give its permission to publicize the data in a form which is useful to the researcher(s)? There must be some concrete guarantees that the company will allow publications. If this is not forthcoming, the advice must be to look elsewhere for applied research opportunities. Until this particular piece of work, TC had not blocked any publications. They gave their permission only after revisions had been made to an earlier draft of the chapter. (A more detailed account of the political and ethical issues surrounding the publication of potentially sensitive data can be found in Barnes, 1979.)

Conclusion

This chapter has sought to describe a general hermeneutic methodology for the analysis of company documentation and an example of its application in one organization. No one should be in any doubt that accessing, analysing and verifying these kind of data is time-consuming and difficult. The usefulness of these data depends greatly on the care and skill employed in their handling, since many of these cannot be taken at face-value. They can never be analysed in isolation and can only be fully understood in the context of a holistic view of the organization and of other types of analyses.

However, if the analysis of company documentation illuminates the meanings of the life-worlds of individuals and groups in organizations, then that is justification enough for using this method. The analysis of company documents *can* bring fresh insights to our understanding of organizational behaviour. These can graphically highlight the interactions between different sub-groups and the political legerdemain which is an integral part of modern corporate life. If effective use is made of these, they can certainly cast new light on individual, group and collective behaviour in occupational research.

Appendix

Action taken by TC in 1990 in response to recommendations made in the *Final Report*: (Forster, 1990)

1 Report to be circulated to senior personnel managers and divisional directors.
2 Recommendations on the introduction of a career counselling programme.
3 Review of internal application form.
4 Review of interview check-list to include:
   (a) job performance expectations in new job;
   (b) relocation issues.
5 Review of appointment letters to include reference to job performance expectations in new job.
6 Review internal recruitment policy to allow minimum period for employee to consider a job before declaring acceptance.
7 Proposal to bring forward the date when appointees to new stores are identified to give longer lead time before appointment date.
8 Recommendations on improving employee awareness of training and development opportunities.
9 Code of practice on the responsibility of general store managers for training and follow-up by controllers.
10 Recommendations to include additional home-finding visits for prospective appointees and spouse prior to acceptance of job offer.
11 Check-list of practical action points for managers accepting job moves with relocation.
12 Procedure for regular follow-up of relocating managers by regional personnel managers.
13 Update all store job descriptions via training specialists.
14 Local information pack to be collated by senior personnel managers for use by relocating managers.

Notes

1 The restrictions placed on this access were: strategic planning documentation for the year 1990–1; personal performance appraisal documentation, which I was allowed to examine but not copy.

2 For further information on the significance of mission statements in the management of cultural change in the supermarket/retail sector, see Ogbonna and Wilkinson (1988).

3 This was repeated, almost word for word, in a conversation with this executive when presenting the findings of the report at HQ. This document had been forwarded to me by a personnel manager in one of TC's London stores.

References

Atkinson, P. (1990) *The Ethnographic Imagination: Textual Constructions of Reality*. London: Routledge.

Barnes, J. (1979) *Who Should Know What: Social Science, Privacy and Ethics*. Harmondsworth: Penguin.

Billig, M. (1978) *Fascists: a Social Psychological View of the National Front*. London: Harcourt Brace Jovanovich.

Clark, B. (1958) *Adult Education in Transition*. Berkeley: University of California Press.

Cummings, T. and Huse, E. (1989) *Organization Development and Change*. St Paul, MN: West.

Dalton, M. (1959) *Men Who Manage*. New York: Wiley.

Durkheim, E. (1952 [1897]) *Suicide*. London: Routledge & Kegan Paul.

Engels, F. (1968 [1845]) *The Condition of the English Working Class in 1844*. Oxford: Oxford University Press.

Filmer, P., Philipson, M., Silverman, D. and Walsh, D. (1972) *New Directions in Sociological Theory*. London: Collier Macmillan.

Forster, N. (1990) *Career Development, Job Mobility and Relocation Project: Final Report*. (Report presented to the collaborating company, TC.)

Forster, N. (1991) 'Developing the role of the personnel function in the management of job mobility', *Human Resource Management Journal*, 2 (1): 60–71.

Giorgi, A. (1970) *Psychology as a Human Science*. New York: Harper & Row.

Glaser, B. and Strauss, A.L. (1967) *The Discovery of Grounded Theory: Strategies for Qualitative Research*. Chicago: Aldine.

Goffman, E. (1971) *The Presentation of Self in Everyday Life*. Harmondsworth: Penguin.

Gurwitsch, A. (1964) *The Field of Consciousness*. Pittsburgh: Duquesne University Press.

Haire, M. (ed.) (1959) *Modern Organization Theory*. New York: Wiley.

Katz, D., Macoby, N. and Morse, C. (1950) *Productivity, Supervision and Morale in an Office Situation*. Ann Arbor: University of Michigan, Institute for Social Research.

Krippendorf, K. (1980) *Content Analysis: an Introduction to its Methodology*. London: Sage.

Kuhn, T. (1971) *The Structure of Scientific Revolutions* (2nd edn). Chicago: University of Chicago Press.

Luckmann, T. (1978) *Phenomenology and Sociology*. London: Penguin.

Marx, K. and Engels, F. (1970 [1846]) *The German Ideology*. London: Lawrence & Wishart.

Merleau-Ponty, M. (1962) *Phenomenology of Perception*. London: Routledge & Kegan Paul.

Merleau-Ponty, M. (1964) 'Phenomenology and the sciences of man', in J. Edie (ed.), *The Primacy of Perception*. Evanston, IL: Northwestern University Press.

Munton, A.G. and Forster, N. (1990) 'Job relocation: stress and the role of the family', *Work and Stress*, 4 (1): 75–81.

Ogbonna, E. and Wilkinson, B. (1988) 'Corporate strategy and corporate culture: the management of change in the UK supermarket industry', *Personnel Review*, 17 (6): 10–15.

Radnitzky, G. (1970) *Contemporary Schools of Metascience*. Gothenburg: Akademieforlaget.

Saussure, F. de (1974 [1915]) *Course in General Linguistics*. London: Fontana.

Schutz, A. (1964) *Collected Papers*. The Hague: Nijhoff.

Selznick, P. (1949) *TVA and the Grass Roots*. Berkeley: University of California Press.

Storey, J. (ed.) (1989) *New Perspectives on Human Resource Management*. London: Routledge & Kegan Paul.

Silverman, D. (1985) *Qualitative Methodology and Sociology*. Aldershot: Gower.

Weber, M. (1922) *The Sociology of Religion*. London: Methuen.

Wertz, F. (1983) 'From everyday to psychological description: Analysing the moments of a qualitative data analysis', *Journal of Phenomenological Psychology*, 14: 197–241.

Wood, S. and Peccei, R. (1991) 'Preparing for 1992: business versus strategic human resource management', *Human Resource Management Journal*, 1 (1): 63–89.

Zimmerman, D. (1974) 'On the everyday world as a phenomenon', in R. Turner (ed.), *Ethnomethodology*. Harmondsworth: Penguin Books.

10

Tracer Studies

Pat Hornby and Gillian Symon

Tracer studies are a method of identifying and describing organizational processes (such as decision-making and communication) across time and stakeholder group by the use of 'tag(s)' (such as documents or meetings). The researcher uses the 'tag(s)' as a way of: following the unfolding process through the organization; prompting the discussion of the process with organizational members; and identifying further important sources of information. The tracer study can therefore primarily be seen as a qualitative *data-sampling and collection framework*, within which a number of different sorts of specific techniques may be utilized (for example, document analysis, interviews, repertory grids and questionnaires).

In this chapter, we concentrate on the method as sampling framework rather than going into a detailed account of the analysis of the data resulting from specific techniques (the reader is referred to other relevant chapters in this book, for example Forster and King, Chapter 9 and 2 respectively).

Background to the method

In this section, we describe some general characteristics of the tracer study (partly drawing on its use in other disciplines) and outline related research methods (such as informant sampling and network analysis), illustrating the differences between these strategies and the tracer study.

General characteristics

All tracer studies include the identification of a 'tag' or 'tags' which is/are used to focus the attention of the researcher on critical features of a process. For example, in geography (Mossman et al., 1991), tracers have been used to investigate processes such as river flows by the introduction of a tag (often coloured dye) into rivers and streams. In a similar fashion, radio-opaque fluid has been introduced into the human bloodstream (a technique termed arteriography) by neuropsychologists interested in outlining the circulation system in order to identify lesions of the nervous system (for example, Walsh, 1978). In contrast, rather than introducing an artificial tag, the organizational researcher is usually more concerned with identifying the most effective 'natural' tag(s) to use for the study of a given process (however, see outline of Henry, 1990, below). Tags may already exist as part of the normal organizational procedures associated with the process under investigation. For example, many organizations have clearly defined procedures for carrying out the design and develop ment of a computer-based system or methodologies for managing particular projects. In these instances, possible tags include documentation and formal prescribed meetings (such as project planning meetings). As an example of an organizational tracer study, Symon and Clegg (1991) used the method as part of a wider case study which concerned the evaluation of a computer-based system integrating the organizational departments of design and manufacturing. The researchers identified approximately 100 products as their tags. These products were traced from their receipt as customer orders, through their design and into the methods engineering section of the manufacturing department, with the objective of ascertain-ing the (differential) uptake of the computer-based system in the two departments. The tracer was accomplished both by studying computer print-outs of products currently in the production process and through interviews with key participants in this process. It was thus discovered that 95 per cent of all new products were being designed on the new system, while only 5 per cent of these designs were being programmed by methods engineers for production purposes (the majority of the other 90 per cent being programmed on the old computer system). The interviews allowed the researchers to consider possible explanations for this situation.

All tracers are concerned with elucidating processes and so, by definition, tracers are associated with the description of activities over time – tracing may be carried out concurrent with the process as it occurs, and/or retrospectively. Concurrent tracing has advantages over retrospec-tive tracing for all of the same reasons that apply to any other psychological investigation (for example, employee recall of events). However, in educational research, tracing has normally been associated with the investigation of historical events (for example, Huberman, 1990). Furthermore, it is likely that in trying to elucidate current processes some reference will be made to the past.

It is important to note that tags are employed both as a source of data *and* as a means of sampling key participants in a process. Indeed, tracing is *primarily* concerned with data-gathering and more particularly with data-sampling as opposed to data analysis or reporting. Document analysis (see Forster, Chapter 9, this volume) is one of a number of techniques that is likely to be utilized during the tracer study. Techniques such as structured and/or unstructured interviews (see King, Chapter 2, this volume) are also likely to be employed to examine the perceptions, motives and differential levels of influence of the various participants in the process under investigation. Depending on the instruments employed, various forms of analysis and reporting may result; however, the data will describe patterns in the broadest sense rather than in terms of causal relationships.

Related methods

Tracer studies are a form of *non-probability sampling*. Thus the purpose is not to establish a random or representative sample but rather to identify those people who have information about the process. It is a search not for a 'generalizable person' but for a specific group of *relevant* people, documents and sub-processes: 'probability sampling . . . yields the researcher a representative picture of various features of the population . . . nonprobability samples yield a small number of informants who provide representative pictures of aspects of information or knowledge distributed within the population' (Johnson, 1990: 23).

The concepts of representativeness and distribution (and this may be distribution across time) described in the quote from Johnson are highly relevant to the conduct of tracer studies, suggesting as they do the relevance of the information obtained and the dispersal of relevant information across place, time and persons (rather similar to the currently popular notion of distributed cognition, see Hutchins 1991).

From a positivist perspective (see Cassell and Symon, Chapter 1, this volume), the major problem with non-probability sampling is the inability to generalize across respondents. Reliability and validity of the results are called into question because the sample size is small and 'skewed' and it is concluded that the results may therefore be biased. Our view is that it seems more appropriate to the questions we are asking to gather specific information from specific informants who are knowledgeable about the process under consideration. We are interested in building up a holistic picture of the process by taking into account a number of *different* perspectives and experiences. '[The] use of [non-probability] samples in fieldwork is predicated on the researcher's interest in the *system* of behaviour rather than in the way that behavioural traits or individuals with specific characteristics are distributed in a known universe' (Honigmann, 1982: 83).

Non-probability sampling in ethnographic studies is usually utilized to identify *key informants* – individuals who have special detailed knowledge which they are willing to communicate and who can smooth the access to other possible respondents in the social setting. In contrast, tracer studies in organizations involve the sampling of documents and meetings which then lead to the identification of informants.

Tracer studies are also similar to the form of non-probability sampling termed *snowball sampling* (Burgess, 1982), where the researcher uses one informant to identify further informants and so forth. A classic example of this type of sampling is described in McCall (1980). McCall was interested in the experiences of women artists in St Louis, USA. However, as they were not a cohesive group, nor were they operating from any particular organization, the sample was difficult not just to access but to *find*. McCall had contact with one artist (a friend) who then told him the whereabouts of other women artists. At each subsequent interview,

McCall made a point of inquiring for further contacts. Eventually, as he became more familiar with the art world (for example, through attending exhibitions and meetings), he was able to have more personal control over his sampling strategy. Hoffman (1980) similarly emphasizes the importance of contacts in gaining access to informants. In her case, the problem was one of status. Her relationship (through family ties) with the social élite of Quebec (who were members of hospital Boards of Directors) enabled her to access this very exclusive group. Once she had interviewed all those she could contact through personal ties, she asked for referrals to other members of the group. In this way, she was able to identify and gain access to a wider sample.

So snowball sampling is a particularly useful strategy to utilize when the sample required is difficult to access. In tracer studies, this aspect of sampling is useful in that the initial tag may only reveal 'formal' organizational roles involved in the process; interviewing this initial sample may lead to other 'invisible' participants.

The most obvious difference between simple informant sampling/ snowball sampling, and tracer studies is that the temporal relationships associated with the tracer study tag are critical – the organizational process happens over time and the tag may change and develop over time as well as constantly adding to the elucidation of the process under investigation.

In ethnography, a distinction is made between '*judgement*' and '*opportunistic*' non-probability sampling (Honigmann, 1982). In the latter case, informants are interviewed because they are available and willing (that is, they are not deliberately chosen by the researcher). Snowball sampling is of this kind. However, in the case of judgement sampling, informants are identified in accordance with the interests of the researcher because they will shed light on a particular aspect of the behaviour under investigation. This is similar to Glaser and Strauss' concept of '*theoretical* sampling': 'Theoretical sampling is the process of data collection for generating theory, whereby the analyst collects, codes and analyses his [sic] data and decides what data to collect next and where to find them, in order to develop his [sic] theory as it emerges' (1967: 45). In Glaser and Strauss' conceptualization, therefore, the sampling strategy is driven by theoretical considerations. However, judgement sampling is a broader concept. Although theory may inform the strategy, it may also result from pragmatic considerations or be informed by the researcher's experience in similar situations or his or her practical knowledge of the area. Similarly, tracer studies may be driven by a combination of factors, including theoretical considerations. For example, the organizational context may suggest possible fruitful samples and sampling techniques.

Another research method with which the tracer study has some similarities is *social network analysis* (Scott, 1991). Social network analysis is a method for investigating the relational aspects of social structures, that is, the ties and connections that relate people one to another. Social network analysis enables the researcher to analyse the strength, direction and nature of ties between individuals and to describe configurations of networks of people. Social network analysis is different to snowball sampling in that the focus for the former is on the ties within and between groups and individuals, rather than using these ties for the purpose of sampling a population. We believe that tracers fall somewhere between snowball sampling and network analysis, being more than simply a means of sampling (though certainly that), but not concerned with analysing in any great detail the nature of the connectedness of the individuals in the study. Tracers are concerned with shedding some light on the process in which a group of individuals has taken part. This means that the focus of the study is not (as is the case with social network analysis) the connections between people but the context within which these connections take place in relation to a given process. Tracers are not about providing a detailed analysis of relationships but are a means of exploring the attitudes and ideas of individuals in relation to a process in which they have all participated in some way.

In summary, the tracer study shares elements with a number of related methods: informant sampling, snowball sampling and network analysis. It is similar to informant sampling in the notion of seeking relevant knowledge which it is known will be differentially distributed throughout the population (and across time). It is similar to snowball sampling in its use of informants to access other informants (particularly those who may be difficult to identify from formal sources). Finally, it can be compared to network analysis in that connections between individuals are used to identify the sample (in the case of tracer studies, these are often formal, organizationally defined connections).

Description of the method

Here we describe the process of conducting a tracer study in general terms. In the section that follows we illustrate this general description with examples from a small tracer study carried out in a government agency, in which we were concerned with following a change process within the organization (specifically a change to a computer system which led to changes in working practices).

Identification of tag(s)

The tracer study commences with the listing of possible tags associated with the process to be traced. A potential tag is anything which records evidence of the participation of various people at a point in the process. This may be documentation completed as a matter of course during a process (for example, a requirements specification, a feasibility report or a planning document), or it could be a meeting or minutes of a meeting. The number of potential tags is very often limited by the formal procedures laid down by the organization. However, for some processes (for example, systems development) and for some particularly bureaucratic organizations, there may be more tags available than the researcher can practically or usefully use. What is needed, therefore, are some clear criteria for selecting the most appropriate and effective tag(s). We have no hard and fast rules but below is a list of considerations which we have found helpful:

- *Organizationally defined criteria.* The procedures associated with the process may themselves suggest which documents or meetings are the most critical. For instance, in the example discussed later in this chapter, we were interested in tracing system design decisions with a view to exposing points in the design process where errors could have been avoided. Logically, we felt that problems in the design coming to light at some later date may be marked by a request for a change to be made to the system. It was, therefore, sensible to consider the documents relating to change requests as possible tags.
- *Theoretical framework.* It may be helpful to consider some theoretical perspectives associated with the process – such as theoretical frameworks describing the process which indicate critical features of phases (for example, with regard to decision-making processes, this may be the specific phases and activities identified by Nutt [1984]). It may be useful to select a tag(s) on the basis of its/their relation to such a framework. (See the previous discussion on theoretical [Glaser and Strauss, 1967] and judgemental sampling [Honigmann, 1982].)
- *Level of analysis.* It may help to consider the focus of the research question. Is the purpose to describe the process in its entirety or particular aspects of the process? For example, is the issue how the process allows for error recovery in decision-making or the description of the decision-making process more generally?
- *Informal processes.* One may wish to identify tags which are not formally identified by the organization. For example, one may wish to tap into informal forums (Pava, 1986) established by organizational members who wish to short-circuit or even subvert the usual organizational procedures (for example, 'informal' meetings between specific individuals who form a sub-set of the overall group involved in the process). Obviously identifying this sort of tag will require far more groundwork in the organization than the more formal approach we have described so far and probably a close relationship between the researcher and the informants.
- *Artificial tags.* It is possible that (as with the natural sciences) the researcher may wish to introduce a tag artificially. For example, Henry (1990), in a study of interdepartmental communication within a hospital, attached a recording sheet to patient case notes asking

anyone dealing with the notes to sign the sheet every time the document passed through their hands. The purpose of this inter-vention was to trace the passage of the case notes themselves (in response to a perceived problem within the hospital of missing case notes) but also to identify key hospital staff in the process of dealing with patient treatment who were later circulated with a questionnaire concerning communication within the hospital.

Sampling criteria

After identifying the appropriate tag(s), the next step is to formulate criteria for sampling specific cases of the process under investigation. At this stage it is important to re-examine the objectives of the research. Specific objectives help to reduce the size of the population of possible cases. Where research objectives are less helpful, one may wish to examine theoretical perspectives, that is, models or frameworks that have been used previously to inform the research question in the literature.

Examination of specific tag(s)

Once having identified tag(s) and sample cases, the researcher moves on to examine the specific tag(s) (usually documents or meetings/forums) selected. At this point, the intention is to place the tag(s) into some context and so questions such as: what is the history of the tag?; what is its espoused function?; and where does it originate? are all useful here. Answering these questions should help the researcher to confirm or reject the relevance of the tag. Examining the tag in this way may highlight deficiencies in it (for example, its exclusion of individuals one has identified as important from informal discussions) which may suggest rejecting it or including an additional, informal tag, such as attendance at informal forums. Examination of tags also helps in the research aim of describing the process as the very existence of the tag may tell us something of how the process is conceived formally or informally by various participants in the process.

'First-pass' identification of relevant informants

Having answered these questions, the researcher then moves on to examine the tag with a view to identifying individuals in the organization who have had an input into the functioning of the tag. These individuals form the initial cohort of participants in the tracer study and should, at this point, be interviewed as to their involvement in the process under investigation.

Data-gathering and identification of further information sources

The content of interviews or observation notes will differ, of course, according to the process under investigation. One issue which researchers will need to address at this stage for all tracer studies, however, is who else needs to be contacted. In effect all participants in the first 'trawl' should be asked who else they have had contact with in relation to the process under investigation and the particular case being sampled. In this way, the cohort of participants in the tracer should grow, naturally, so that all key participants in the process are included in the study. Also, an initial analysis of the interview and observation data collected at the first 'trawl' should be carried out and the results of the analysis examined to see whether further participants are suggested on the basis of these data.

Ending the study

The time to stop collecting data, in the case of a retrospective study, is when all participants identified from the original tag (and iterative process described above) relating to the specific cases under consideration have been included. One way of knowing when it is time to stop collecting data in the case of a concurrent study is when the process, as it relates to a specific case identified by the researcher, has concluded. This suggests that the researcher is able to identify, beforehand, the points at which the process starts and ends for a particular case. Sometimes this will be possible, for example when one is using the formal procedures to define the process. In this instance, the procedures normally signal the start and end of a case. However, we believe that the method is flexible enough to be applied both when the process can be tightly defined and for more loosely defined cases when the start- and end-points are less clear. In this instance, the decision to end data collection is based on indicators other then the procedural start and end. For example, when theoretical and/or practical considerations determine the point at which to stop data collection or when no further useful information is emerging: 'saturation point' (Glaser and Strauss, 1967).

Application example

We outline in this section a retrospective example of a tracer study we carried out in a government agency. The agency had recently introduced an automated system to perform much of the clerical work formerly carried out manually by large numbers of clerical staff. Our research team was interested in evaluating the current use of the clerical system in order to identify (retrospectively) particular design activities during the development process which had led to specific outcomes (both positive and negative) in everyday use of the system. The aim of this part of the study (as a sub-set of the overall objective) was to isolate those system features which in everyday use were found to be problematic, therefore leading to changes to the original design of the system, and to evaluate this change process.

As we had already been involved for some time with this organization, we had formed a relationship (particularly with the User Support Group) which allowed us to be quite demanding as a research group! We were allowed to examine (relevant) documentation without restriction and to contact and talk to whomever we wanted (as long as they themselves agreed). This may be partly because, unlike other areas of the agency's business, the system development process was not seen as particularly contentious or in need of protection. Our main contact and informant was the head of the User Support Group (who managed the relationship between Computer Branch staff and users). As such, she had overall responsibility for managing and processing changes to the computer-based system. Clearly, this sort of contact is extremely helpful in providing access, privileged information and in managing the 'social' side of our activities in the organization. More than this, the User Support Group itself was a relatively new section in the organization and a 'maverick' in comparison with other groups – with less rigidly defined internal roles and relationships. Members of this group were able to move about more freely and talk to other employees (including the head of the organization) with less regard to status because of the nature of their work. Consequently, we were able to adopt similar sorts of roles, which, together with our 'privileged' status as academics, allowed us considerable latitude in our activities.

One of the reasons why a tracer study seemed so appropriate here was that many processes were (at least superficially) formalized (as befits most civil service operations), and the amount of documentation available meant that many processes were recorded in detail. We were anxious to take advantage of these rich sources of data already available in the organization in pursuing our research interests.

Identification of tag(s)

Our first task, then, was to identify possible tags. Clearly, we needed some way of identifying changes to the original system and the people who had been involved in the change. In this study, we utilized the formal project management methodology used by the agency to identify an appropriate tag.

In order to keep control over the procedures and avoid being over-whelmed with requests, the User Support Group requested that all ideas for change from users be sent as memos through their line manager to the Group. These requests are then stored on a suggestions database. Periodically, the contents of this database would be reviewed by the line managers, who would prioritize requests and pass this 'master list' on to the User Support Group. At this point, all changes to the system required a formal Change Request Document to be completed in accordance with the project methodology. The User Support Group then recorded the request on to the Change Proposal Register, processed it and eventually noted the final decision (whether or not to proceed with the change) against the original entry on the Register.

As our aim was to examine possible weaknesses in the development process which had led to the design of features which needed to be changed at some later date, we decided that the change request form was an appropriate tag in this instance. Other tags may have included any of the specific documents or attendance at relevant meetings or examination of minutes of project meetings. Clearly, one possible sampling problem in this study is the fact that a perceived need for change may not always result in a formal change request. This may result in a 'needed' change never being made or a 'needed' change being made but not recorded. We attempted to account for this here by talking to people 'on the shop floor' prior to carrying out the study to ascertain what they considered to be important issues relating to the computer system they were using. We used this information to guide the selection of some cases.

Sampling criteria

Having decided on the tag, we then obtained a copy of the listing of all possible change request tags (the Change Proposal Register) from our main informant in the organization. From this point, we needed some criteria for selecting cases. As we indicated above, it may be useful at this stage to re-examine the research objectives. An examination of the research objectives in this study enabled us to more clearly define the sample population of changes in which we were interested and the following criteria emerged to guide our selection:

- *User orientation.* We were interested in the impact of the design process on users as well as designers. The clear implication here is that our sample of cases should include only changes to the computer system that had had or potentially would have some visible effect on users. Purely technical changes could, therefore, be excluded from our potential sample immediately.
- *Unsuccessful change requests.* The 'change request' process can be viewed as a sub-system of the larger system design process. As we were interested in examining potential weaknesses in the entire system design process, including the change request process, it was apparent that excluding unsuccessful change requests from our sample would have meant missing out on important aspects of the change process. Cases that were difficult to deal with because of weaknesses in the process could have been systematically excluded from our sample.

Consequently, rejected as well as successful change requests needed to be represented in the sample.

- *Completed requests for change.* Finally, as the research was retrospective (that is, the system was already operational as the research commenced), we needed to include changes that may have been requested and actioned in the early days of the system going live. Ignoring these changes raised the possibility of our including only those requests of relative unimportance to the user, as the most important user requests were likely to have come in the early days of system operation. We therefore felt it necessary to include examples of completed requests for change (that is, those for which final decisions had been made and carried through) as well as current, ongoing requests.

These are not mutually exclusive sampling activities and so one case may represent more than one of the criteria mentioned above. The other limiting factor on our sampling of cases was, as always, the practical issue of resources available to carry out the work. Given the time limits on our access to the organization and the high resource demands of the data collection techniques (primarily semi-structured interviews), we had to limit our final number of case studies to three:

- *The issuing of reminder letters.* The new system was set up in such a way that at a certain point in the processing of client data, a number of pre-formatted letters were automatically printed out reminding clients to provide information which initially had not been supplied (according to the computer records). However, it was often the case that shortly after this clients would send in this information anyway. Knowing this, clerical staff in this department would delay sending out the reminder letter for approximately one month. Consequently, many of these letters would be by that time unnecessary and clerical workers spent a considerable amount of time sorting out these reminders and *throwing the letters away.* A change request had been filed for immediate action and had been successfully processed.
- *The implementation of a special function key.* The system had been set up to support two different kinds of interaction: by the clerical staff and by the professional staff. The clerical staff used the system to carry out one function on a number of different client cases; consequently, they would be continually inputting different client reference numbers but only using a small amount of the system functionality. Conversely, the professional staff used the system to carry out a number of functions on one particular client case at a time. For them, the system was set up such that they did not have to continually rekey the client reference number to access different functions; however, this was achieved by predetermining the sequence of the functions to be utilized. The professional staff claimed that they did not always use these functions in the specified order and that to

access functions individually they had to rekey the client reference numbers (in the same way as the clerical staff). Consequently, they requested the implementation of a special key which, when pressed, would invoke this number automatically as they moved around the functions. This change proposal was unsuccessful.

- *Development of a pc-based system for the professional staff* (which would be linked to the 'clerical' mainframe system). It was argued that professional staff needed a further computer-based system which would enable them to carry out a number of their specific tasks more effectively. This is clearly a change request of a different magnitude but we felt an appropriate one (at this early stage the change process was the same). This case covered our third criteria of being a current and ongoing change.

For the purposes of this chapter, we intend to outline only the first case described here – that of the reminder letters. In the third case, the process turned into a major independent project currently being pursued by one of the authors (G.S.).

Examination of specific tag(s)

Our first task was to glean what information we could from an examination of the Change Proposal Document itself (see Figure 10.1). This had been signed by one of the User Support Group as 'Originator', so, clearly, he was one of the first informants to interview. However, it was also important to note the priority status of the proposed change; what other associated documents could be examined; and how the change is described (this latter can then be used for comparison purposes with representatives of other interest groups in the organization).

The Change Proposal Document, however, is only the impetus for the change process and leads to the production of other documents. Of particular significance here is the Impact Analysis Document (see Figure 10.2). This document is used to assess (as the name suggests) the likely impact of the instigation of the change process on different departments involved and on the agency as a whole (for example, in terms of client satisfaction and number of work days needed to complete). Analysis of the Impact Analysis Document gave us a statement of the expected costs and benefits which the respondent 'formally' puts forward – which could then be compared with the total criteria described during later interviews (which included 'informal' reasons).

Examination of these documents (provided by the User Support Group) led us to the Business Assurance Coordinator and the Technical Assurance Coordinator (formal roles dictated by the project management technique) who were each responsible for completing an Impact Analysis Document.

CHANGE PROPOSAL		
1. System:	2. CP No.:	
3. CP Title:		
4. Priority*: Routine/Emergency Latest Implementation Date:		
5. Reasons for Change:		
6. Statement of Benefits: Documentation Attached* Yes/No		
7. Description of Change: Documentation Attached*: YES/NO		
8. Impact Analysis Only*: YES/NO		
9. Category of Change* Note: Identify only one category per CP Legislation Enforced Requirement (ENREQ) Requirements Omission (REQOM) Requirements Clarification (CLARI) User Requirement (UREQ) Design Error (DESER) Design Change (DESCH) Conversion (CONV) PRL Item (PRL)		
10. Related Change Proposal No(s).:		
11. Related Problem Reports:		
12. Originator:	Signature:	Date:
13. UAC:	Signature	Date:

Figure 10.1 *Change Proposal Document*

CHANGE PROPOSAL IMPACT ANALYSIS			
1. System: CP No.: CP Title:			
2. To: 3. Impact Analysis Due:			
4. Statement of Impact	Man Days	Staff Type	£
i) Preparing Change			- - - - - -
ii) Requirements/Logical Design & QR			- - - - - -
iii) Implementing Change			- - - - - -
iv) Hardware/Computer Costs	- - - - - - -	- - - - - - -	
5. Documents Affected – Title, Reference, Version.			
6. Baselines Affected – CI Reference			
7. Effect on Schedule in man days/hours:			
8. Other Functional Areas Affected:			
9. Other Comments:			
10. Name of Analyser:	Signature:		Date:
11. Manager	Signature:		Date:

Figure 10.2 *Impact Analysis Document*

Data-gathering and identification of further information sources

The next stage was to contact the individuals identified from the documents. In contacting them for interview, we informed them how we had obtained their names and what the interview was about. Each interview lasted from 30 minutes to one hour and took a semi-structured form covering (in no particular order) the areas of: the respondents' role in the process; others involved in this particular instance; evaluation criteria used (that is, in deciding whether the change should proceed or not); the respondents' historical recall of events; their evaluation of these events; and their evaluation of the process in general.

Interviewing this sample immediately provided information about both the specific change under discussion and other employees who had been involved. Thus, we discovered that, because it was perceived to be a highly technical document, the formal Change Proposal Document would be filled out by one of the User Support Group rather than the user who had actually requested the change. Interviewing the User Assurance Coordinator allowed us to identify the users who had actually been affected by the system design fault and had reported it. Furthermore, the Technical Assurance Coordinator led us to the technician who had actually programmed the change to the system and his immediate manager (who was responsible for allocating the work).

Iteration

Having gathered our first 'trawl' of information, we now instigated our second round of interviews – which can be considered at a deeper level in the sense that we were now going beyond the formal documentation and formal roles. We were also now widening our inquiry to include the specific work carried out in achieving the change.

Our previous interviews had led us to two 'users' (in this case, in fact, not 'hands-on' users but the line manager of the actual users and her own line manager) who had raised the issue of the reminder letters. We were also led to explore the work practices of the Computer Branch by interviewing the programmer (and his line manager) who had actually been involved in changing the existing computer program (that is, writing new code). The interview questions covered the areas of: others involved in this particular instance; the respondents' historical recall of events (including their own input); their evaluation of these events; and their evaluation of the process in general (a sub-set of the previous interview questions). This iteration led us to further interviewees – the clerical staff who had been responsible for disposing of the unwanted letters and were displaced by the technical change to the system.

Withdrawal and example results

In this case, we relatively quickly exhausted the possible pool of informants because the change under investigation was reasonably minor. Having exhausted the pool, the tracer study was at an end.

This particular tracer study provided us with information in two important areas. First, *the content of the change request process as a decision-making activity*. From our interviews, we categorized the respondents into four main 'stakeholder' groups (see Burgoyne, Chapter 11, this volume) which were only partially defined by the formal organizational roles: the users; the user representatives; the technical staff; the business representatives. The evaluation criteria of the different groups involved differed, to some extent, according to their role in the activity. Thus, users were concerned with procedural efficiency, staff displacement and relationship with external clients, while the user representatives (with their broader view of the system) were concerned with: relationship to other changes; enabling the even representation of changes across departments; and the image of the system to internal clients (that is, the users). The technical staff were concerned with: logical integration; maintainability; and work effort involved. Finally, the business assurance reps considered financial viability; usability; and the possibility of a manual solution.

Second, *the actual operation of the change process*. Our sampling criteria led us to isolate three 'typical' cases which we wanted to examine (as described above). The very process of doing this revealed an interesting finding about the process itself. Because the formal process is quite lengthy and resource-demanding, an initial assessment of the proposal is made by the User Support Group, such that change requests which are 'likely' to result in rejection are not processed through the formal procedures (that is, including Impact Analysis Documents, etc.). This assessment is based on their collective experience with previous changes to the system. Conversely, changes which seem clearly necessary to the User Support Group (like the reminder letters) may go straight to Change Proposal status without the intermediary line management assessment from the suggestion database. Thus, when change requests are sent through the formal procedures, it is assumed by those who receive them that they are already acceptable – it is simply a question of indicating how many work days will be required to make the change. In this way, the formal decision-making process was adapted to a more 'manageable' activity. These findings led us to question the nature of the formal decision-making process itself and agree with March and Shapira (1982) that to some extent decision-making can be viewed as a symbolic process intended to demonstrate to other organizational members that proper procedures have been followed.

It is evident that the formal process takes no account of the 'behind the scenes' negotiations associated with making and implementing changes to a system of this sort. How many changes never make it to the change request stage because they are not in the interests of more powerful stakeholder groups than the end-users, or because knowledge of their existence is restricted to stakeholders with a vested interest in not making change? In the case described here, having been excluded from the original design process, hands-on users had adapted to the inefficiencies in the system – in this case, the processing of the unnecessary letters. Special clerical jobs had been created to manually correct the errors deriving from the inefficient systems procedures. Although aware of the inefficiency, the users had not in fact immediately requested a change. Such a move would not have been entirely in their interests as correcting the system would potentially have led to the loss of two clerical posts. Line managers were particularly concerned about this because, to some extent, numbers of staff in the department were an indication of organizational power. Some negotiation between line managers, senior managers and the User Support Group was needed to ensure that the change would not decrease the number of clerical posts in this particular section.

So, in relation to our original aim of describing problems in system use which could be linked with weaknesses in system development processes, we can suggest that hands-on user involvement in the original design could have prevented the inefficiency in the procedures to support it. Many of the changes requested reflected the fact that design features did not reflect the experience and ways of working of the users. However, the organization had moved shortly after the system was implemented and consequently the users were not always the same people who had been in post at the time of the development of the system. It is also clear that imposing standards and methods in the formal processes does not necessarily ensure quality of design. Formal procedures, even when documented, may inaccurately reflect the true nature of the process.

Evaluation of the method

We have found the tracer study method a very useful method of sampling for the purposes of analysing complex organizational processes. However, could the procedure as we have described it in our example here be used in other contexts? System development has many tags associated with it because it tends to be a heavily controlled organizational process. Other less formulated change processes may be more difficult to describe in such terms. Furthermore, as we already suggested, government agencies are generally bureaucratic organizations (in this case, to use Mintzberg's [1979] terminology, a mixture of machine and professional bureaucratic forms), with a significant amount of documentation and number of formal meetings from which to select. Perhaps more flexible and informal organizations would not offer such opportunities? Further work may shed some light on these issues.

We are also aware that we had, we felt, privileged access in this particular organization. Perhaps other organizations would not be so accommodating? In this last case, we feel that the tracer study may actually be an appropriate method for organizations where access and research *is* more difficult. Given it follows procedures already in place, it does not necessarily involve any more work for participants (although establishing a key informant at the beginning, as in all organizational research, may be helpful).

Because the (real-time) tracer study involves the identification of 'tags' which are recurrent throughout a process or which pass through a number of 'hands' in their development, we are enabled to follow organizational processes as they unfold. We believe that tracer studies uniquely allow the investigator to study complex processes over time, observing the interconnectedness of episodes and issues and examining participants' ideas, motives, meanings and perceptions as opposed to simply measuring their attitudes to outcomes or the relationships between members of temporary groupings. A more quantitative approach may have identified individual or group attitudes to particular system outcomes or to identifiable points in the process. It may even have given us some measure of the strength or type of relationships between and within stakeholder groups. However, it is unlikely that such an approach would have allowed us to examine the interconnections between individuals and ideas throughout the process.

Thus tracer studies lend themselves to the analysis of change and development in organizations in contrast to cross-sectional samples. In the retrospective example described here, of course, the distinction is blurred. We were sampling at one time-point. However, our use of documents which had followed a sequence of events across time meant that we could attempt to re-create the time-dependent nature of the process.

It could also be argued that the tracer study assumes a certain sequentiality of organizational processes. In carrying out the tracer study, we could be implying a sequentiality which organizational members are then constrained to reproduce for us. In the context in which we were working, the change process was depicted (graphically) by the organization itself as consecutive because of its concern to uphold formal processes. However, we recognize that, in other contexts, the nature of the tracer study may create the research circumstances, although we believe that this is inherent in the research endeavour, whatever the method (Woolgar, 1988).

As has already been suggested, one of the advantages of the tracer study as a form of non-probability sampling is that it allows the researcher to select appropriate informed sources – that is, people who are involved in the process and who are knowledgeable about it. Conversely, of course, a drawback of this strategy may be failing to select from those impacted by the process but not actually involved in it. Such informants *should*, however, be revealed by the iterative nature of the tracer study, as in the example described above where the role of the clerks previously involved in coping with the inefficient system was revealed during our study, although they had not been directly involved in the change process. It is likely that in a real-time study this problem may not arise as the researcher is able to observe the unfolding process him-or herself to some extent and consequently note the people involved.

It could be claimed that the focus on organizationally determined procedures may limit the types of information it is possible to obtain. The researcher is unable to 'go behind the scenes' as it were. From the example described above, we believe we have demonstrated that it is possible to go beyond formal procedures using the tracer study. Furthermore, we feel that combining the organizational perspective with the theoretical and experiential elements of judgemental sampling enables a wider perspective on the issue than the organization itself may provide.

It is possible that other 'tags' would have revealed a different sample and different criteria. This is undoubtedly true. With access to more resources, we would have preferred to examine a number of cases within the change proposal system. However, it was appropriate to our purposes at the time (given the study was part of a larger evaluation exercise). Perhaps if we had not selected the change proposal documents but, rather, for example, attended a number of information technology project meetings (as our tag) and followed particular decisions (as our cases), we would have gathered different material. As we suggested earlier in outlining the criteria for selecting particular tags, the usefulness of a particular tag depends on the question to be answered and the level of analysis required. As long as the researcher is clear about this, the issue would seem to be unproblematic. On a larger scale, however, it may be useful to utilize a number of sources of information as tags about one particular process. In the current (workstation) project, regular meetings, specific ongoing activities and documentation are being followed, together with the completion of activity diaries by the participants.

Conclusion

In conclusion, we would emphasize that the tracer study be particularly regarded as a non-probability sampling strategy which complements the other methods described in this book. It is a particularly useful method for examining ongoing organizational processes and for capitalizing on existing organizational procedures. As a qualitative approach, it has the advantage of allowing the identification of knowledgeable (as opposed to random) informants and allowing the observation of the construction of the process across time between organizational actors (rather than restricting the research to a representation of a static situation).

We suspect that what we have described may be familiar to many as 'sort of what we do anyway'. However, we feel that expressing the approach more formally and beginning to examine some of the ground rules may validate the approach for those who 'sort of' already use it, as well as introducing it to the uninitiated.

Acknowledgement

Thanks to Cathy Cassell and the head of the User Support Group for their comments on an earlier draft of this chapter.

References

Burgess, R.G. (1982) 'Elements of sampling in field research', in R.G. Burgess (ed.), *Field Research: a Sourcebook and Field Manual*. London: George Allen & Unwin.

Glaser, B. and Strauss, A.L. (1967) *The Discovery of Grounded Theory: Strategies for Qualitative Research*. Chicago: Aldine.

Henry, P. (1990) 'User needs in information technology: a hospital case study and methodology'. MSc dissertation, MRC/ESRC Social and Applied Psychology Unit, Sheffield.

Hoffman, J. (1980) 'Problems of access in the study of social élites and boards of directors', in W. Shaffir, R. Stebbins and A. Turowetz (eds), *Fieldwork Experience*. New York: St Martin's Press.

Honigmann, J. (1982) 'Sampling in ethnographic fieldwork', in R.G. Burgess (ed.), *Field Research: a Sourcebook and Field Manual*. London: George Allen & Unwin.

Huberman, M. (1990) 'Linkage between researchers and practitioners: a qualitative study', *American Educational Research Journal*, 27 (2): 363–91.

Hutchins, E. (1991) 'The social organization of distributed cognition', in L. Resnick, J. Levine and S. Teasley (eds), *Perspectives on Socially Shared Cognition*. Washington: American Psychological Association.

Johnson, J. (1990) *Selecting Ethnographic Informants (Qualitative Research Methods Series, Vol. 22)*. Newbury Park, CA: Sage.

McCall, M. (1980) 'Who and where are the artists?' in W. Shaffir, R. Stebbins and A. Turowetz (eds), *Fieldwork Experience*. New York: St Martin's Press.

March, J. and Shapira, Z. (1982) 'Behaviour decision theory and organizational decision theory', in G. Ungson and D. Braunstein (eds), *Decision-making: an Interdisciplinary Inquiry*. PWS: Kent.

Mintzberg, H. (1979) *The Structuring of Organizations*. New York: Prentice-Hall.

Mossman, D., Holly, F. and Schnoor, J. (1991) 'Field observations of longitudinal dispersion in a run-of-the-river impoundment', *Water Research*, 25 (11): 1405–15.

Nutt, P. (1984) 'Types of organizational decision processes', *Administrative Science Quarterly*, 29: 414–50.

Pava, C. (1986) 'Redesigning sociotechnical systems design: concepts and methods for the 1990s', *The Journal of Applied Behavioral Science*, 22 (3): 201–21.

Scott, J. (1991) *Social Network Analysis: a Handbook*. Beverley Hills, CA: Sage.

Symon, G. and Clegg, C. (1991) 'Technology-led change: a study of the implementation of CADCAM', *Journal of Occupational Psychology*, 64 (4): 273–90.

Walsh, K. (1978) *Neuropsychology: a Clinical Approach*. Edinburgh: Churchill Livingstone.

Woolgar, S. (ed.) (1988) *Knowledge and Reflexivity: New Frontiers in the Sociology of Knowledge*. London: Sage.

11

Stakeholder Analysis

John G. Burgoyne

Stakeholder analysis can be fundamentally described as a research approach based on the view that any phenomenon of interest in organizational psychology has a number of 'stakeholders', or interested parties, who affect, are affected by, experience and conceptualize it. Stakeholder analysis proceeds by identifying some, many or all of these stakeholders and collects data about their actions, perceptions, behaviours, experiences and thoughts in relation to the phenomenon. This can be done at a point in time or over time, and generates a multidimensional data matrix as material for analysis in a variety of inductive, deductive or comparative ways.

This chapter locates stakeholder analysis in the spectrum and history of research methods, and describes the main steps in its application. The chapter also explores a general example and introduces some of the more fundamental theoretical and practical issues that relate to it.

Stakeholder analysis: concept and context

The term 'method' is varied in its application, to the extent that some commentators question the usefulness of the term (Feyerabend, 1993; Morgan, 1983). It is used to label: general data-gathering approaches, for example interview (see King, Chapter 2, this volume); technologies based on particular theories, for example psychometrics (Guilford, 1954); and theory-specific methodologies, for example repertory grid as the methodological expression of construct theory (Bannister, 1970; and Gammack and Stephens, Chapter 5, this volume). Method may also be used to label broad research philosophies, for example phenomenology (Schutz, 1967) and ethnomethodology (Benson and Hughes, 1983). However, the variety of meanings of the concept does appear to have two underlying dimensions on which stakeholder analysis can be located:

1 how tactical (specific tool) or strategic (research philosophy) a claimed method is; and
2 how theory-specific or free it is.

Stakeholder analysis is 'middle range' on both these dimensions. It can be used within a variety of broad research philosophies, taking on a different meaning and emphasis as it does so. Equally, a variety of the more specific/technical methods can be used within it. On the theoretical dimension, a stakeholder interpretation is itself a broad middle-range theoretical proposition, but one within which more precise theoretical formulations can be located and developed.

Stakeholder analysis is a broad organizing principle for research, with which it is possible, indeed necessary, to use the more tactical research methods – for example, questionnaire, direct observation of behaviour. However, stakeholder analysis does not claim a grand, unique or particularly coherent base in a specific epistemological and ontological world-view, in contrast to, say, phenomenology. Nor is it the direct manifestation or application of a particular theory in the manner of repertory grid and personal construct theory, or, say, the Myers-Briggs Type Indicator as the methodological offspring of a union between psychometrics and Jungian theory. In this sense, stakeholder analysis may have something in common with case studies (see Hartley, Chapter 12, this volume), tracer studies (see Hornby and Symon, Chapter 10, this volume) and intervention research (see Fryer and Feather, Chapter 13, this volume), but they are not alternatives: all of these approaches could be structured on stakeholder lines.

Stakeholder analysis can be seen as belonging with, or sympathetic to, a broad family of theoretical approaches which favour a constructionist (rather than realist), pluralist (rather than unitary) view of reality (Berger and Luckmann, 1966; Daft and Weick, 1984; Denzin, 1989; Lincoln and Guba, 1985). Furthermore, the stakeholder concept 'turns up' in some specific theoretical formulations, for example the concept of 'role set' in role theory (Biddle, 1979).

Arguably the 'middle-range' status of stakeholder analysis is one of its advantages and attractions, as well as perhaps being one of its sources of frustration. It may have something to offer those who want neither to get lost in mindless and narrow empiricism, nor disappear into a speculative realm of meta-theory. It can be applied at a simple and robust level – as a framework for a handful of interviews in a pilot study – or as the infrastructure for a vast database for a worldwide longitudinal survey. Stakeholder analysis does not, and probably should not, seek to offer itself as a 'research theology' to belong to. It may not be possible to 'be' a stakeholder analyst in the way it is possible to 'be' an ethnographer (Fetterman, 1989), a phenomenologist or even a psychometrician.

Presenting stakeholder analysis as an approach to qualitative research has some interesting implications. The qualitative/quantitative issue can be taken at least at the tactical and strategic levels discussed.

At the tactical level, the issue is one of methods to get at the presumed qualitative as opposed to quantitative aspects of reality (Hamilton, 1977). At this level, stakeholder analysis may in practice often involve a substantial amount of descriptive/qualitative data about the interests, experiences, thoughts and feelings of stakeholders, but this does not arise from any necessity of principle. In stakeholder analysis, it would be wrong not to count the countable. If hours of attendance, exchange of money goods and services and the like are part of the stakeholder interaction and relevant to the phenomenon under investigation, they should certainly be counted. If it is pragmatically useful and justifiable to express some data quantitatively, even if their basic form is not necessarily quantitative (as in opinions and opinion-rating scales), then it may be the best thing to do. In this sense, stakeholder analysis is not a purely qualitative method. It can be argued that too much is made of the quantitative/qualitative distinction: both words and numbers are kinds of language, and ones that are often mixed and indeed need each other – pure qualitative or quantitative statements are difficult to achieve! However, at the strategic level, stakeholder analysis aligns with a number of key propositions that are related to the 'qualitative' view:

1   The subjective nature of (some?) reality – hence different stakeholders do experience the nominally 'same' phenomenon differently, and this is not perversity (Berger and Luckmann, 1966). Investigations themselves have stakeholders and social contexts (Brenner et al., 1978), and are not neutral or value-free in the problems they address, the ways they frame them, the data and interpretations that they select.
2   Situations are not necessarily manifestations of single purposes and plans, but may be created by the interaction of multiple purposes and multiple agendas for achieving them (see Dreyfus, 1987).
3   The post-structuralist rather than structuralist view of the generation of behaviour, that is, that much/all behaviour is the manifestation of *cultural software* that actors have internalized, rather than *hardware of a basic structure of human personality* as a fixed reality across people and over time (see Sturrock, 1979).

Sources and origins

It is not clear whether stakeholder analysis has a single or multiple origins as a concept and method, either in everyday lay usage or as a research method. Like the invention of the wheel, it may have a single point of origin from which it has been copied and disseminated, but perhaps more likely it may have been discovered or invented relatively independently in many different situations.

Inspection of dictionaries suggests that the term 'stake' originates from physical stakes, as in wooden poles driven into the ground, to mark a piece of territory. The 'holder' of the stake makes a claim to the exploitation of the territory (and perhaps, interestingly, usurping the interests of others having a less possessive relationship to it!). From there has probably developed the usage of the term as a gamble or bet.

The term 'stakeholder analysis' and the underlying concept has probably been taken from this everyday usage and applied in various theoretical and methodological ways in the social and behavioural sciences.

The general area of role theory (Biddle, 1979) probably represents one of the broadest uses of the idea, allowing role to be conceptualized as a combination of expectations of a person's behaviour by stakeholders. The concept is widely used in evaluation research, from where many of the examples in this chapter are taken (Easterby-Smith, 1986; Hesseling, 1966). The concept is also widely used in the area of social responsibility of business (Toffler, 1986) to emphasize and locate interests in business beyond the profit motives of owners. Mitroff (1983) provides a particularly interesting and early application of the concept in organizational analysis.

Another clear influence is the emergence of political modes of analysis of organizational and behavioural phenomena (see Morgan, 1986; Pettigrew, 1973) where the dominant approach, presumably borrowed from political science, is to interpret events as the unfolding interactions of competition and collaborations of interests, taken as entities at least across the range from the individual to the nation-state, and their forms of power.

Elaborating the concept and basic frameworks for its application

To elaborate the concept of stakeholder analysis as initially presented at the beginning of this chapter, and to reach a position in which enough has been said to allow the formulation of an application in a particular situation, three issues need to be explored:

1 the nature of stakeholders;
2 what might count as data, and in what categories;
3 what procedural steps are generally involved in carrying out a stakeholder-based investigation, and, within that:
    (a) what are the ways in which research situations arise, and the implications of this for the approach;
    (b) what analysis and theoretical and/or practical outcomes are intended.

The nature of stakeholders

Stakeholders are actors, agents, interested parties, interests, interest groups. From the theoretical point of view, stakeholders are of interest because their needs, wants, desires, perceptions and conceptualizations are different. The source of these differences is a fundamental question. The main possibilities have been mentioned – the structuralist interpretation in terms of individual human motive, or the post-structuralist view of evolving cultural ideologies manifesting through people. Mitroff (1983) provides a particularly interesting analysis of the interaction between the supposedly intrapsychic stakeholders of Jungian archetypes and the supposedly macro, societal stakeholders.

For the fieldworker stakeholders may present themselves as people (Joe), as role occupants (the Personnel Manager), as groupings (the cricket club), as occupational groupings (the medical profession), as pressure groups (the environmental lobby) and many more. Many situations present themselves to some extent as already structured in terms of stakeholders, for example a strike may present itself with a management and union side, possibly a police interest and a media interest. The fieldworker may not need to worry too much about the structuralist/post-structuralist issue in deciding what data to collect from whom, though it may suggest some interesting lines of inquiry and pose some interesting questions in the later analysis. Identifying stakeholders in a particular situation can itself be an empirical process, and there are two questions involved: who is to count and at what level of aggregation to take them. The general guide-line on the former is that a stakeholder is any interest affected by or affecting the phenomenon. The guide-line on the latter is that a stakeholder is a grouping with a relatively consistent experience and point of view.

Practically, if an imagined stakeholder interest (for example, the medical profession) seems to have significant internal differences of opinion in relation to the phenomenon, then perhaps it needs to be broken down. If a group of people, say the personnel managers in a series of operating plants, seem to be saying more or less the same thing about, say, the usefulness of assessment centres, then it may be safe to treat them as a single stakeholder interest. Identifying the coherent sets of interest is one of the things that can emerge in the process of collecting data in stakeholder analysis. The practical process of doing stakeholder analysis, as is arguably the case with all research, involves making a continuous stream of skilled researcher craft judgements – whom to talk to, what to ask, what to probe, etc. Stakeholder analysis, as a mode of research, is perhaps more like unfolding detective work than the implementation of a detailed prestructured experimental design (see Easterby-Smith et al., 1991, for this and other styles of research). As in detective work, collecting data from one interested party will tend to identify other stakeholders, which can then be followed up. One approach to the practical question of identifying stakeholders is therefore to follow a similar logic to that of sequential sampling rather than predetermined sampling – collect data until nothing new turns up (see Hornby and Symon, Chapter 10, this volume). In this situation, the guide-line would be to immerse oneself in the situation until no new stakeholders are identified. However, this may be to some extent a purist principle. In practice, researchers will have to 'draw a line' somewhere, in the context of their research purpose and such practical issues as their research access and the time and resources at their disposal.

Whom to count as stakeholders is a delicate issue, and ultimately one that cannot be detached from the orientation of the researcher and the research. There are two general issues to bear in mind. First, stakeholders with power and influence over the phenomenon and other stakeholders are more likely to be easily identified than those affected by it but with less influence – children in a marital dispute, displaced residents in a property development scheme, the villagers living under the fall-out from the polluting factory and so on. Second, the research(er) may start with an allegiance to one or more of the stakeholder interests, and will indeed be a stakeholder themselves.

Occupational and organizational psychologists may tend, to some degree, to be aligned with the interests of the personnel/human resource management function in organizations, for example. Furthermore, in any kind of applied research, the project will be sponsored by, and intended to serve the interests of, one or more of the stakeholders. This does not invalidate the approach, but the researcher needs to be aware of this, and the way in which it may condition the conclusions. In the context of applied research, and subject to ethical limits and standards, there may be nothing wrong with acknowledging that the research is from a certain point of view, and to serve certain interests, and indeed stakeholder analysis arguably makes it possible for the researcher to make this clear.

Data: what counts and what kinds

As a 'middle-range' research method, within which the full range of data collection techniques can be used, there is nothing special in stakeholder analysis in terms of what counts as data. The same range of practical, technical, theoretical and philosophical issues apply to this question as apply to any occupational psychology/social science investigation.

However, as a practical guide-line, it may be useful to consider data in the following categories, and to code any given data item according to this categorization in collecting a stakeholder analysis data set:

1   data that are personal/subjective: an opinion, perception, experience, point of view, personal theory from one individual;
2   data that are interpersonal/intersubjective, that is, opinions or views that are shared in more or less the same form by a set of informants;
3   data that are subjective or intersubjective but also grounded in some verifiable evidence ('I think I am fairly fit, because I finished the London Marathon, and here is a picture of me crossing the finishing line!');
4   data that are, for practical purposes, objective, factual and non-controversial.

Such categorization is made up of 'pure types', so judgement is needed in their application, and the categorization is open to question from more philosophical points of view (for example, 'all data are intersubjective', 'only objective data count'). However, from a pragmatic point of view, some such data-coding may be useful when it comes to analysis.

In stakeholder analysis, it is important to be continuously doubtful of apparently factual, non-controversial data, since these can often be constructions of powerful groups of stakeholders which exclude others. It is questioning these 'taken for granteds' that can lead to the identification of other stakeholders and interests.

Procedures, starting-points and analysis

In general, and again as an ideal model, the pattern of steps in a stakeholder analysis research investigation are:

1 to identify the phenomenon of interest, the theoretical and or practical/applied research question, and the general research approach (inductive, deductive, comparative);
2 to deduce a likely initial set of stakeholders, collect initial data, identify other stakeholders;
3 to collect fuller data, construct a multidimensional database, and fill it out until complete enough for the intended analysis;
4 to analyse data to address the research question(s);
5 to write up, present, publish and disseminate conclusions − a process which itself poses stakeholder questions of audience, in the sense of why and how to reach and address them.

As with all such research prescriptions, the actual doing of research will to some extent reflect these broad steps, but in practice they will tend to overlap and often cycle back to earlier stages. Again, as a middle-range approach, the details of implementation will vary from situation to situation, but some general points can be made about these steps.

Research can, of course, begin from all kinds of starting-points. For the purpose of this discussion, it is worth considering the relatively theoretical and the relatively practical, on the one hand, and the relatively specific or relatively open-ended on the other (see Figure 11.1).

A theoretical and fairly specific starting-point might be, for example, the proposition that culture is extremely stable and resistant to change in organizations. This might lead to a stakeholder analysis of a number of organizations that claim to have implemented culture-change programmes, collecting data from those that claim to have perpetrated the change and also those affected by such programmes. In this case, the study would be partly deductive − to define what data would count as evidence of culture change and look for them, and partly comparative − compare the claimed,

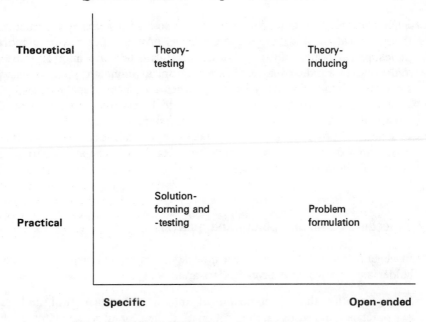

Theoretical	Theory- testing	Theory- inducing
Practical	Solution- forming and -testing	Problem formulation
	Specific	**Open-ended**

Figure 11.1   *Research starting-points*

intended, anticipated organizational processes, as seen by the culture-change perpetrators, with the experiences/observations of other parties.

A theoretical/open starting-point might be a general interest/curiosity about, say, conflict in organizations, and lead to a stakeholder investigation in organizations which are thought to be interesting from a conflict point of view. Here the researcher would be collecting data with a fairly open mind both about stakeholders and about issues, but with the concept of conflict in mind. Analysis would be much more likely to be inductive, looking for interesting patterns in terms of conflict, which would hopefully emerge from the data.

A practical/specific starting-point might start from, say, a personnel manager who is implementing a new payment system based on some practical theory and view of the situation that he or she has, but who wants to check and if necessary correct this as it is implemented. Here the starting approach can be to create a fictitious 'as if' map of stakeholders, what happens to them and what they do in the terms of its perpetrator's vision. This ideal/intended scenario can then provide the template for an actual stakeholder investigation, initially to guide what data to collect from whom, and then as a basis for a comparison of 'intended' with 'actual', so that conclusions can be drawn from the points of both match and mismatch.

A practical/general starting-point might be a general sense, in an organization, that, say, the appraisal system is 'not working' but with no explicit or shared view as to what the problem is: a sense of something being wrong without knowing what. Here a stakeholder analysis might proceed with open-ended questions to the obvious stakeholders, the following up of some less obvious stakeholders, leading to analysis of the agreements, disagreements, clustering of opinions around broad questions of what the appraisal scheme should be for, how it should work, what is going on in its name, and so on.

In initially setting up a stakeholder analysis in one of these ways, the subsequent questions of whom to look at as stakeholders, what data to collect, whether they should be 'point in time' or longitudinal, and how to analyse them begin to be addressed. The general research design should anticipate the form that the data analysis will take to address the research question. Getting this right is arguably the most important step in the practical business of carrying out good stakeholder analysis. The research planning questions are:

1   What research question am I trying to answer?
2   What analysis will provide a useful response to the question?
3   To conduct this analysis what data do I need and from whom?
4   What are the practical steps to get and record these data?

These questions are important in all research, but particularly so in stakeholder analysis. This is because the number and variety of stake-holders that can be linked to any phenomenon, and the potentially relevant data that one could collect, are, for practical purposes, infinite – stakeholder situations have no natural outer boundaries. For this reason, a tight vision of the minimal set of data and the minimal set of stakeholders needed to address the research question is of great use in setting priorities in terms of data to collect. If the research starting-point and purpose, in the terms of Figure 11.1, is specific, then potential data can be evaluated in terms of whether they are needed for the analysis and are likely to make a difference to the conclusions. In the more open-ended situation, the criteria have to be relevance and novelty, while recognizing that the researcher's perception of these will evolve as he or she becomes familiar with the situation.

The issue of 'point in time' versus longitudinal will arise here. There are three possibilities:

1   *'Point in time'*: data at a point in time about a current state of affairs, as in a survey of current mutual role expectations in a working team.
2   *Retrospective longitudinal*: collecting data in a finite period, but trying to collect data, for example through accessing memory and records (see Webb et al., 1966, for an imaginative exploration of approaches), about events over a period prior to data collection. This option has attractions as a compromise between the desirability of longitudinal approaches and the convenience of 'point in time' data collection. However, there are difficulties and dangers. Historical data may be

only selectively available, and hence subject to bias, and those who conduct real-time longitudinal studies (for example, Pettigrew 1985) would argue that they have a quality of data that could not be accessed through retrospective accounts. Historical studies, therefore, pose particular challenges to finding informative sources, and cross-referencing and validating historical data.

3   *Real-time longitudinal research*: following through a sequence of events and stakeholders' involvement and experiences as they happen. Such studies in many ways yield the most satisfactory data from the point of view of sound analysis, but obviously they call for more elaborate data collection programmes, and by definition there will be something of a lead time before conclusions can be drawn – often a negative factor, particularly in applied research where there is some urgency to inform practical decisions.

When time-based processes, or cause and effect relationships, are of interest in the research, then longitudinal data are likely to be more satisfactory from an analytical point of view. In this context (2) and (3) can often be used together, following an event for a certain period but also collecting data on its history. However, the practicalities of research often dictate that 'point in time' research is easier, more affordable and achievable in a given research timetable.

The identification of stakeholders is an iterative process. The starting definition of the problem is likely to contain an initial definition of relevant stakeholders. On the detective work principle, data collection from some stakeholders is likely to lead to the identification of others (see also Hornby and Symon, Chapter 10, this volume). As the researcher begins to understand the research situation, he or she may be able to identify the less visible stakeholders: the less powerful but affected parties. The data themselves may suggest which generic stakeholders might need splitting into sub-interests, and which individual stakeholders could be aggregated on the grounds of common interest.

Researchers need to approach data collection with three considerations in mind:

1   A balance of specific questions arising from the definition of the research question, open questions to pick up other relevant data, and questions orientated to identifying other stakeholders.
2   A view as to what count as data, and their status, in terms of subjective, intersubjective, grounded and objective as discussed above.
3   Given the concept of stakeholder as influencer/influenced, a general set of questions that will take on specific form depending on the problem:
    (a) what is your interest/concern/purpose/hope/fear in relation to the phenomenon?
    (b) what are your plans for dealing with it and/or expectations on how it will function in relation to your interests?

(c) what action are you taking/have you taken/will you take in relation to it?

(d) what specific experiences of the impact of it on you are you having/have you had/will you have?

(e) what do you see as general outcomes, consequences?

Since there is no point in collecting data that will not be used in analysis, data-recording and storing is not a trivial issue. Data need to be stored in their natural form – qualitative, quantitative. Data may need 'reducing' (Ehrenberg, 1975) – numbers to averages, interview transcripts to summaries – just as with any kind of research. Stakeholder analysis data need to be captured in a multidimensional matrix containing the data set. The likely dimensions are:

1 the identity of the stakeholder;
2 the data in terms of intention/hope, action/experience, outcome/effect;
3 the data in terms of their 'status' – subjective, grounded etc.;
4 the data on one or more dimensions of topic/theme relating to the research issue.

Happily, for the technically inclined, modern commercial microcomputer programs are, as computer software goes, quite close to what is needed in stakeholder analysis for recording, retrieving and manipulating the data. Database programs that accommodate reasonable amounts of textual material are useful, but in the author's experience simple is often best, and well-organized and indexed word-processing files and all-purpose programs like Works can be very useful in searching and browsing through data, 'cutting and pasting' for content analysis (see also King, Chapter 2, this volume, for possible software.)

The general modes of analysis have been explored as part of formulating the research problem. They come down to the deductive –formulating an 'ideal' or 'imagined' data set on the basis of a theoretical prediction or practical aspiration, and assessing this against 'actual' data in a hypothesis-testing exercise – or inductive – looking for the patterns of stakeholders and their interests – or comparative – investigating the agreements and contrasts in the different stakeholders' aspirations, experiences, actions and felt consequences. One of the advantages of stakeholder analysis is arguably its flexibility in relation to these different approaches, and the opportunity it offers to mix them in one investigation.

Application example

The evaluation of education, training and development provides a good example of what stakeholder analysis has to offer to occupational and organizational psychology and social science research.

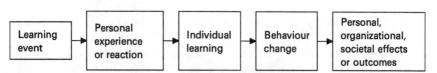

Figure 11.2   *Chain of consequences from a learning event*

Much of the theory and practice of evaluation research is based on a cause–effect chain model (Easterby-Smith, 1986; Hamblin, 1974; Hesseling, 1966; Warr et al., 1970) – see Figure 11.2. To this tends to be added the logic of experimental design regarding the learning event as a 'treatment' given to people, to be assessed by before–after measures at one or more of the different levels in the effects chain, contrasted with control groups and so on (Campbell and Stanley, 1966; Glaser, 1962). Although this approach has been widely advocated, there are relatively few examples of its application, and these tend to be limited. The reasons span from the practical to the theoretical to the philosophical. The practical difficulties are those of achieving an experimental design (difficult enough in a laboratory setting) in a field research context. At the more design/theoretical level is the effect of other influences than the training/ development intervention on the outcome – variables that to all intents and purposes are impossible to control in the field setting. More philosophically, there is the assumption that the trainees/learners are passive/deterministic elements in the system, whose behaviour is deter- mined by the treatment interacting with prior conditions. Contrasting this is the observation that reactions to and consequences of education, training and development vary widely even when the treatment is the 'same', and that learners have widely differing personal strategies for how they use, and manage themselves in, learning situations.

In addition to this, the classical approach makes the assumption, implicitly at least, that there is one right purpose/objective/function for the learning event which is either intrinsic to it, or is given to it by some official source of legitimization that is itself beyond question. It is perhaps this point that distinguishes the traditional approach from the stakeholder approach, both in evaluation research and in more general applications. In the traditional approach, learning events are deemed to have or be given purposes in their own right, the assessment of the achievement of which is the business of evaluation research. In the stakeholder view, events in themselves do not have purposes, but people or stakeholders have purposes, or ambitions or aspirations for them, and these may differ widely. This does not deny that learning events are often described as 'having purposes', but from a stakeholder analysis point of view such statements are to be interpreted as a bid to capture the event for the aspiration/agenda by one of the stakeholders, or perhaps as a 'proposal' in an implicit political negotiation between stakeholders about the

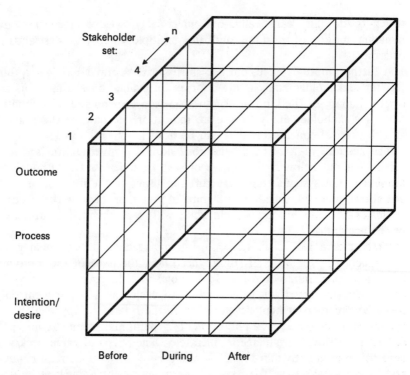

Figure 11.3   *General data framework of stakeholder evaluation study*

conditions under which they will mutually agree to support the event (Legge, 1984; Palumbo, 1988). Another way to look at this is to consider that purposes are negotiated or contracted between stakeholders in a training or development situation (Stuart, 1978).

From a stakeholder analysis point of view, an interesting feature of the evaluation of a learning event as a research project is that it tends to have as a central phenomenon a time-bound event – the learning event itself. This means that a likely general framework for a stakeholder evaluation study can be a three-dimensional data matrix, as shown in Figure 11.3. The *time* and *intention/desire – outcome* dimensions are different, although formulating purpose is likely to be a significant antecedent process, action an event process and so on. Purposes and aspirations do exist before, during and after, and do in fact change in these different phases.

In addition to these three main dimensions, data collected can be coded on two additional variables, which means that in effect a five-dimensional data matrix is in play. The first would be the 'data status' scale described in the general section above, the second would be the 'consequence level' described in Figure 11.1. This means that stakeholder analysis is not 'throwing out' the potentially useful aspects of the classical approach, either in its underlying model, or in its aspiration to map causes and consequences. What it is doing is developing a broader framework in which to do this realistically, one which acknowledges the plural and dynamic nature of purpose and the multiple intertwining strands of causality.

A further, more detailed, but necessarily brief example may give a fuller feel for stakeholder analysis in action in an evaluation setting. This is a brief summary of the kind of account that can be rendered of a situation from a stakeholder analysis, and an indication of some of the practical and theoretical conclusions that can be drawn.

The account of a research question, situation, investigation and conclusion set out below is illustrative of a stakeholder study. Although the account is not systematically structured in terms of the main steps as set out above, they did, together with some of the other frameworks discussed in this chapter, guide the research. These will be commented on at the end of the account.

As part of a general investigation of management development policy and practice in British Rail (Burgoyne, 1985), the issue of the usefulness of a particular course on 'New Technology for Management' arose. The concept first occurred when the Personnel Development Department put a new plan for management development to the Board for approval, which was in the main based on a philosophy of general management courses for different levels in the managerial hierarchy. The proposal came back with general approval, together with a number of suggestions/requirements. One of these was that 'the issue of the management of new technology and the impact of new technology on management be addressed'. The Personnel Development Department discussed this, found that they were not sure what it meant, so instituted informal inquiries with the Board through the Personnel Director. The response was that it was a priority that a few members of the Board thought was missing, and that it was hoped that the Department would be capable of operationalizing it. The Department discussed it again and decided to seek inspiration by writing a specification couched in very general terms of the importance of new technology to management, and putting this out to tender to a variety of colleges and management consultancies as a short course. The resulting proposals were all judged to fall into one of two categories: proposals to do with new developments in engineering, which were judged not to have much 'managerial' content; and proposals to do with specific skills in using information technology – microcomputers and associated software – which were judged to be too much skills-specific training to fit in with the overall philosophy of the management development programme. All the tenders were rejected, and the experience used as a basis for informal discussion and search, mainly with colleges and providers that were delivering the general management programmes.

This resulted in an introduction to a particular member of staff at one of the colleges who had a particular enthusiasm for, and vision of, management and new technology, and who was personally keen to create training work for himself in this area in the college. Consequently, a course was proposed, and accepted, which dealt with both engineering innovation and information technology from a managerial point of view, and dealt with the latter in terms of both conceptual understanding and skills development.

The course, which was residential, took place in a relatively high-tech environment in terms of teaching aids: videos, projected computer images, micro-computers for every two to three participants, various white-boards, flip charts, etc. for participative work. It used a variety of inputs (personal and recorded): for example, case studies of technological innovation-based organizational and business changes and development; and participative work exploring the participants' own experiences of managing innovation-based change situations. Running through the course was a team-based simulation/game based on the development of a business and implementation plan to exploit the potential of a technical innovation in the transport industry. The simulation was structured to require the participants to use a multi-function software package of word-processing, database, spread-sheet and graphics. Briefing and training in the use of this was part of the preparation for the simulation.

In terms of 'reaction'-level evaluation, the programme was experienced in a very positive way from the beginning and throughout by all the participants. The tutor, who ran the course more or less single-handed, with a few visiting speakers, was enthusiastic and energetic throughout, but also exhibited a certain amount of concern and anxiety about the participants' satisfaction, which he explored in a daily brief evaluation session. He was quick to respond, and be seen to respond, to individual difficulties and concerns. Not surprisingly, the participants, including the tutor (and evaluator who was sitting in as a participant/observer), rapidly became a cohesive social group.

On the final morning of the one-week course, a formal evaluation session was conducted by one of the senior college staff members. This took place the morning after a final dinner permeated by mutual goodwill, congratulation and elaborate plans for reunions. The tutor was absent from the formal evaluation session, the external participant evaluator was present. The session lasted 30 minutes, of which the first 20 were devoted to 'domestic' issues like the quality of the food, and a seemingly inordinately long debate about the pros and cons of providing televisions in the bedrooms. The external evaluator's personal sense of this situation was that there was, at this stage, a mutual avoidance and embarrassment about discussing the actual process, content and learning from the course, and the tutor himself. When the topic was broached, by the college staff members, the participants' comments were universally positive.

Follow-up interviews with participants six to eight weeks later found that participants still had non-specific positive feelings about the course. Asked about learning from it, and application of the learning in their work, participants typically claimed to be able to 'think more broadly about things', particularly in relation to the theme of the course, and felt that 'this had a generally positive effect on their judgement and decision-making', though it would be 'hard to prove this'. Pressed further by the interviewer with the behaviour-change level of consequence in mind, the only specific and 'grounded' change-claim that was made came from about one-third of the participants who reported, and were often able to show physically, the use of a micro-computer-based spread-sheet analysis on some management problem/decision in their domain. In about half of these cases, participants had done this themselves; in the other half, they had had a member of their staff do it. In about half of each of both kinds of these cases again, this had involved actively acquiring hardware and/or software; in the other half, it involved using resources that were already readily available.

A further source of post-course data was the comments that the Personnel Development Department invited back from the divisions and departments from which the participants came. These generally came in free-form letter format in response to a fairly open-ended letter of inquiry, and came from either local personnel officers or line managers. In both cases, the people replying to the letter appeared to be doing so on the basis of a talk with the participant, probably stimulated by the letter inviting comments. What struck, and surprised, the external evaluator about these comments was that they almost universally took what could be called a 'course as performance commentary' stance ('my delegate found the course stimulating and interesting, and the material professionally presented'), rather than a 'work performance contribution' stance ('my delegate has been able to add some useful elements to our plans to restructure the division as a result of ideas picked up from the course'). This observation partly reveals a preconception on the part of the evaluator of how development 'ought' to impact organizations, and how evaluation 'ought' to track this. It can also be read, from a research point of view, as an indicator of how education, training and development are really thought about in the organization culture in general, outside the Personnel Development Department.

As part of the practical, applied research aspect of this study, the reaction and follow-up data were fed back to and discussed with the Personnel Development Department. The debate that ensued focused on two issues. First, the extent to which the general participant claim to be 'making generally better decisions and judgements' was sufficient to justify the not insubstantial cost of the course. This debate itself had two modes: the general issue of cost benefit and how benefit can be judged, and the more 'political' debate as to what the Board could be asked to accept as, or be presented with as evidence of, good use of a management development budget. It was interesting to note that the Personnel Development Department had arranged the structure of the situation so that they wrote the overall evaluation report to which the Board would have access, and that they were the recipients of the external evaluator's report, the course director's report and the participants' sponsors' report mentioned above.

The second issue revolved around the more substantial evidence of a limited adoption of the use of spread-sheets. One line of argument was that this could be a useful byproduct of the programme, but was not what it was really intended for. A related argument was that if that was the main objective then there would be much cheaper and more effective ways of doing it. A counter-point to this was that middle to senior managers would regard keyboard skills training as beneath them, and that this was the only way to achieve such change, which could also be taken as an indicator of increased general willingness and ability to innovate technically as well as something useful in its own right. As with the meeting several months before when the to-be-rejected tenders were reviewed, it seemed that outcome evidence, like the tenders, was used rather more to clarify what the objectives were/should/could be than to assess whether some clear aim had been met.

In this example, stakeholders emerged sequentially. First, there was the Personnel Development Department who presented themselves as a client, and in doing so created the author as an evaluation research consultant in the situation. Within the Department, individuals emerged as sub-stakeholders with their varying and differing opinions. The Board, demanding and reacting to plans, established themselves as a powerful stakeholder. The putting of the course out to tender produced a temporary array of new stakeholders as management development course-providers. As things progressed, one particular person in one particular providing institution became a critical actor, and his place in the stakeholder network of his institution became significant. From here on the programme participants and later their managers became of interest for their communalities and differences of opinion and action. At this level of description, stakeholder-mapping seems common sense, but it is the contrasting realities and interactions of these meanings that provide the subtlety in stakeholder analysis.

In terms of the main steps in stakeholder analysis set out above, the initial phenomenon of interest (1) emerged primarily from the applied interest in giving advice on future training initiatives in the area of the course studied. Related to this were some of the researcher's interests in the theoretical issues discussed above. The initial research orientation was a comparative one in terms of the varieties of aspirations and outcomes for the programme, with the applied aim of interpreting the situation back to the sponsor who is one of the stakeholders. The likely initial set of stakeholders (2) suggested themselves both from general experience with training events, and, in this situation, because the research project was part of a larger research programme within which the interested parties had become apparent. Data collection and organization (3) covered a range including interviews, analysis of documentation, participant obser-vation and questionnaires including simple statistical analysis of responses. Physically the data were obviously filed by source, time of origin and issue. Beyond that, the evaluation data 'cube' in Figure 11.3

was used primarily as a mental organizer for making the comparative analysis implied in the research approach. The case study above shows something of the kind of account and conclusion-drawing (4) that such an organization of data can be used for.

As well as making a contribution to practical and policy decisions and thinking, as a piece of applied research, this case example of a stakeholder account hopefully shows how useful conclusions of a more theoretical kind can emerge. As an example, the account allows some interesting inferences to be made about how goal-setting and clarification functions in the context of the planning, implementation and review of training and development initiatives. First, as has been shown, the goals, as seen by the initiators, change, evolve and are clarified alongside, rather than prior to, the event. Second, there are circumstances in which the goals stay broadly and vaguely defined because it is in several parties' interests that they do so, or because it avoids conflict that might occur if they were more specifically determined. Such observations can be taken, for example, as support for the view that certain organizational processes serve defensive functions (Menzies, 1960). Under a unitary approach, lack of goal clarity or late goal formation would have appeared as technical inefficiency rather than understandable phenomena. Such an approach does, perhaps above all, make it clear that evaluation can never be simply a technical matter. There are differing interests and concerns that can only be resolved by a mixture of technical and political process (Fox, 1989).

Standing back further from this as an example of a research account or case study (Beukenhamp and Boverhoff, 1972) of a situation that can be 'read off' from a longitudinal stakeholder data set, a number of points can be made. First, it is possible to mix a number of different research 'modes' in the analysis: a 'case-reporting' style with a relatively detached researcher account of the antecedent processes; a relatively 'ethnographic' phase where the researcher is fairly fully immersed in the situation as a participant/observer in the course, hopefully achieving a degree of involved detachment to understand and report the situation; a relatively detached objective evidence collector in the follow-up stage, counting applications of spread-sheets. In addition to this is the reflexive mode of interpreting the situation the researcher is in, first, by recognizing that the researcher is a stakeholder him/herself with views on development and evaluation that can be 'confirmed' or 'shocked' (the course as performance assumption in evaluation reports), and second, by the locating and use of the researcher's work in the political structure of the situation. This mixing of research styles is arguably an advantage of the stakeholder approach, though not exclusive to it, as is its middle-range non-aligned status. It is perhaps also interesting as a demonstration of how both applied and purer research conclusions can be derived from the same study and data, by a kind of interlinked parallel processing of the material.

Conclusions

This chapter describes stakeholder analysis as a general research approach. It has been presented as a 'middle-range' method, between technique and philosophy, demonstrating how it can be a meeting-ground of different approaches and a framework in which they can, to a degree, be reconciled. The approach is also, to a degree, neutral as regards the kinds of theory or theoretical orientation within which it might be employed.

At a more fundamental level, however, the stakeholder approach and concept does have its theoretical emphasis, and something to offer more fundamental debates. As has been discussed earlier, the question of the origin of stakeholders' interests leads straight to the structuralist/post-structuralist debate about the basis for interest, desire, ideology, ethic and motive: perhaps the social sciences' equivalent of the origin of the universe/Big Bang debate.

In an obvious sense, the stakeholder concept aligns with a political, interactionist, constructionist, intersubjectively created view of reality. However, in another respect, it can be reconciled with more structuralist, functionalist, systems, machine-metaphor (Morgan, 1986) views that stakeholders may negotiate/agree to function as a unitary system and hence behave in this way. In so doing, the approach can accommodate quantitative and objective or highly intersubjectively agreed data.

If stakeholder analysis has a disadvantage, it is perhaps that there is an array of judgemental choices to be made by the researcher at each stage of implementation – the issue, the stakeholders that matter, the data to collect, the interpretations to make. While orientating advice can and has been given on these judgements, obviously the outcome of the research can be very significantly shaped by these often quite fine judgements. This may be disappointing and disturbing if research is to be expected to yield stable and predictable outcomes, but this is rarely the case in practice, and perhaps stakeholder analysis is simply clearer than many other forms of research about these difficult but crucial underlying choices.

The concluding remark about stakeholder analysis is therefore that one of its virtues is that it travels well and fits in with most of what it encounters. It applies to very grounded situations and at the frontiers of meta-theory and philosophy. It fits across a wider range of substantive issues, and is able to use a variety of more specific modes of data collection and analysis, compatible with both theoretical and applied research aspirations and able to pursue them together. It is able to accommodate deductive and inductive, hypothesis-led and curiosity-led research. As theories, methods, underlying research philosophies in occupational and organizational psychology and related behavioural sciences diversify, and the gaps between researchers who are inexperienced or experienced in different kinds of ways grow, stakeholder analysis can hopefully provide a common ground, meeting-point and location for continuing discussion and joint work.

References

Bannister, D. (ed.) (1970) *Perspectives in Personal Construct Theory.* New York: Academic Press.

Benson, D. and Hughes, J.A. (1983) *The Perspective of Ethnomethodology.* London: Longman.

Berger, P. and Luckmann, T. (1966) *The Social Construction of Reality.* Harmondsworth: Penguin.

Beukenkamp, G.J. and Boverhoff, G.J. (1972) 'Case method and case research in European marketing education', *Management International Review*, (6): 115.

Biddle, B.J. (1979) *Role Theory: Expectations, Identities and Behaviours.* New York: Academic Press.

Brenner, M., Marsh, P. and Brenner, M. (1978) *The Social Context of Method.* London: Croom Helm.

Burgoyne, J.G. (1985) 'Management development policy: the British Rail case', in C.W. Clegg, N.J. Kemp and K. Legge (eds), *Case Studies in Organizational Behaviour.* London: Harper & Row.

Campbell, D.T. and Stanley, J.C. (1966) *Experimental and Quasi-Experimental Designs for Research.* Chicago: Rand McNally.

Daft, R.L. and Weick, K.E. (1984) 'Towards a model of organizations as interpretation systems', *Academy of Management Review*, 9 (2): 284–95.

Denzin, N.K. (1989) *Interpretive Interactionism: Applied Social Research Methods (Applied Social Research Methods Series, Vol. 16).* London: Sage.

Dreyfus, H.L. (ed.) (1987) *Husserl: Intentionality and Cognitive Science.* Cambridge, MA: MIT Press.

Easterby-Smith, M.P.V. (1986) *Evaluation of Management Education, Training and Development.* Aldershot: Gower.

Easterby-Smith, M.P.V., Thorpe, R. and Lowe, A. (1991) *Management Research: an Introduction.* London: Sage.

Ehrenberg, A.S.C. (1975) *Data Reduction.* London: Wiley.

Fetterman, D.M. (1989) *Ethnography – Step by Step (Applied Social Research Methods Series, Vol. 17).* Newbury Park, CA: Sage.

Feyerabend, P. (1993) *Against Method* (3rd edn). London: Verso.

Fox, S. (1989) 'The politics of evaluating management development', *Management Education and Development*, 20 (3): 191–207.

Glaser, R. (ed.) (1962) *Training Research and Education.* New York: Wiley.

Guilford, J.P. (1954) *Psychometric Methods.* New York: McGraw-Hill.

Hamblin, A. (1974) *Evaluation and Control of Training.* London: McGraw-Hill.

Hamilton, D. (ed.) (1977) *Beyond the Numbers Game.* London: Macmillan.

Hesseling, P. (1966) *Strategy in Evaluation Research.* Assen: Van Gorcum.

Legge, K. (1984) *Evaluating Planned Organizational Change.* London: Academic Press.

Lincoln, Y.S. and Guba, E.G. (1985) *Naturalistic Inquiry.* Beverly Hills, CA: Sage.

Menzies, I.E.P. (1960) 'A case study in the functioning of social systems as a defence against anxiety', *Human Relations*, 13: 95–121.

Mitroff, I.I. (1983) *Stakeholders of the Organizational Mind.* San Francisco: Jossey-Bass.

Morgan, G. (ed.) (1983) *Beyond Method.* Beverly Hills, CA: Sage.

Morgan, G. (1986) *Images of Organization.* Beverly Hills, CA: Sage.

Palumbo, D.J. (1988) *The Politics of Programme Evaluation.* Beverly Hills, CA: Sage.

Pettigrew, A.M. (1973) *The Politics of Organizational Decision-making.* London: Tavistock.

Pettigrew, A.M. (1985) *The Awakening Giant: Continuity and Change in ICI.* Oxford: Basil Blackwell.

Schutz, A. (1967) *The Phenomenology of the Social World.* Evanston, IL: Northwestern University Press.

Stuart, R. (1978) 'Contracting to learn: a perspective on the dynamics of management development activities', *Management Education and Development*, 9 (2): 75–84.

Sturrock, J. (ed.) (1979) *Structuralism and Since: from Lévi-Strauss to Derrida*. Oxford: Oxford University Press.

Toffler, B.L. (1986) *Tough Choices: Managers Talk Ethics*. New York: Wiley.

Warr, P., Bird, M. and Rackham, N. (1970) *The Evaluation of Management Training*. Aldershot: Gower.

Webb, E.J., Campbell, D.T., Schwartz, R.D. and Sechrest, L. (1966) *Unobtrusive Measures: Non-reactive Research in the Social Sciences*. Chicago: Rand McNally.

12

Case Studies in Organizational Research

Jean F. Hartley

Case studies are widely used in organizational studies in the social science disciplines of sociology, industrial relations and anthropology. Within organizational psychology, however, case study methodology is an under-utilized research strategy. Although there are many descriptions and practical guides about, for example, designing questionnaires or multi-variate statistical analyses, we have much less information about the theoretical, methodological and practical aspects of case studies.

Yet case studies can be theoretically exciting and data rich so it is important to analyse their strengths and weaknesses as well as provide a practical guide on how to conduct and manage them. This chapter examines what case studies are, the circumstances in which they may be used, the relation of method to theory and the challenges to the researcher as a person in conducting case study research.

There exists a simplistic argument which says that case studies are 'meaningful' and 'rich' compared with the sometimes 'dustbowl empiric-ism' of quantitative techniques. They can shed light on the fine-grain detail of social processes in their appropriate context. The counter-argument (equally simplistic) is that case studies are lacking in rigour and reliability and that they do not address the issues of generalizability which can be so effectively tackled by quantitative methods. However, this level and type of argument is totally outmoded. There is nothing about a method *per se* which makes it weak or strong. The argument about the method depends on two factors. First, the relationship between theory and method, and, second, how the researcher attends to the potential weaknesses of the method.

Fortunately, the methods, strengths and weaknesses of case study method raised by some researchers (for example, Miles, 1979) have been increasingly addressed since the late 1970s. There is an increasingly sizeable literature about how to conduct and analyse data from case studies (Campbell, 1975; Eisenhardt, 1989; Gummesson, 1991; McClintock et al., 1979; Rose, 1991; Yin, 1981, 1989).

What is a case study?

Case study research consists of a detailed investigation, often with data collected over a period of time, of one or more organizations, or groups within organizations, with a view to providing an analysis of the context and processes involved in the phenomenon under study. The phenomenon is not isolated from its context (as in, say, laboratory research) but is of interest precisely because it is in relation to its context. Of course, case studies can also be concerned with individuals (for example, Abrahamson, 1992; Bromley, 1986; Freud, 1933) and here the overall approach is similar – generally inductive analysis focusing on processes in their social context – but with a different level of analysis.

A case study approach is not a method as such but rather a research strategy. As Yin (1981) notes, because the context is deliberately part of the design, there will always be too many 'variables' for the number of observations made: consequently the application of standard experimental and survey designs and criteria are not appropriate, although issues of validity and generalizability have to be addressed.

Within this broad strategy, a number of methods may be used – and these may be either qualitative, quantitative or both, though the emphasis is generally more on qualitative methods because of the kinds of questions which are best addressed through case study method. Participant observation is one possibility, as in the research of Burawoy (1979), where the researcher took a job on an assembly line in order to answer questions about how consent to workplace practices is created between workers and supervisors (and see Waddington, Chapter 7, this volume). Observation but in the role of researcher not as active participant is also a technique which is widely used. This forms the basis of the case study research I conducted with colleagues on the organization of strikers during a national strike (Hartley, 1989; Hartley et al., 1983). A further technique is to use interviews with a variety of informants in the organization. These may range from semi-structured to relatively unstructured (see King, Chapter 2, this volume), following issues as they become pertinent to the research. The work of Edwards and Scullion (1982) on the different forms of industrial conflict in seven workplaces illustrates this approach. The case study may also involve the use of questionnaires with members of management or the workforce in addition to a detailed investigation through observation and interviews. This combination of methods has been used in a number of situations, for example in a study of job insecurity (Hartley et al., 1991). In addition, a case study researcher is likely to take advantage of other sources of data within the organization, some of it opportunistic and some of it deliberately sought out: for example, analysis of documentary materials (see Forster, Chapter 9, this volume), attendance at meetings, conversations in corridors or in cars between locations. Indeed, one can argue that all the qualitative methods described in this book, and some quantitative techniques too, may be of use to the case study researcher. Many case study researchers, in their pursuit of the delicate and intricate interactions and processes occuring within organizations, will use a combination of methods, partly because complex phenomena may be best approached through several methods, and partly deliberately to triangulate (and thereby improve validity).

A case study, therefore, while often including qualitative methods, cannot be defined through its research techniques. Rather, it has to be defined in terms of its theoretical orientation. This is not necessarily substantive theory but rather the emphasis on understanding processes alongside their (organizational and other) contexts. The distinction between interviews carried out as part of a case study and interviews carried out as part of a survey is a matter of degree, but in the first situation interviews are used more to explore and probe in depth the particular circumstances of the organization and the relation between organizational behaviour and its specific context, whereas in survey interviews the emphasis is likely to be primarily on comparisons of the prespecified phenomenon across organizations (or groups within the organization). Case study methods, therefore, are likely to be better able to adapt to and probe areas of original but also emergent theory.

The value of theory is key. Although case studies may begin with (in some situations) only rudimentary theory or a primitive framework, they need to develop theoretical frameworks by the end which inform and enrich the data and provide not only a sense of the uniqueness of the case but also what is of more general relevance and interest. In some situations, grounded theory (Glaser and Strauss, 1967) may lead to emergent theory, while in other situations the researchers may have some clear propositions to explore. Either way, without a theoretical framework, a case study may produce fascinating details about life in a particular organization but without any wider significance. Indeed, a case study without the discipline of theory can easily degenerate into a 'story'. There may be a great deal of description and a blow-by-blow account of activities, conflicts and decisions, but these are of little interest to those outside the action if the detail does not convey ideas about fundamental social or organizational processes. Of course, in any case study there are unique features due to organizational characteristics and the personalities and roles of individuals. These can give the case study a richness, immediacy and graphic quality which engages the mind and the imagination of the reader in a way which is often more difficult with concepts as operationalized in a questionnaire. The point is that without a theoretical framework, the researcher is in severe danger of providing description without wider meaning.

For example, my own work with colleagues on the 1980 national steel strike, as played out in Rotherham, would have been deficient had it simply given a blow-by-blow account of the negotiations, the pickets, the victories and the defeats of the militant Rotherham steel strikers. The case study is interesting to the extent that it analyses and illuminates the organizational processes of an emergent and immanent organization. It rendered problematic issues of leadership and decision-making through showing that leadership requires, to greater a or lesser degree, the consent of the governed. These processes of change, leadership and decision-making are of wider relevance to organizational studies, providing insights not only for those organizations such as voluntary and public bodies with distributed leadership, but also for private organizations where leadership is *apparently* a matter of one-way control.

Case studies may also be distinguished by their approach to theory-building, which tends generally (but not exclusively) to be inductive. The opportunity to explore issues in depth, in their context, means that theory development can occur through the systematic piecing together of detailed evidence to generate (or perhaps replicate) theories of more general interest. The method, it has been suggested (Yin, 1981), is akin to that of the detective who must sift evidence (some of it relevant and some of it not) to build a picture of motive, opportunity and method. In case study research, such detective work is undertaken not only to understand the particular and unique features of the case(s) but also to draw out an analysis which is applicable on a wider basis.

Case study methodology has a long history of intermittent use in organizational psychology, though it has been used more widely within sociology, industrial relations (see, for example, Edwards, 1992) and organizational behaviour. The case study is an important method in industrial relations and industrial sociology (see, for example, Batstone et al., 1977, 1978; Beynon, 1988; Burawoy, 1979; Edwards and Scullion, 1982; Flanders, 1964; Pollert, 1981) because it has allowed for the complexity of processes of conflict and cooperation, especially among sub-cultures in the organization, to be described and analysed in ways which have not predetermined what constitutes conflict and cooperation for particular groups.

Case studies have also been widely used in studies of organizational behaviour, especially in understanding organizational innovation and change, as shaped by both internal forces and the external environment (for example, Biggart, 1977; Burns and Stalker, 1968; Lawrence and Lorsch, 1967; Pettigrew and Whipp, 1991; Pettigrew et al., 1992). Case study analysis has allowed the tracking of change over time, as a response both to historical forces, contextual pressures and the dynamics of various stakeholder groups in proposing or opposing change.

Although less well developed as a method in psychology, case studies have been significant in understanding formal and informal processes in organizations. A stream of research has been conducted on technological change (see, for example, Blackler and Brown, 1980; Cassell and Fitter, 1992; Symon and Clegg, 1991), with much of the socio-technical systems research having been conducted through case study methodology (see, for example, Gyllenhammar, 1977; Rice, 1958; Trist and Bamforth, 1951). Action research generally has often favoured case study methods to elucidate meanings and changes (see, for example, Jones, 1987; Marshall and McLean, 1988). Case studies have also been used to investigate informal or emergent organizations (see, for example, Brown and Hosking, 1989; Hartley et al., 1983; Waddington, 1987).

However, case studies have largely been a minority taste. One reason for this may be that it is a labour-intensive method and also that it is harder to fit within the standard journal format for research. Many case studies, in sociology and psychology, have been written as books (or chapters) rather than journal articles. On the other hand, teaching materials based on the case study approach have become very popular (for example, Clegg et al., 1985; Gowler et al., 1993), although the cases may be based not on case study methodology as such but on other research strategies which are later put into context for teaching purposes.

Questions which can be addressed using case studies

The strength of case studies lies especially in their capacity to explore social processes as they unfold in organizations. By using multiple and often qualitative methods including observation, the researcher can learn much more about processes than is possible with other techniques such as surveys. A case study allows for a processual, contextual and generally longitudinal analysis of the various actions and meanings which take place and which are constructed within organizations. The open-ended nature of much data-gathering also allows for processes to be examined in considerable depth. This contrasts with survey methodology where although associations may be found between variables it is harder to tease out what processes lie behind the correlations. In the steel strike case study (Hartley et al., 1983), we were able to examine relationships within the local strike leadership which, among other things, revealed the complexities of how decisions were made and information used in developing strategies for prosecuting the strike. Interviews alone would not have captured this because the espoused and enacted behaviours were on occasion different and revealed the political nature of much decision-making in the strike committee. We were also able to see how decision-making developed and changed over time.

Case studies are also useful where it is important to understand those social processes in their organizational and environmental context. Behaviour may only be fully understandable in the context of the wider forces operating within the organization, whether these are contemporary or historical. For example, examining job insecurity in the context of organizational decline enabled a more thorough exploration of what job insecurity is and means to different employees and how it is promoted by organizational actions than would be the situation if a survey alone had been carried out (Hartley et al., 1991). In the steel strike study, the political aspects of decision-making of the strike committee become comprehensible in the context of the fast-changing and hostile environment faced by the strikers and the huge investments of financial and emotional resources in the strike.

Case studies are tailor-made for exploring new processes or behaviours or ones which are little understood. In this sense, case studies have an important function in *generating* hypotheses and *building* theory. They have a high likelihood of generating new theory, and, furthermore, the emergent theory is likely to be testable with constructs that can be measured and hypotheses that can be falsified (Eisenhardt, 1989) because the theory-building has largely been inductive. This is not to suggest that researchers go into the case study with no theory at all – they would quickly become overwhelmed with data – but the key point is that the initial identification of research questions and theoretical framework will work best where it is tentative – with a recognition that the issues and theory may shift as the framework and concepts are repeatedly examined against the data which are systematically collected. For example, Sutton (1987) developed a framework for understanding people's responses to impending organizational death: the issue was too new for relevant or validated frameworks to be available. Eisenhardt (1989) notes that although a common stereotype of case studies is that researchers 'find what they want to find', in fact the opposite may be the case: that realities which conflict with expectations 'unfreeze' thinking and allow for the development of new lines of inquiry and the modification of existing theory.

Case studies can be used where the intention is to explore not typicality but unusualness or extremity with the intention of illuminating processes. The exaggerated example, where processes may be more stark or clearer, may suggest processes which are occurring in more mundane or common settings (where they may be harder to observe). The research by Pettigrew et al. (1992) in health authorities chose deliberately to focus on 'high change' rather than 'average change', partly because managerial actions would stand out in sharper relief under such conditions. This is perhaps the organizational equivalent of using the study of human neuroses to understand the commonalities of human emotion and cognition. Case studies of strikes and other industrial action have been revealing of the ordinary processes of industrial 'peace' as well as 'war'.

Case studies can be useful in capturing the emergent and immanent properties of life in organizations. A survey may be too static to capture the ebb and flow of organizational activity, especially where it is changing very fast. The establishment of a totally new organization to prosecute the strike in Rotherham, or the weekly changes in organization due to distributed leadership in a women's organization (Brown and Hosking, 1989) can probably only be captured through the regular and dedicated presence of the researcher.

Case study is also a useful technique where exploration is being made of organizational behaviour which is informal, unusual, secret or even illicit. While exploration of such issues is not confined to case study method (skilful interviewing may achieve the same end), the trust which develops over a period of time between researcher and organization members means that gradually information may be provided which would not be made public to the researcher in a one-off interview. For example, during the steel strike research we were privy to many aspects of planned tactics, including illegal aspects of picketing, which the strike committee discussed behind locked doors. Indeed, almost all our knowledge of strikes comes out of case studies because other techniques lack both the dynamism and the sensitivity to capture the complexity of action in a hostile environment (see also Batstone et al., 1978; Karsh, 1958; Lane and Roberts, 1971; Waddington, 1987, and see also his chapter in this volume). Case study can also be used to understand more everyday practices which would not be revealed in brief contact: for example, how absenteeism is experienced by employees (Edwards and Scullion, 1982) or how collusion between employees and supervisors develops in certain workplace practices (for example, Brown 1973; Burawoy, 1979).

Finally, detailed case studies may be essential in cross-national comparative research, where an intimate understanding of what concepts mean to people, the meanings attached to particular behaviours and how behaviours are linked is essential. A survey may find a difference in, say, organizational commitment but a comparative case study can tease out what commitment means to a Japanese worker compared with a British or German worker. Gallie (1978) conducted detailed comparative case studies of French and British oil refinery workers indicating different attitudes to militancy and the union, which he placed in a historical and sociological context.

Case studies: research design

A single case study, the result of weeks or years spent by a researcher in one organization, can provide valuable information about the research question. Such a study may be the only feasible option for research if resources or opportunities preclude a wider study. In single case studies, however, the disentangling of what is unique to the organization from what is common to other organizations can be difficult. The research may be strengthened by the addition of a second case (or more: consensus appears to indicate that managing more than a dozen case studies is not feasible or weakens the method). Alternatively, the researcher can develop contrasts within the case. For example, in our study of the Rotherham strike organization, we spent a few days at both the Sheffield and Scunthorpe strike committees. These were particularly informative contrasts, because we were able to tease out, from a similar geographical location and prior level of union organization, that the form of organization and decision-making in Rotherham was not inevitable but arose from the presence of certain officials prior to the strike and to the dynamics of the strike committee during the strike.

Where it is feasible to undertake only a single case study, then it can be helpful to seek out possible contrasts within the case: for example, do employees in certain departments perceive the situation differently from colleagues in another department, and if so why (see also Chapter 11 above by Burgoyne on stakeholder analysis)?

A useful research design can be to use both case study and other research strategies in different phases of a research project. For example, one company-level industrial relations survey (Marginson et al., 1988) found that many companies had a formal human resource management policy and that some companies communicated this policy to employees. In addition, case studies were conducted by Morris and Wood (1991) which were drawn from the same sample. They found that, in practice, many managers acted without reference to the policy and in some companies were not aware that it existed. This combination of survey and case studies was able to establish not only formal procedures over a large sample but also an indication of practice on the ground. In this case, the intensive case study method worked well with the survey which was able to use a much larger sample. Other research might start with case study research and test the theory developed there in wider survey-based research.

Undertaking case study research

This section looks at some of the practical steps and plans which may be needed in order to conduct case study research. As so little has been written about this area, the following text is based largely on my own experiences and on conversations with colleagues who have also under-taken case study research. However, useful commentary on case study methodology is available also in Eisenhardt (1989), Rose (1991) Yin (1981, 1989). Some comments concern any organizational research but are particularly pertinent to case study research because of the need to maintain continued access to the organization. The edited collection by Bryman (1988) and the work of Schatzman and Strauss (1973) are useful here.

Choosing the case study

Assuming that the researcher has decided on why a case study is seen to be an appropriate way to tackle the research question (as opposed to other methods of inquiry), an initial issue is how to choose the case study organization. First, what kind of organization is the researcher looking for? Is it intended to be typical of the phenomenon to be studied? Or an extreme example? Has the researcher the resources and interest in undertaking more than one case? In which situation, how might the cases contrast each other ideally? Locating the case study might be opportunistic or planned (I have experienced both), but the researcher needs to be clear about what kind of organization would fit the criteria for the research.

Using contacts in industry, academia and friendship circles can be helpful, first, in establishing what the *population* is of organizations you might draw the case study from, and then how to choose the case(s). Interviews with employers' representatives (for example, CBI, Engineering Employers' Federation) or with trade unions nationally or locally (full-time officials especially are likely to have knowledge of the sector you are interested in) can be useful in finding out about certain organizations before you make a direct approach. Academics with contacts from research or consultancy can be helpful or a useful contact may come from your social circle. Reading the specialist and trade press is informative too. Draw up a shortlist of organizations you would like to approach – and make sure it is larger than the actual planned study: some may refuse to become involved for a variety of reasons, while some may be willing but turn out to be unsuitable.

Gaining and maintaining access

Unless you are already known in the organization or the industry, you are likely to be in the position of 'cold calling' the organization. I have found that this is made easier by two devices. The first is to be introduced through a third party, for example a trade union official or another researcher or through someone you know in the company. The second is to conduct a broad-ranging interview with a senior personnel manager in the organizations you think may be suitable. At this stage, this is a genuine exploration of the issues that interest you and an opportunity to see if the organization is suitable and would be receptive to a later approach to undertake a case study. For example, in the research on job insecurity I approached several potential cases, saying that I was researching management and trade union responses to the recession in the region and asking for an interview. Of these, around half appeared in practice to be suitable and so I returned to make an approach about doing case study-based work.

Deciding on who are the critical 'gate-keepers' to organizational research is important. These are the people (there may be several) who are influential in deciding whether you will be allowed access, for how long, and who can introduce you to useful informants. Initially, as an organizational psychologist, your contact is likely to be a personnel or human resource manager. But you need to establish quickly who are the other significant people in the organization who might affect the progress and success of your research. In a production-driven organization, getting to know the production manager can be important. Meeting the Chief

Executive or influential members of the Board can be important. Some research will run aground if the local union is not involved. In some cases, setting up a working party in the organization to sponsor and oversee the research can be a way of ensuring that it is supported by the organization. If you rely on one person, your position is unstable. If that person is sacked or promoted (I have had both happen!), you need to have links elsewhere in the organization for continued access. As well as gate-keepers, who tend to be individuals, it is also useful to think about who are the stakeholders in your research (see Burgoyne, Chapter 11 above). Clearly you need to have a keen (and continuing) sense of the politics of the organization.

Gaining access is one thing but maintaining it requires continual attention. Changes in personnel or the fortunes of the company, changes in views about how much organizational time you are tying up, changes in the perceived value of the research – these mean that access has to be worked for. Regular reporting back and discussions with the principal sponsor in the organization can be useful (see also Buchanan et al., 1988).

Choosing an initial theoretical framework

Depending on the state of the published literature concerning your field of study, the initial focus of the case study may be very broad and open-ended. However, some focus is needed to structure the study to avoid the twin dangers of being overwhelmed by data and being drawn into narrative- rather than theory-building. Because the case study strategy is ideally suited to exploration of issues in depth and following leads into new areas or new constructions of theory, the theoretical framework at the beginning may not be the same one that survives to the end. Theory-building is key to case study analysis but to do this there has to be theory to examine, contest, find supporting or conflicting evidence for. Even the most open-ended approach to theory-building – grounded theory (Glaser and Strauss, 1967) – argues for an initial framework which is then tested against the data gained in the study.

The theoretical framework may be very broad. In the steel strike research, we started with a conceptual model developed by Kelly and Nicholson (1980) of intergroup relations between management and unions during a period of industrial conflict, but we became more interested in examining the local strike organization as a new and emergent organization, with all the issues of the management and motivation of members evident in organizations; an area we had better opportunity to research.

Collecting systematic data

Given the variety of sources of data potentially available to the researcher – documents, observation, interviews, attendance at meetings – and the variety of people who might be suitable informants for the research, how do you start?

The first strategy might well be to get a general overview of the structure and functioning of the organization. This might consist of half a dozen 'orientation' interviews in which the researcher learns something of the history and present functioning of the organization. Obtaining an organization chart (assuming an up-to-date one is available) is useful in ensuring that you are aware of the work of the principal departments. It can be valuable to be 'walked round' the organization following the workflow and observing the work being undertaken. In this way you can map out where you think the principal sources of data are likely to be and you will not be surprised later on by the existence of a department you had no idea existed. You will probably also gain an idea of when are the best (and worst) times and occasions on which to talk to people and this will help you plan your work. Some organizations are frantically busy at month-end and others have seasonal periods of activity and slack.

Having gained an overview, you can plan out the people and groups you want to talk with/observe and the research methods you want to use. These should be tentative in that the strategy may be modified in line with new sources of information or new constructs which are developed in the research. However, the emphasis, despite flexibility and opportunity, is to develop the research evidence systematically. This includes an emphasis on triangulated methods where possible: is the theory supported by evidence gained in different ways, from different groups, in different situations or with different researchers in the research team? The search, as with all systematic inquiry, is for a broad array of evidence which looks for and takes into account disconfirming as well as confirming data.

The data collected need to be systematic rather than ad hoc. It is useful to ask yourself certain questions as you set up interviews and observation periods: have I sampled this behaviour/process from a wide enough set of informants? Are there other people who might have a different view or explanation of this? Are there any data which do not support my current hypothesis?

There is *some* place for ad hoc or opportunistic data collection: a conversation with a receptionist as you walk in one morning, or a chance meeting by the coffee machine may give you new ideas which then need to be incorporated into your research design and investigated more thoroughly. A case study researcher has to retain some flexibility to follow leads and invitations.

There is a myth that scientific activity (and organizations) are wholly rational. But intuition can be important in collecting systematic data. Working in an organization and getting to know its members and activities (indeed in any research setting) gives rise to all sorts of feelings about people and hunches about the quality and type of data you are getting. These feelings can be harnessed, either impulsively to follow a lead without initially quite knowing why, or else by using that intuition to reassess the explicit knowledge already gained. This is not to say that scientific research should be interpreted and analysed on the grounds of intuition, rather this can be a spur to further systematic investigation. Is there another way you can get that person to tell you what is really going on? Can someone else shed light on the phenomenon? Are there documentary records you can check? What starts as an intuition may crystallize as an observation which can then be tracked for its significance. For example, during the steel strike committee meetings, I started to feel that the white-collar steelworkers on the strike committee were not being taken seriously compared with the manual workers. I commented on this to my colleague and we then observed carefully that during meetings less time was spent on their suggestions and less positive comments made about their views. This led us into some interesting theorizing about the espoused values of the strike committee and we came to the conclusion (based on other data collected too) that decision-making was primarily political rather than rational. The functions of this for the committee and the strike organization were then investigated.

Managing data collection

While it is easy in a case study to go on collecting more data, to interview just one more person, thought has to be given to the opportunity costs and to the management of the data collected. Will a further interview or period of observation add significantly to what you already know? Will it allow the testing of tentative ideas about the phenomenon? Does it allow you to be reasonably certain there is no disconfirming evidence in the organization? At some point you have to decide to stop collecting further data. Saturation point is reached when you feel you are not gaining significantly new knowledge or ideas about the focus of your study.

I will not discuss here in detail the recording of data because that is covered in other chapters and in other articles. However, thought must be given to how you will record data and how you will prevent yourself being overwhelmed by the data. In many organizations, as a participant or observer, tape-recording will be both impractical and inadvisable for a variety of reasons and it is likely that recording by notebook will be best. Glaser and Strauss (1967), Schatzman and Strauss (1973) and Turner (1988) give many ideas about how to record data within organizational settings. Impressions, insights and theoretical musings need to be noted as well as observed and recorded data about the organization itself. Glaser and Strauss (1967) make distinctions between observation notes, method notes and theoretical notes, all of which need to be recorded.

Unless you are a full participant observer, continual presence in the organization is unlikely to be beneficial. Considerable time needs to be given to writing up notes of interviews and impressions and this needs to be done as soon as possible after the event. Some distancing from the organization is also advisable so the researcher is not overloaded with impressions and does not get so close to the data that he or she is unable to see their wider significance. During the steel strike research, we spent about 50 per cent of the day with the strikers, and later in the 13-week strike, as activities stabilized, the two field researchers took it in turns to cover the strike. During the case research on job insecurity, during a six-week period of intense observation and interviews, I spent three days a week in the plant (having arranged an office near the shop floor for my use).

I have not spent time on the politics of case study research, although this is especially important in this type of research because the researcher develops close links with the organization and its members and is likely to hold information which is or may be prejudicial to the interests of certain individuals and groups within the organization. Other writers cover these aspects (Beynon, 1988; Bryman, 1988; Waddington, Chapter 7, this volume) as well as issues of contracting and research confidentiality.

Analysing the data

How researchers get from the recording of data to their interpretation and the conclusions is the part of (especially qualitative) research which is least well described in research methodology. However, some researchers are trying to provide more details of the methods they use in analysing data using primarily inductive techniques (Eisenhardt, 1989; Glaser and Strauss, 1967; Marshall, 1981; Strauss and Corbin, 1990; Yin, 1981, 1989).

Data analysis and data collection are developed together in an iterative process. As noted, this can be a strength as it allows for theory development which is grounded in empirical evidence. However, the danger is that the researcher reaches premature closure, having been unduly influenced by particularly vivid, unusual or interesting data. There are several ways to guard against such tendencies.

The first is careful description of the data and the development of categories in which to place behaviours or processes (see Yin, 1989). The data may be organized around certain topics, key themes or central questions. Then the data need to be examined – 'interrogated' in Strauss' terminology – to see how far they fit or fail to fit the expected categories. Use of tables to search for patterns, or grouping of similar topics, helps to explore the data. Initial interrogations of the data may lead to unexpected or unusual results which may mean that the categories need refining or that the event needs to be interpreted in a different way. Questions lead to further questions. All the time the researcher is alert to the possible presence of disconfirming data and the existence of paradoxes and contrasts. These can be welcomed (however inconvenient!) as indicating that further theory-building needs to occur.

Yin (1981) notes that final explanations should fit several criteria. The explanatory case study should be an accurate rendition of the facts of the case, there should be some consideration of the possible alternative explanations of these facts, and a conclusion drawn based on a single explanation (ideally) which appears most congruent with the facts. Eisenhardt (1989) adds that the writing up of the research should provide enough evidence for each construct used to allow readers to make their own assessment of its fit with theory. Not so different from traditional deductive research in fact!

A mistake in writing up case studies is to believe that the narrative is the most interesting aspect of the study. Narrative alone is unlikely to be of interest to those outside the organization and every effort has to be made to draw out the wider implications of the study while giving a strong sense of the particular circumstances of the case. I have found that a first draft may often follow narrative more than the wider themes, as this helps me get 'the storyline' straight. In the second draft, I can move on to the broader implications of the study. Sometimes a brief description of the main events – perhaps in a tabulated diary form – can help get past the need to set the events chronologically while also wanting to pursue themes in the case.

The careful checking of constructs and theory against various sources of evidence helps prevent being biased by early impressions. Other means of increasing the internal validity of the research exist too. The use of research teams can help, with the similarities in data – but also the contrasts – being carefully explored. We used this as a deliberate part of our research strategy in the steel strike, as did Pettigrew et al. (1992) in their work. Having other people you can bounce ideas off is also valuable. These may be other researchers, friends or even the 'reader' of your own written commentary on what you are doing. During the steel strike research, our data collection and interpretation were enhanced by having two researchers in the field and one researcher back in the university. There were several occasions when as fieldworkers we reported back on events and impressions as vivid experiences and our interpretation was enhanced by the office-based colleague saying 'but why did that happen?' Non-plussed and unable to answer, we were able to return the next day to investigate that aspect further. Harris and Sutton (1986) call this the 'devil's advocate' strategy. It was very helpful in our own research and allowed the combination of closeness and distance which is essential to good research.

Finally, the analysing of data is enhanced by reference to the existing literature and using this to raise questions about whether the researcher's findings are consistent with or different from extant research. Sources of difference need to be examined and can be the source of creative theory development.

Leaving the case study

When you have collected enough data (or when the strike has finished), you will have to leave (see also Buchanan et al., 1988). You should clarify at that stage what you plan to do with the data and how long you expect it will be before results are available. You may want to offer a report on the findings to the organization. (A short report to all members? Longer for key informants such as the personnel department and the trade union?) There may be other offers you can make in recognition for the help you have received: interactive sessions to discuss the findings, policy recommendations. You may also want to give the organization the opportunity to check that it is satisfied that it has been sufficiently disguised in any publications (if that is an issue: this should be clarified at the contracting stage of the case study). Care needs to be taken with information which was offered to you 'off the record'. Are individuals disguised or in other ways protected?

It can be emotionally difficult to leave a case study when you have built up good working relationships with people in the host organization. Paying careful attention to this is important both for you and for your informants. (See also Waddington, Chapter 7, p. 107 above.)

Being a researcher

We get no training as psychologists in how to *be* while we are doing research. We get extensive training in scientific method and statistical data analysis and in how to use computers, but not in how to relate to people in research settings. Yet this can be a very personally challenging aspect of doing organizational research (I remember vividly the first day of the strike research: standing in a busy strike office surrounded by noisy, burly male manual workers and feeling small, female, nervous and excited, and very shy). We also know that the relationship between researcher and researched affects the type and quality of data obtained (Rosenthal, 1966). There is no justification for ignoring this aspect of research in organizational research. What is the point in being trained in the finer details of, say, sampling or survey question design if you cannot put an informant at ease during an interview or understand how your own psychology may be influencing your perceptions and interactions? Yin notes 'the demands of a case study on a person's intellect, ego and emotions are far greater than those of any other research strategy' (1989: 62).

Over the last decade, there has been a growing awareness of the impact of social role characteristics on the research process, for example the impact of gender and ethnicity (Oakley, 1981; Pettigrew, 1981). This may be a source of strength as well as limitation. During the steel strike research, conducted by a female and a male researcher, each of us had access to data which were not so readily available to the other. For example, the steelworkers gave me blow-by-blow accounts of the current state of the national negotiations, which was spared my colleague (they presumed he understood) but which gave important insights into morale and confidence among the strikers.

The social skills of listening, interviewing and observing can be taught and get better with practice. What is less talked about is the emotional reality of being a researcher and how this affects research. Two areas in particular need more discussion: first, how one's interactions with and perceptions of the organization affect the observations made (for example, through projection, introjection and so forth); and second, how to attend to and manage the feelings which arise in the course of doing case study work (for example, curiosity, excitement and concern as well as anxiety, fear or anger).

As researchers, we are encouraged to concentrate on our thoughts and symbols. Indeed, this is the essence of science: the application of rationality to the external world. This has its place and has led to important insights about human beings and their world. But to believe that only rationality is important in understanding the world is to live in a half-light. This is especially the case in the social sciences, where we are dealing with human beings with their self-reflective, emotional and symbolic complexities.

Some approaches to research are encouraging the explicit acceptance of ourselves as researchers with feelings and emotions which can be drawn on to make sense of our research (for example, new paradigm research: Reason and Rowan, 1981). There also exist frameworks for understanding how the inner world of the individual makes contact with the external world, for example in Gestalt psychology (Hinksman, 1988) or transactional analysis. Space precludes much exploration of these issues but they can provide a basis for understanding and communicating among researchers about using our wider faculties in undertaking case study research.

Attention to the boundary between the inner and outer world is especially useful in the context of case study research, where by dint of being in regular interaction with members of the organization the researcher comes to operate in an *organizational* boundary position: partly insider, partly stranger; partly accepted and partly not; partly understanding the culture and partly still being able to question it.

I will simply give an example. Gestalt uses the concepts of 'figure' and 'ground' to help understand what is of importance to an individual at any time. Attention may switch between feelings, senses and thoughts as each becomes, sometimes only momentarily, 'figure' (dominant for the individual at that moment). For example, in a meeting with a chief executive, I might be aware not only of the content of the interview but also of my physical comfort, my feelings about the interview, about him/her and about myself at that point. Rather than filtering out these sources of information which are additional to the interview content, my interview may be enriched by such a broader awareness and may be the source of important intuitions which can then be tested in more scientific terms. Furthermore, the 'figure' may change as the interview progresses. For example, I may become aware that the figure is changing from the content of the interview to a sense of boredom. Rather than tick myself off for not paying more attention, I can treat this as new material: is it that the person is not giving me the information that I am looking for? Is it that I don't like this person? Is it that his or her views are rather similar to what I already know from other people in the organization? All these possibilities give me clues to the processes at work in myself and the organization and therefore what steps I can consider taking next. This is not to say that one acts on feelings: instead, they provide a rich source of data which can be used imaginatively to contribute to the systematic investigation. Awareness of feelings may also limit the effects of projection, introjection and so forth.

Awareness of the feelings which arise as a result of being in the organization and interacting with its members can be helpful in managing those feelings. It is quite likely that in the course of doing the case study you will meet people you like and people you do not, you will encounter situations that make you feel angry (say, over attitudes towards women or the treatment of redundant employees) and situations that make you feel anxious (what shall I do here? how shall I react?) as well as situations that make you curious (interesting to watch the interaction between the managers at a meeting: why does everyone ignore Joe?) and enthusiastic (sharing an experience with people in the organization). Your feelings may or may not be for sharing or expressing in the organization: that is your choice. If they are not finished with, they may become 'figure' next time you are in the organization (and get in the way of fresh and clear perceptions). In this situation, you may find it helpful to 'offload' some of the stronger feelings with colleagues or friends outside the situation. Some feelings may be for sharing in the organization: saying how you react to certain events may generate further useful data as people explain to you their reactions too, or the reasons why such and such has occurred. The point is that you are a person with all kinds of data about self and environment to draw on in your study of the case. This can be used to generate systematic investigations and to manage yourself in the organization.

Generalizing from case studies

Once data have been collected and analysis is being undertaken, how can one write a case study in a way which is insightful not only about the case itself but also more generally about organizational behaviour and processes? In other words, how does one generalize from a case study?

It is conventional wisdom to say that case studies are weak in their capacity to generalize to other situations. This, supposedly, is in contrast to quantitative studies, where it is possible to generalize from the data by the detailed analyses of means, correlations and other methods. One can say, from a quantitative survey, what is likely to happen in a 'typical' or 'average' situation (assuming this exists other than as a statistical construct). By contrast, how can one decide which are the unique and which are the general features when one is dealing with the idiosyncracies of a case study?

This 'problem' can be tackled in two ways. The first is to question what we mean when we talk about generalizing from data. This may mean slightly different things in qualitative and quantitative research in *technical* terms, although be very similar in *epistemological* terms.

For a quantitative researcher, generalizing is achieved through such techniques as sample size, sampling frame and so on. The idea is to be able to sample cases (respondents, organizations) which are typical in specified ways of the population. If the sample is correctly drawn, then the results are deemed to be applicable (generalizable) to the specified population (see also Chapter 10 by Hornby and Symon for a discussion of sampling techniques).

This is a useful aspect of generalizing but it is not without difficulties. Using a quantitative approach one can only make generalizations about the sample to the population. But what happens when the sample is not typical? This is particularly an issue with organizations, where it is hard to get large samples and where the organizations can be very heterogeneous. What is a 'typical' organization? If a quantitative study takes place in the food industry in small workplaces, how certain can you be that the findings apply in large engineering companies – or anywhere else? In addition, because quantitative studies rely on the dispersion of variables in statistical relationships, one cannot be certain about the processes underlying those relationships.

Of course, this is not to suggest that generalizing from case studies is easier or less problematic but rather to suggest that while generalizing from case studies can be difficult, *the same is true for quantitative studies*. Just because there are established techniques for generalizing does not make it any easier where there is heterogeneity and where the processes have not been elucidated.

This is where case studies can be useful. The detailed examination of processes in a context can reveal processes which can be proposed as general or as peculiar to that organization. The detailed knowledge of the organization and especially the knowledge about the *processes* underlying the behaviour and its *context* can help to specify the conditions under which the behaviour can be expected to occur. In other words, the generalization is about theoretical propositions not about populations. For example, in the steel strike case study we observed that decision-making by the strike committee was primarily political, which we attributed partly to the need to ensure the cohesion of the strikers and to encourage their continuing commitment to the strike in a hostile environment. From this observation from a single case study, we can make several predictions: that where there is a hostile environment, such decision-making will be more likely to occur; that where the cohesion of a group or organization is important, then this will also be the case; and that such decision-making has to appear to be open to ideas from the whole organization because of the tenuous nature of authority in a voluntary organization. We even suggest that authority is not secure even in private organizations. Thus the basis of the generalization is not primarily about the typicality of the organization (cases may have been chosen deliberately to be untypical in order to bring to the surface processes hidden in more usual settings). Rather, the argument is about the existence of particular processes, which may influence behaviours and actions in the organization. Understanding the contingencies (context) in which those processes occur is important.

The value of specifying processes rather than variables (at least on some occasions) is seen in situations where there is rapid change. In fact, there may be too few examples of the type of organization to do a quantitative study (emergent forms of organization for example). Also, where change is occurring rapidly, the statistical generalizations might be out of date or irrelevant by the time they are unravelled. Here, an understanding of processes can be vital.

The second approach to the 'problem' of generalizing is to follow the lead of Yin (1981) in tackling the statistical issue head on. Yin argues that case studies as analytic units should be considered on a par with whole experiments. In other words, there are repeated observations within a particular environment. This approach gains particular value in the context of research which includes multiple cases.

There are certain actions which a researcher can take to ensure that generalizations are as strong as possible. Clearly, the measures for ensuring the internal validity of the research (covered in the section on analysing data) are important so that the case study itself is well argued and presented and examines alternative explanations of the data.

In generalizing from the case study, using existing literature to assess the extent of generalizable findings is important (see Eisenhardt, 1989). The aim of writing with a clear conceptual framework rather than a narrative will also help to relate theory to the literature and aid generalization. Where the researcher has been able to undertake more than one case study, this clearly increases confidence in the findings, though it is unlikely that the sample size will ever be large and single case studies can have authority in their own right.

Conclusions

Case study research is a heterogeneous activity covering a range of research methods and techniques, a range of coverage (from the single case study through carefully matched pairs to up to a dozen cases), differing lengths and levels of involvement in organizational functioning and a range of different types of data (including both quantitative and qualitative kinds). Reaching conclusions about it as a research strategy is inevitably difficult.

However, the key feature of the case study approach is not method or data but the emphasis on understanding processes as they occur in their context. The emphasis is not on divorcing context from the topic under investigation but rather to see this as a strength. Much case study research, because of the opportunity for open-ended inquiry, is able to draw on inductive methods of research which aim to build theory and generate hypotheses rather than primarily to test them. This is not an excuse for unsystematic work: a conceptual framework is essential, even if the researcher knows that the framework may change as a result of the data which come to light.

Researchers have been less proficient at explaining the techniques which lie behind inductive research methods but the picture is changing as more researchers are able to describe their methods and reasoning. We still need to consider the role and experience of being a researcher in this strategy. Encouragingly, confidence is growing in the ability to generalize from case study research. It is a method with a long history and an optimistic future.

Acknowledgement

Thanks to John Kelly and the editors for comments on an earlier draft of this chapter.

References

Abrahamson, P.R. (1992) *A Case for Case Studies*. London: Sage.

Batstone, E., Boraston, I. and Frenkel, S. (1977) *Shop Stewards in Action: the Social Organization of Workplace Conflict and Accommodation*. Oxford: Basil Blackwell.

Batstone, E., Boraston, I. and Frenkel, S. (1978) *The Social Organization of Strikes*. Oxford: Basil Blackwell.

Beynon, H. (1988) 'Regulating research: politics and decision-making in industrial organizations', in A. Bryman (ed.), *Doing Research in Organizations*. London: Routledge.

Biggart, N.W. (1977) 'The creative-destructive process of organizational change: the case of the post office', *Administrative Science Quarterly*. 22: 410–26.

Blackler, F.H. and Brown, C.M. (1980) *Whatever Happened to Shell's New Philosophy of Management?* Farnborough: Saxon House.

Bromley, D. (1986) *The Case Study Method in Psychology and Related Disciplines*. Chichester: Wiley.

Brown, H. and Hosking, D. (1989) 'Organizing activity in the women's movement: an example of distributed leadership', in B. Klandermans (ed.), *Organizing for Change: Social Movement Organizations in Europe and the United States*. Greenwich, CT: JAI Press.

Brown, W. (1973) *Piecework Bargaining*. London: Heinemann.

Bryman, A. (ed.) (1988) *Doing Research in Organizations*. London: Routledge.

Buchanan, D., Boddy, D. and McCalmam, J. (1988) 'Getting in, getting on, getting out and getting back', in A. Bryman (ed.), *Doing Research in Organizations*. London: Routledge.

Burawoy, M. (1979) *Manufacturing Consent*. Chicago: University of Chicago Press.

Burns, T. and Stalker, G.M. (1968) *The Management of Innovation* (2nd edn). London: Tavistock.

Campbell, D.T. (1975) 'Degrees of freedom and the case study', *Comparative Political Studies.* 8: 178–93.

Cassell, C. and Fitter, M.J. (1992) 'Responding to a changing environment: an action-research case study', in D.M. Hosking and N. Anderson (eds), *Organizational Change and Innovation*. London: Routledge.

Clegg, C.W., Kemp, N. and Legge, K. (1985) *Case Studies in Organizational Behaviour.* London: Harper & Row.

√ Edwards, P.K. (1992) 'Comparative industrial relations: the contribution of the ethnographic tradition'. Unpublished paper, Industrial Relations Research Unit, University of Warwick.

Edwards, P.K. and Scullion, H. (1982) *The Social Organization of Industrial Conflict.* Oxford: Basil Blackwell.

Eisenhardt, K.M. (1989) 'Building theories from case study research', *Academy of Management Review*, 14: 532–50.

Flanders, A. (1964) *The Fawley Productivity Agreements: a Case Study of Management and Collective Bargaining.* London: Faber.

Freud, S. (1933) *New Introductory Lectures on Psycho-analysis*. London: Hogarth Press.

Gallie, D. (1978) *In Search of the New Working Class*. Cambridge: Cambridge University Press.

Glaser, B. and Strauss, A.L. (1967) *The Discovery of Grounded Theory: Strategies for Qualitative Research.* Chicago: Aldine.

Gowler, D., Legge, K. and Clegg, C.W. (1993) *Case Studies in Organizational Behaviour.* (2nd edn). London: Paul Chapman Associates.

Gummesson, E. (1991) *Qualitative Methods in Management Research*. London: Sage.

Gyllenhammar, P. (1977) *People at Work.* Reading, MA: Addison-Wesley.

Harris, S.E. and Sutton, R.I. (1986) 'Functions of parting ceremonies in dying organizations', *Academy of Management Journal*, 29: 5–30.

Hartley, J.F. (1989) 'Leadership and decision-making in a strike organization', in B. Klandermans (ed.), *Organizing for Change: Social Movement Organizations in Europe and the United States*. Greenwich, CT: JAI Press.

Hartley, J.F., Kelly, J.E. and Nicholson, N. (1983) *Steel Strike: a Case Study in Industrial Relations*. London: Batsford.

Hartley, J.F., Jacobson, D., Klandermans, B. and Van Vuuren, T. (1991) *Job Insecurity: Coping with Jobs at Risk*. London: Sage.

Hinksman, B. (1988) 'Gestalt group therapy', in W. Dryden (ed.), *Group Therapy in Britain.* Milton Keynes: Open University Press.

Jones, S. (1987) 'Choosing action research: a rationale', in I. Mangham (ed.), *Organizational Analysis and Development*. Chichester: Wiley.

Karsh, B. (1958) *Diary of a Strike*. Urbana University of Illinois Press.

Kelly, J.E. and Nicholson, N. (1980) 'The causation of strikes: a review of the literature and the potential contribution of social psychology', *Human Relations*, 33: 853–83.

Lane, T. and Roberts, K. (1971) *Strike at Pilkingtons*. London: Fontana.

Lawrence, P.R. and Lorsch, J. (1967) *Organization and Environment*. Cambridge, MA: Harvard University Press.

McClintock, C., Brannen, D. and Maynard-Moody, S. (1979) 'Applying the logic of sample surveys to qualitative case studies: the case cluster method', *Administrative Science Quarterly*, 24: 612–29.

Marginson, P., Edwards, P., Martin, R., Purcell, J. and Sisson, K. (1988) *Beyond the Workplace: Managing Industrial Relations in the Multi-establishment Enterprise*. Oxford: Blackwell.

Marshall, J. (1981) 'Making sense as a personal process', in P. Reason and J. Rowan (eds), *Human Inquiry: a Sourcebook of New Paradigm Research*. Chichester: Wiley.

Marshall, J. and McLean, A. (1988) 'Reflection in action: exploring organizational culture', in P. Reason (ed.), *Human Inquiry in Action: Developments in New Paradigm Research*. London: Sage.

Miles, M.B. (1979) 'Qualitative data as an attractive nuisance: the problem of analysis', *Administrative Science Quarterly*, 24: 590–601.

Morris, T. and Wood, S. (1991) 'Testing the survey method: continuity and change in British industrial relations', *Work, Employment and Society*, 5: 259–82.

Oakley, A. (1981) 'Interviewing women: a contradiction in terms', in H. Roberts (ed.), *Doing Feminist Research*. London: Routledge.

Pettigrew, A.M. and Whipp, R. (1991) *Managing Change for Competitive Success*. Oxford: Blackwell.

Pettigrew, A.M., Ferlie, E. and McKee, L. (1992) *Shaping Strategic Change*. London: Sage.

Pettigrew, J. (1981) 'Reminiscences of fieldwork among the Sikhs', in H. Roberts (ed.), *Doing Feminist Research*. London: Routledge.

Pollert, A. (1981) *Girls, Wives, Factory Lives*. London: Macmillan.

Reason, P. and Rowan, J. (eds) (1981) *Human Inquiry: a Sourcebook of New Paradigm Research*. Chichester: Wiley.

Rice, A.K. (1958) *Productivity and Social Organization: the Ahmedabad Experiment*. London: Tavistock.

Rose, H. (1991) 'Case studies', in G. Allan and C. Skinner (eds), *Handbook for Research Students in the Social Sciences*. London: Falmer.

Rosenthal, R. (1966) *Experimenter Effects in Behavioural Research*. New York: Appleton-Century-Crofts.

Schatzman, L. and Strauss, A. (1973) *Field Research: Strategies for a Natural Sociology*. Englewood Cliffs, NJ: Prentice-Hall.

Strauss, A. and Corbin, J. (1990) *Basics of Qualitative Research*. Newbury Park, CA: Sage.

Sutton, R.I. (1987) 'The process of organizational death: disbanding and reconnecting', *Administrative Science Quarterly*, 32: 542–69.

Symon, G. and Clegg, C.W. (1991) 'Technology-led change: a study of the implementation of CAD/CAM', *Journal of Occupational Psychology*, 64 (4): 273–90.

Trist, E.L. and Bamforth, K.W. (1951) 'Some social and psychological consequences of the longwall method of coal-getting', *Human Relations*, 4: 3–38.

Turner, B. (1988) 'Connoisseurship in the study of organizational cultures', in A. Bryman (ed.), *Doing Research in Organizations*. London: Routledge.

Waddington, D.P. (1987) *Trouble Brewing: a Social Psychological Analysis of the Ansell's Brewery Dispute*, Aldershot: Gower.

Yin, R.K. (1981) 'The case study crisis: some answers', *Administrative Science Quarterly*, 26: 58–65.

Yin, R.K. (1989) *Case Study Research: Design and Methods* (rev. edn). Beverley Hills, CA: Sage.

13

Intervention Techniques

David Fryer and Norman T. Feather

What is intervention research?

> None of our researchers should be . . . a mere reporter or outside observer.
> Everyone was to fit naturally into the communal life by participating in some
> activity generally useful to the community. (Jahoda et al., 1972: 5)

It is insufficient to describe intervention research simply as research which
involves an intervention. Whether the researcher acknowledges it or not,
most empirical social research methods involve intervention in some form
or other. Even a doorstep survey interviewer, for example, intervenes in
the informant's world in the sense of creating a new and different social
situation with implications for the informant. It thus potentially affects
what the informant will think, say and do, both during the research itself
and subsequently. Moreover, much of occupational and organizational
psychological research involves manifest or intended intervention. The job
(re)design literature exemplifies this (see, for example, Wall, 1987). Action
research may perhaps usefully be considered to be research in which a
central feature of the research design is the explicit intention jointly to
optimize the quality of research information and effectiveness of the
system under investigation. Much occupational psychology has, however,
been conducted within a unitarist frame of reference (see Fox, 1973;
Hartley, 1984) which tends to make managerial assumptions about the
'effectiveness' of systems under investigation and to accomplish change by
further empowering certain already relatively powerful interest groups
whilst further disempowering others (Kelly, 1978). In this chapter, we
describe research which intervenes to redress rather than amplify power
differentials by furthering the interests of informants who are normally
disadvantaged. This intervention is a central part of the research process
which simultaneously optimizes the quality of research information. To
distinguish this type of research from action research we call it
intervention research.

Broader concerns of intervention researchers

In developing intervention research techniques, we are motivated by the
desire to discover and then use ethically viable ways for persons as

researchers to relate to persons as research informants, whilst simultaneously enhancing the accuracy and detail of our understanding as researchers of our informants' assumptive social worlds.

Our intervention research design is based upon the following assumptions. We believe that recognizing and furthering informants' interests can legitimately be a central part of research design rather than necessarily being excluded from it as a source of bias. We believe that the extent of informants' control over the research process should be maximized rather than minimized wherever possible. We believe that the relationship between researchers and informants should be developed and enhanced wherever possible as a means of information enrichment rather than minimized as a source of data pollution.

As intervention researchers, we are particularly concerned to encourage informants to participate in our research studies who would otherwise be very reluctant, and very unlikely, to become involved in psychological investigations. We also believe that it is vital to develop methods to investigate material which is inaccessible by conventional methods and to maximize the extent and accuracy of disclosure of exceedingly complex and sensitive material by informants. As intervention researchers, we are thus attempting to reconcile a number of methodological and ethical dilemmas. Whilst for ease of exposition it is convenient to consider these separately, they are normally inextricably intertwined in actual research.

Methodological concerns of intervention researchers

All researchers are concerned to use methods which are appropriate to the particular research questions being posed and to the nature of the subject matter being investigated. For some questions in occupational and organizational psychology, quantitative techniques are preferable. These use standardized procedures, large numbers of subjects, validated questionnaire measures and powerful computer packages to establish the statistical significance of associations between precisely measured variables in tightly controlled environments. For other questions, qualitative techniques are preferable. These use flexible, individually tailored procedures with smaller numbers of informants and interpretative analysis to describe and make sense in detail of the precise meanings to particular persons of phenomena occurring in their usual social contexts. The relative merits of quantitative and qualitative methods are fully explored elsewhere in the literature, so these issues will not be pursued further here.

However, for some research questions neither of these alternatives is practicable or sufficient to allow the researcher adequately to develop understanding of a phenomenon.

Informants who are low in confidence, who have limited communication skills, who are confused, demotivated, apathetic, emotionally fragile, distressed, suspicious of – or hostile towards – research, perhaps regarding it as manipulative or humiliating, are unlikely to get constructively involved in research of an orthodox kind. This is especially true where the issues to be investigated are private, sensitive, complex, difficult to access and where informants' experience is frequently characterized by confusion, inconsistency, ambivalence and defensiveness. Yet to exclude such issues and such informants' experience from psychological research is to exclude from the field a great many important issues and a massive proportion of its potential informants. This is especially true in occupational and organizational psychology, where psychological consequences of labour market experience (employment-related psychological strain, unemployment-related mental health problems, etc.) still tend to affect those lower down the socio-occupational hierarchy disproportionately. Such people are frequently already disadvantaged in terms of educational achievement, relative poverty, housing, base-line mental health, etc.

The difficulties of gaining access to do research with close-knit groups consisting of several people (work groups or families, for example), where each member can veto the entire research project, are especially great. In these cases, maximization of participation becomes vital.

Ethical concerns of intervention researchers

Many researchers who work with those whose distress arises principally from social and material deprivation feel somewhat uncomfortable about the research they do and how they carry it out. For example, it is difficult to avoid pondering the morality of being oneself advantaged by a well-paid and satisfying job as a researcher whose own work is directly a result of others' disadvantage as relatively poor and unemployed; where, moreover, the research outcome is unlikely to play a part in eliminating the source of distress.

In part, such disquiet stems from the researcher's impotence in the face of such distress. The researcher's position is not conventionally that of the good Samaritan. As an articulate informant put it to Ullah: 'It's just like you walking down the street. You see a man on the road and he's been stabbed a hundred times. You don't go up to him and say "how does it feel?"' (1987: 117). Yet, conventional psychological research methods frequently restrict one to doing virtually that.

As intervention researchers, we are also concerned with further ethical dilemmas relating to the nature of the research process. What really is an ethically acceptable way for persons (in the role of research psychologists) to relate in a research capacity to persons (in the role of research informants)? How can one carry out systematic social scientifically acceptable research whilst avoiding research relationships which do not further distress, alienate or further disadvantage already disadvantaged people?

An empathic, respectful, trusting and supportive investigator/informant relationship is a necessary condition of intervention research and as intervention researchers we attempt to use non-threatening, non-judgemental, non-invasive methods whose purpose is transparent to informants, which imply no sense of routine passive processing. But is it sufficient? As intervention researchers, we believe not, and also attempt to exercise power more cooperatively with research informants than is usually the case in research, giving the informant as much control over the research process as possible and trying to ensure that the informant's control is as far as possible increased both objectively and subjectively as a consequence of participation in the research. Specifically, we intentionally set out to intervene in informants' circumstances in ways which increase their opportunities to gain both personally and collectively, and preferably in a very tangible form, as part and parcel of the research process.

Intervention techniques in unemployment research

We can explicate the nature of intervention research more clearly if we discuss it in connection with substantive research questions rather than in the abstract. To do this, we diverge briefly to give an account of relevant recent research on unemployment and mental health.

Unemployment is responsible for psychological change and for very many people this change is negative. This has been established beyond reasonable doubt in large part by the use of quantitative methods. Average scores on measures of anxiety, depression and reported cognitive difficulties, for example, have all been demonstrated to be higher, and average scores on measures of self-esteem, activity level and affective well-being measures to be lower, in groups of unemployed people than in judiciously chosen comparison groups of employed people. Moreover, longitudinal studies using well-validated, reliable, self-report measures following groups across employment status transitions (such as from school to unemployment, training scheme or employment [Feather, 1990] or from employment to unemployment [Fryer and McKenna, 1987, 1989]) have demonstrated that unemployment is causally responsible for the documented distress.

The methods used in this research have many important positive features. Standardized procedures allow comparability across studies. The established reliability of the measures used allows us to retest samples longitudinally with confidence. The use of validated measures provides agreed bench-marks of mental health and thereby allows us to know different researchers are referring to the same phenomenon when they talk, for example, of 'depression' or 'anxiety'. Large numbers of subjects combined with powerful statistical computer packages allow us to make between-group mean comparisons which obliterate the 'noise' of within-group variation and to carry out increasingly complex statistical analyses.

However, these methods also impose limitations on research. The unemployment research literature is dominated by studies carried out by survey research organizations using off-the-shelf scales and single-item operationalizations.

It is notoriously difficult to persuade unemployed people to take part in survey research, so the question arises of the representativeness of those who do so. Refusal rates are seldom published. When they are, whilst some reassurances are available regarding comparability, survey respondents remain unlikely to be representative of those unemployed people lowest in confidence, with poorest communication skills, most confused, demotivated, apathetic, emotionally fragile, distressed, suspicious and hostile. It is self-evident that these people will be amongst those least likely to figure amongst survey informants. Concern is heightened by the fact that diminishing confidence, emotional lability, apathy and distress are amongst the most frequently reported outcomes of being unemployed.

Most survey interviewers, whilst no doubt working according to high professional standards, are likely to have little personal commitment to any particular research project. Our experience of fieldwork is that some of the places where and times at which one needs to interview, as well as the conditions under which one might be required to do this, can be very demanding. It would not be surprising if commercial survey interviewers chose to concentrate in the field on areas which were likely most easily to yield completed survey returns, areas in which they felt comfortable and which they perceived as relatively safe.

Another concern about survey research in this field relates to the possibility that it might actually exacerbate unemployed people's distress. We know from qualitative studies that many unemployed people experience being benefit claimants as involving invasion of their privacy, especially with regard to sensitive financial matters. Such studies suggest that many unemployed people feel passively processed, powerless, de-individualized and marginalized in their interactions with the state, in a suspended limbo of alienating bureaucracy, confusing regulations and both information and material poverty.

Yet, the conventional survey research interview is in many respects isomorphic with the benefit interview. In both cases, the flow of information is in one direction, highly structured, controlled by an employed professional who self-discloses as little as possible whilst expecting the interviewee to self-disclose in great detail. In both cases, the interaction is bureaucratized, standardized and characterized by an imbalance of power over both process and outcome.

A fascinating insight into the respondent's experience of a structured survey interview is provided by Young (1987), who reports on depth interviews conducted by trained qualitative interviewers with respondents who had recently taken part as respondents in a highly structured survey.

Generally favourable reactions were reported to the survey as a whole but below we concentrate on some of the concerns uncovered. The depth-interviewees reported uncertainty and apprehension in advance of the survey. Specifically, they feared that their ignorance would be exposed, that they would give 'incorrect', insufficiently definite or non-valuable views and answers. Almost all interviewees reported difficulty understanding at least some questions during the survey, difficulty in concentrating and a tendency to prefer to answer haphazardly rather than ask the survey personnel for help or to admit to not knowing something they felt they were expected to know. Frustration with closed questions, unease that their views had not been accurately captured, that they had (inappropriately) no opinion on some topics, experienced pressure to hurry with answers, discomfort in talking with a stranger about sensitive issues, were all raised by depth-interviewees with respect to their experience of being survey respondents.

If this is true even of the relatively innocuous material of the survey in question and with a cross-section of informants, how much more concern should one have about the sensitive and personal material investigated in much unemployment research with people who are disproportionately likely to be already distressed, disadvantaged and vulnerable?

In psychological research, the researcher is usually in a relatively powerful position compared with the researched-upon. This is in part a reflection of structural social factors in terms of social class, gender, race, education, affluence, professional role and technical expertise (Bhavnani, 1991). This can clearly have negative consequences for research as the researcher who is perceived by the informant as wielding power may intimidate, confuse and mystify the informant. The unemployment literature predominantly presents a picture of unemployed people as powerless, dependent, passive and reactive. Is it entirely fanciful to wonder if the powerless reactivity reported in the unemployment literature could be in part a reflection of the research process itself? Even more disquieting, Holman (1988) suggests that research 'for' or 'on' the poor and unemployed often reinforces rather than diminishes the differences between powerful institutions, such as research units and universities, and poor and unemployed people.

How is intervention research actually done?

Below we discuss the use of one particular intervention technique developed in our research designed to contribute to an understanding of the role of social psychological aspects of income in the experience of employed and unemployed members of families living on very low incomes.

The central intervention feature of the technique which we have been developing involves the provision to unemployed people of information and advice which is intended to demystify their benefit entitlement and, wherever possible, increase their income.

We draw below upon two studies. In one study, Fryer and Fagan (1993) used a computerized welfare benefits package as the basis of an intervention in a severely deprived area of a large Scottish city. The fieldwork involved use of a portable notebook computer loaded with the Lisson Grove Welfare Benefits Program,[1] with back-up from an advice agency. The Lisson Grove Welfare Benefits Program is a regularly updated menu-driven interactive program which allows the operator to work out all the state income maintenance to which a person is entitled by entering in the personal circumstances of the person. In the other study, we conducted research in South Australia which provided verbal welfare benefit advice, again with back-up from an advice agency.

In both studies reported, we used quantitative and qualitative as well as intervention research methods, with intra-family member triangulation of accounts. Specifically, we used: validated measures of psychological well-being; checklists of consumer durables, fortnightly sources of income and of spending (the quantitative component); depth interviews (the qualitative component); and benefit advice to clarify and demystify benefit arrangements and potentially increase informants' income (the intervention component). We collected data from both 'parental partners' in unemployed and/or low-paid employed families.

Much of the preparation and conduct of this research overlaps with that of other qualitative methods. These include: development and testing of the depth interview topic guide; choice of sampling frame; conducting pilot studies; securing ethics committee approval from appropriate bodies; identifying and negotiating access with gate-keepers, agencies and community organizations; issuing invitations to participate whilst ensuring informants' informed consent; choosing and familiarization with the research fieldwork site; outreach to surrounding areas for comparative purposes; becoming known and 'credible' in the community in which the research is to be conducted. This all takes place before the actual data collection, transcription, collation and analysis. Because these are largely common to other methods discussed in greater detail and with a greater degree of focus elsewhere in the literature, we do not pursue them further here.

Practical outcomes of the intervention

To date, about 80 per cent of those for whom we have provided this facility have been revealed to be getting their full entitlements. However, even amongst these people, informants have reported to us that they were relieved to come to understand why they were getting what they were getting (and not getting what they were not entitled to), that is demystification of benefit receipt is regarded as positive whether or not it actually increases income. Having uncertainties removed and the suspicion that they were being short-changed reduced is reported as being beneficial in itself.

Moreover, some informants have been able to use the intervention facility to make detailed calculations about the financial repercussions of various courses of action. For example, informants are able to work out the financial advantages and disadvantages of going back to employment after illness versus staying on sickness benefit. Other unemployed informants have used the intervention facility to determine accurately the financial repercussions of taking low-paid employment in terms of available income supplements for the low-paid. Some informants used the intervention information to work out in detail the parameters of the benefit trap in order to cope more effectively with it.

We have so far been able to notify about 20 per cent of our informants of entitlements which were their due but which they were not yet getting. These included housing benefit, attendance allowance for looking after ageing parents, and laundry allowance for bed-wetting children.

We have also found ourselves, as intervention researchers, frequently intervening in the lives of our informants in ways not specifically antici-pated in advance but in line with the principles of intervention research in terms of serving useful functions for informants and developing and enhancing the researcher–informant relationship. At the family level, this included helping informants write job applications, fill in official forms and helping informants deal with other matters which they raised. Less formally, as intervention researchers we sometimes became involved in helping out in the domestic and social lives of our informants' families. At a community level, as intervention researchers, we have become involved in community ventures, related voluntary work in the evenings and at weekends, participation in local community groups and so on.

Consequences of using intervention research

In the case of investigating the relationship between unemployment, relative poverty and psychological distress, the method adopted is capable of revealing with precision and in painstaking detail the fine grain of income-related behaviour and experience. This is as true in the micro-economic as in the experiential domain. At the margins of poverty, relatively small amounts of money can be crucially important and the technique adopted is capable of pinpoint accuracy. Moreover, many aspects of the experience of poverty occur at the intersection of individual, social, cultural, community, social-institutional and economic forces which make their explication a particular challenge. Intervention techniques illuminate this intersection and facilitate as far as possible full and accurate disclosure of information by informants who are not always fully in possession of relevant information, and who sometimes find it difficult to access information which they in a sense possess and which they might otherwise on occasion distort or withhold. After all, informants appreciate that benefit advice which might substantially alleviate poverty is only of value if it is based upon full and accurate information. Moreover, the relationship of rapport and trust, facilitated by the understanding that the researchers are working 'on behalf of' the informant, maximizes the likelihood of honesty.

This method encourages participation in the research of unemployed informants who would otherwise be very reluctant to become involved and maximizes the chances of full and accurate disclosure by informants of material which is usually considered exceedingly private and difficult to access: experience of and attempts to cope with unemployed poverty.

An example of results of using this technique

We used the provision of detailed benefit entitlement advice as an intervention research technique to investigate the interrelationship between financial difficulties, employment status and family well-being in families in South Australia. Here we illustrate some of the advantages of using intervention research techniques by reporting on some of the experiences of one of these families. We call them the 'South' family.

The South family

The researcher visited and interviewed Mr and Mrs South independently and then visited the couple for a third time to negotiate accounts. During the research, Mr and Mrs South independently provided background information about themselves and their labour market experience, completed a number of standardized inventories and measures, a checklist of household durables which were owned/rented/hired/or had been repossessed, and also a checklist of all sources of income for the family each fortnight. Mr and Mrs South also each consented to an independent depth interview. Jointly, Mr and Mrs South kept a fortnightly expenditure diary of all spending over a two-week period. This involved a considerable amount of effort and time on the part of the informants. It is unlikely that they would have agreed to this had the relationship built up during the intervention phase not become so intimate.

The South family consisted of Mr South, aged 47, Mrs South aged 38, two daughters, aged 10 and 17, and a son, aged 15. Mr South described himself as having been unemployed for six years. Previously he had been employed on production line work. Mrs South had not been employed since their children were born but had recently secured a part-time job at the time of the interview (she had not up to then received any wages). Both Mr and Mrs South defined themselves as unemployed, although both were studying part-time (a few hours per week) and Mr South was, it emerged during the research, actually employed part-time for several hours per week.

The Souths' financial and material circumstances

Mr and Mrs South gave a detailed breakdown of the family income and outgoings, concurring that the family income was made up of a number of allowances and benefits, earnings from Mr South's part-time employment of several hours per week and a contribution from their elder daughter, who was also in part-time employment. Mrs, but not Mr South also reported that the family relied on drawing upon savings. The (jointly completed) fortnightly expenditure diary revealed a modest total expenditure for the period. Of this, 31 per cent had been spent on mortgage payments; 17 per cent on meeting what were expressed as being emergency or otherwise unavoidable one-off expenses (repair to a domestic heater and a family birthday); 14 per cent on hire purchase repayments; 9 per cent on household fuel; and 4 per cent on petrol. Thus 75 per cent of the income was spent on household 'hardware'. A further 11 per cent was spent on food, 8 per cent on family members' leisure and 4 per cent on personal expenses (largely cigarettes and clothing). The remaining 2 per cent was spent on newspapers, stamps, public transport, etc.

Both Mr and Mrs South reported that the family owned a washing machine, vacuum cleaner, telephone, radio, refrigerator (but not a freezer), all of which they had bought, and a music centre and television which they had been given. They were buying a car on hire purchase. The state of repair of many of these household durables was poor.

Mr and Mrs South's psychological well-being

The scales and measures utilized are designed to be used not individually but in group mean comparisons. However, it is interesting to note that both Mr and Mrs South scored very poorly on affective well-being, high on employment commitment and very high on financial stress and strain. For example, both independently reported that they were 'definitely not' (the most negative response available) able to afford: furniture or household equipment which needs to be replaced; the kind of car they need; the kind of medical care the family should have; or the kind of leisure activities the family wants. Thinking back over the past month, Mrs South reported that she had had serious financial worries 'frequently', whilst Mr South reported that he had them 'all the time'.

Experience of poverty

Analysis of the depth interviews was fascinating. Here, we discuss some of the material relating to the informants' reported experience of family poverty, how they attempted to cope with it and some of the resulting family repercussions.

Hardship in the South family

According to both informants, the family was experiencing considerable hardship. Household income was insufficient to maintain the material fabric of the household. For example, the water heater was damaged, taps were leaking, the refrigerator was working only intermittently and even then inefficiently. The family could not afford to get them repaired. Painting, papering and general decorating had had to be postponed indefinitely and everyday cleaning materials like washing-up liquid were difficult to afford when they ran out. As regards clothing, the son was having to wait for new school trousers and everyday shoes which needed replacing. The parents simply went without replacing their own worn-out clothing and were unable to afford clothing acceptable to the teenage children. This was a source of repeated conflict within the family.

Finding school lunch money for the children was very difficult and pocket money very problematic indeed, with resulting restrictions on the children's social life. Family outings were of course severely restricted. Petrol costs prohibited social outings by car, whilst commercial entertainments, meals out and family holidays were out of the question. Birthdays and festivals like Christmas had become dreaded events due to the expenses involved. The Souths felt they were having to make do with inferior dental and medical services due to poverty.

How the Souths were coping with the situation

The parents talked at great length about their efforts to cope with the situation. A central strategy revolved around the efficient management of the inadequate financial resources they had, and in particular avoiding the possibility of 'impulse spending'. Cash kept in the house and particularly cash carried by family members was kept to an absolute minimum. When Mr South went into town, for example, he intentionally took no cash at all with him: only a return bus ticket. Money which was not carried could be neither lost nor spent. All expenditure was very painstakingly planned in advance according to a strict set of priorities: mortgage payments, electricity bills, telephone bills, petrol for essential journeys and the children's needs being priorities.

The remaining priority was food shopping. This was a carefully planned operation. Homework in the family's own and library cookery books was used to plan cheap and nutritious meals. Shopping was done fortnightly for a pre-planned menu for the 14 days' meals. Purchasing involved careful inspection of the prices of everything required for the planned meals in a range of shops, painstaking shopping around for special offers using local knowledge of cheaper retail outlets, and a functional division of family labour. The husband bought meat in bulk whilst the wife bought the other groceries more frequently in smaller quantities. The family produced much of their own food in their large garden. To an extent the family had removed itself, by force of circumstances, from the cash economy. For example, they were able to barter for certain services by 'payment' in garden produce. Members of their extended family had also helped out materially through gifts of furniture, a television and the occasional loan of a vehicle. However, both inter-family and intra-family 'subsidy' was discussed by both informants with some associated anxiety as having 'strings attached': issues of entitlement and reciprocal duties were very prominent.

Most of these issues can be unpacked further from the transcripts and additional sources of information available. For example, the Souths told us that they had experimented with bulk-buying all their groceries. However, whilst this saved money in principle, in practice it was inefficient. Bulk-purchased food which could be eaten with little preparation, such as biscuits, bread, etc., was at risk of being consumed on impulse by the children, especially by the son and his friends, who were at an age when they were frequently hungry and could eat a whole loaf of bread and a pot of jam in one sitting. Dividing out and allocating such bulk-buys over a long period of time and having to 'police' the system was difficult and conflict-prone. Accordingly, repeated purchases of small amounts – an empty larder strategy – served a budgeting function. Meat, on the other hand, could be bought in bulk because, as its preparation time was longer before it could be eaten, it was not as prone to impulse eating. Mr South did the bulk meat buying. Both informants explained this in terms of him being a more knowledgeable meat purchaser, and it is true that background details given indicated that Mr South had been employed as a cook at one time. Meat in bulk is, of course, heavy and awkward to carry, which also partly explains Mr South's role in bulk-buying, but it is interesting to note that other studies (for example, Bostyn and Wight, 1987) have suggested that the provision and consumption of 'butcher meat', as opposed to meat products like pies or sausage or non-meat foods, is important to the masculine identity of some informants in some sub-cultures.

Some other bulk purchases which appeared to allow cheaper unit costs had been discontinued because consumption was so slow that the product was stale or the family bored with it before it was finished.

'Irrational' spending in the South family

The issue of 'impulse' buying or spending recurred for both informants. What has been termed 'irrational spending' has been discussed in the unemployment literature since Jahoda et al. (1972, originally published 1933) first reported that poverty-stricken unemployed people were spending money on coffee, which the investigators pointed out was a drink of virtually no nutritional value, and growing flowers rather than cabbages on their allotments whilst their families were malnourished.

The Souths did report occasional impulse spending (for example, on a second-hand book, a birthday celebration – both confirmed by our expenditure diaries) despite the strategy of seldom carrying cash expressly to avoid this occurring. However, what was far more striking was the way in which the parents regarded themselves as being forced into financial irrationality by their circumstances. For example, their fruit trees cropped around the same time. They wanted to diversify their fruit trees so that the cropping season would start sooner and extend longer. However, they were unable to afford to buy the trees to plant for a harvest in three years' time, although it would be cost-saving in the longer term. Meanwhile, the fruit which cropped simultaneously produced too much for the family to consume. They would have liked to buy a freezer to preserve fruit for consumption throughout the year. Again this was impossible because they had not got the capital to invest in a freezer even though it would have saved money in the long run. Indeed, even the refrigerator was malfunctioning and using more power than it should, yet they were unable to afford to replace it with a more efficient and in the longer term cheaper to run model.

The same story was repeated in other areas of the family members' lives. The children had to be transported to school by the parents. There had been a time when the family car had broken down and they could not afford to have it repaired. In the meantime, they had to pay for a taxi to transport the children to and from school.

As a final example, the son was running competitively for the school team. His running shoes took a lot of punishment from the gruelling training and racing. However, the parents could only afford cheap trainers. These wore out very quickly and were, the parents asserted, poor value for money. However, they could not afford to invest the lump sum in better quality trainers which would have been more cost-effective spending.

South family conflict

Much of the interviews, whose course and content was largely determined by the informants themselves, related to conflict within the family arising out of their relatively poverty-stricken circumstances.

To unpack the running shoes issue further, in effect Mrs South as the clothes purchaser could only with great difficulty afford a cheap pair of trainers, whereas her son wanted a brand name pair which cost ten times as much. The cheaper shoes wore out quickly and were in this respect a poor use of resources. However, the expensive shoes would have been far more than a cost-effective purchase to the son. The expensive brand name trainers would have served important symbolic social functions for the son because of the status bestowed on the wearer in his relations with his peer group.

This point can be illustrated even more clearly in relation to the son's school trousers. The son was required by the school to wear trousers which conformed to certain school regulations in term of colour and style. However, a variety of brands of trousers met the school's requirements. The son, meanwhile, had his own requirements of any trousers, in terms of what he would actually wear to school. This was largely determined by peer group expectations about what brand names of trouser it was acceptable to be seen in. Third, the mother (as purchaser) also had requirements of any trousers she would buy in terms of what she could afford. Briefly, amongst those trousers meeting the school requirements, the mother could only afford inexpensive ones. However, the son would not countenance wearing these. He would only consider wearing trousers of a brand name which met the school's requirements and also (crucially) met with the approval of his peer reference group. These trousers however, were too expensive for the mother to afford. In the meantime, the son was going to school in trousers not meeting the school requirements and the parents were receiving letters from the school pointing out that school-approved trousers were required. The issue of symbolic social as opposed to functional consumption was leading to conflict between parents and child, between parents and school, between child and peers and between parents.

To take one more example of conflict arising through attempts to cope with the financial difficulties of unemployment. Providing a nutritionally adequate diet for growing adolescents was naturally a priority for the Souths. In general, the parents were satisfied that they were doing this. The family diet was characterized by lots of fresh fruit and vegetables, peas, beans and lentils, with little processed food or what the father referred to as 'junk' food. The father regularly made home-made bread, which he talked of as rather a 'social cachet' in some quarters.

However, when the mother was interviewed in depth a somewhat different perspective emerged. She revealed that she and the children were heartily sick of the food provided by the father – characterizing his efforts as primarily to fill them up and fuel them rather than satisfy them. Moreover, the oldest daughter was reported as regarding home-grown and home-made foods as inferior. She hankered after processed and packaged and take-away foods, public consumption of which for her also served symbolic and peer group functions. For her, the home-grown and home-made family food was a source of shame. Meanwhile, the son had reportedly been embarrassed by the parents' restriction of his friends' snacking by the 'empty larder' strategy outlined above. The group of friends were used at their various homes to raiding the larder for food and drinks when hungry. This, combined with the fact that the friends had eight to 10 times as much pocket money as he did, and the daughter's embarrassment with home-made food, led both the son and daughter to curtail their home-based activities with friends. It was preferable to avoid socializing with friends at home than admit that their family could not afford to meet friends' expectations of reciprocal hospitality or risk the embarrassment of friends witnessing the 'inferior' self-provisioning of the parents.

All the children were also reported as being fed up with the narrow range of foods provided by the parents. The children wanted a variety of, for example, breakfast cereals, wanted more snack food like biscuits, etc. which were regarded by the parents as 'junk', and resented the restricted quantity of food available. The son, for example, according to the mother, was frequently hungry for more bread than was his rightful share, with the result that the mother often went without to let him have her portion.

Ironically, the parents attempts to cope effectively were in some respects confounding or exacerbating the family's problems.

Concluding remarks

Like all research methods, intervention research has costs and benefits for both researchers and informants.

Intervention research carries a number of disadvantages for researchers. Relinquishing control over the research process has many stressors implicit within it. The investigator becomes uncertain as to both the process and the outcome of the research. The process of intervention research is expensive in terms of time, energy, personal investment and exposure and it carries risks of psychological strain due to role conflict. When completed, the results of intervention research are difficult to publish, are conventionally regarded as low status and are not therefore an automatic route to career advancement.

Moreover, there are very practical difficulties. In orthodox research funding, the researcher is required to write a research proposal, gain funding and then recruit a research assistant. However, it is evident that for intervention research such as is described above, the qualities and appropriateness of the fieldworker are paramount. Moreover, fieldworkers who are up to the challenges of such intervention research are few and far between. In a reversal of the usual procedure, for intervention research it is frequently more effective to design the research around the strengths of the fieldworker rather than the reverse. The fieldworker must, of course, be technically competent, have the personal qualities required for this gruelling and demanding technique, have credibility in terms of self-presentation within the informant community and crucially have confidence and conviction in the intervention technique. At the very least, the selection of fieldworker, specific intervention technique, field-work site and sampling frame are inextricably intertwined.

Intervention research intentionally can create strong bonds between researchers and informants. Whilst this can be a source of support to the informant, the relationship is, from the researcher's perspective, at least in part and at least initially a research technique. Acceptable limits to the nature of the relationship must be negotiated with the informants and the nature of the actual relationship continuously monitored for acceptability. As in therapy and counselling, the researcher must have constant regard as to how the relationship is to be terminated, without detriment to the informant, even as the research commences. In particular, the researcher must simultaneously guard against exploiting the informant by refusing to allow the informant to develop unrealistic expectations of the relationship and facilitating the informant's role in shaping and ending the relationship.

However, intervention research also has a number of advantages to all parties. A central feature of intervention research is that the furthering of the interests of informants is specifically and intentionally included in research design.

The research aims to import information and material resources into informants' lives. Informants' control over the research process is maximized rather than minimized, their capacity to ask as well as answer questions facilitated. A conscious effort is made to establish an empathic relationship between the researcher and the informant as a source of information enrichment. The informant should therefore benefit in these respects from the intervention.

The researcher, on the other hand, has the modest comfort of knowing that however the research findings come out and however influential or otherwise the research outcomes are regarding policy, at least some disadvantage has been relieved to some extent as a result of the study: that of the particular informants.

Other advantages to the intervention researcher accrue from the detail, accuracy and authenticity of information collected. The high degree of informant commitment to the research which is frequently obtained is likely to lead to minimal drop-out of informants and informant willingness to allow the researcher to investigate otherwise inaccessible issues.

The practice of intervention research overlaps with some of what clinical psychologists, counsellors, organizational psychologists, well-trained social workers and community activists also do. However, from a research perspective, intervention research techniques have the strengths of being suitable both for testing hypotheses derived from psychological theory and for generating new hypotheses and grounded theory.

Intervention research attempts to triangulate information which is typically regarded as the prerogative of differing disciplines. The combination of multi-disciplinary inputs is fraught with difficulty but to attempt it has the advantage of requiring the psychological researcher to go beyond individualistic accounts to treat the aetiology of psychological distress as lying in an 'interaction over time between person and social settings and systems, including the structure of social support and social power' (Orford, 1992: 4).

The material in this chapter poses some very difficult questions with regard to the use of intervention research techniques and we have certainly not attempted to answer them all. Intervention techniques supplement other methods used by psychologists. They are intended to recognize and foster control, autonomy and agency in informants via the research process. Whilst the use of such techniques is not clearly appropriate for all research questions, we believe that it can provide important insights which are difficult if not impossible to obtain by the use of other techniques.

Acknowledgement

We are grateful to: the Flinders University of South Australia for granting the first author a Short Term Visiting Research Fellowship in the Social Sciences during which some of the research reported in this chapter was carried out; the Economic and Social Research Council of Great Britain for financial support for some of the research reported in this chapter; and the University of Sussex for granting the first author a Visiting Research Fellowship in the School of Social Science during which parts of this chapter were written. Marie Jahoda, Rose Fagan and Cathy Cassell offered valuable feedback on earlier drafts of this chapter.

Note

1 Details available from Department of General Practice, St Mary's Hospital Medical School, Imperial College of Science, Technology and Medicine, Lisson Grove Health Centre, Gateforth Street, London NW8 8EG.

References

Bhavnani, K.K. (1991) *Talking Politics*. Cambridge: Cambridge University Press.
Bostyn, A.-M and Wight, D. (1987) 'Inside a community: values associated with money and time', in S. Fineman (ed.), *Unemployment: Personal and Social Consequences*. London: Tavistock.
Feather, N.T. (1990) *The Psychological Impact of Unemployment*. New York: Springer.
Fox, A. (1973) 'Industrial relations: a social critique of pluralist ideology', in J. Child (ed.), *Man and Organization*. London: Allen & Unwin.
Fryer, D. and Fagan, R. (1993) 'Coping with unemployment', *International Journal of Political Economy*, 23 (3): 95–120.
Fryer, D. and McKenna, S. (1987) 'The laying off of hands: unemployment and the experience of time', in S. Fineman (ed.), *Unemployment: Personal and Social Consequences*. London: Tavistock.
Fryer, D. and McKenna, S. (1989) 'Redundant skills: temporary unemployment and mental health', in M. Patrickson (ed.), *Readings in Organizational Behaviour*. Sydney: Harper & Row.
Hartley, J.F. (1984) 'Industrial relations psychology', in M. Gruneberg and T. Wall (eds), *Social Psychology and Organizational Behaviour*. Chichester: Wiley.
Holman, R. (1988) 'Research from the underside', *Community Care*, 18 February: 24–6.
Jahoda, M., Lazarsfeld, P.F. and Zeisl, H. (1972 [1933]) *Marienthal: the Sociography of an Unemployed Community*. New York: Aldine-Atherton.
Kelly, J.E. (1978) 'A reappraisal of sociotechnical systems theory', *Human Relations*, 31 (12): 1069–99.

Orford, J. (1992) *Community Psychology: Theory and Practice.* Chichester: Wiley.

Ullah, P. (1987) 'Unemployed black youths in a northern city', in D. Fryer and P. Ullah (eds), *Unemployed People: Social and Psychological Perspectives.* Milton Keynes: Open University Press.

Wall, T. (1987) 'New technology and job design', in P. Warr (ed.), *Psychology at Work.* Harmondsworth: Penguin.

Young, P. (1987) *The Survey Respondent's Experience of a Structured Interview.* London: SCPR report 23/010.

Index